DATE

Oc

The Failure of Criticism

The Failure of Criticism

EUGENE GOODHEART

HARVARD UNIVERSITY PRESS

Cambridge, Massachusetts, and London, England   1978

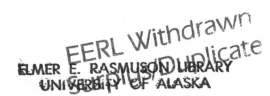

Library of Congress Cataloging in Publication Data

Goodheart, Eugene.
    The failure of criticism.

    Includes bibliographical references and index.
    1. Criticism
I. Title
PN85.G595   801'.95   77-29055
ISBN 0-674-29115-8

For Joan

Acknowledgments

Several chapters in this book are revisions of essays originally presented to the Cambridge Humanities Seminar, an interinstitutional and interdisciplinary seminar which I direct jointly with Alvin Kibel of the Massachusetts Institute of Technology. I am grateful to the members of the seminar both for their support and for their healthy skepticism. The National Endowment for the Humanities deserves special thanks for the financial and moral support it has given to the seminar. Wayne Booth, Joseph Frank, and Alan Trachtenberg read the manuscript in its penultimate version and made substantive suggestions which found their way into the final draft of the book. I am especially grateful to another friend, Daniel Aaron, for his astute and meticulous reading of the manuscript. He saved me from many an error. My wife, Joan Bamberger, proved an indispensable editor before the manuscript went to press. What remains is incorrigible.

I wish to thank the editors of *The Centennial Review, Clio, New Literary History, Salmagundi,* and *The Yale Review* for their hospitality to earlier versions of chapters in this book. Excerpts from the poetry of T. S. Eliot and from *The Family Reunion* are reprinted by permission of Harcourt Brace Jovanovich, Inc.; copyright, 1936, by Harcourt Brace Jovanovich, Inc.; copyright, © 1943, 1963, 1964, by T. S. Eliot; copyright, 1971, by Esme Valerie Eliot. I wish also to thank Faber and Faber, Ltd., for permission to quote from *The Collected Poems, 1909-1962,* by T. S. Eliot, and F. R. Leavis, Denys Thompson, and Chatto & Windus, Ltd., for allowing me to quote from *Culture and Environment*. Excerpts from *The Triumph of the Therapeutic* by Philip Rieff, copyright © 1966 by Philip Rieff, are reprinted by permission of Harper and Row, Publishers, Inc., and the author.

The Graduate School of Boston University generously provided the necessary funds for preparing the manuscript. One could not ask for more competent and more patient typists than Donna Scripture and Vicki Worona.

Contents

The Failure of Criticism

Introduction

THE DECLINE of critical standards can be dated no more precisely than the fall of man or the dissociation of sensibility. Anyone who takes it upon himself to complain of the failure of criticism at the present time will be reminded that the failure has been remarked upon for a long time. F. R. Leavis in 1933 lamented the disappearance of "a living tradition" that once "constituted a surer taste than any individual as such can pretend to." With "no center and no authority," Leavis wrote, critics as different as "Mr. Eastman, Mr. Nicholson, Mr. Priestley or Mr. Walpole can assume authority without being in the eyes of the world ridiculous,"[1] and he invidiously contrasted the situation in 1933 with that in Matthew Arnold's time. "The centre—Arnold's 'centre of intelligent and urbane spirit,' which, in spite of his plaints, we can see by comparison to have existed in his day—has vanished."[2]

Is it a matter of degree or absolute difference? Was it merely worse in 1933 than it was in 1869? Is it still worse today? Or are we now in a radically new situation? It is difficult to know how to answer these questions or to be sure that the questions are properly formulated. It is clear, however, that the "plaints" of Arnold and Leavis correspond to a condition of modern life and literature, a condition which is the subject of this book. It is also clear that what Arnold described as "this strange disease of modern life"[3] can no longer be diagnosed with such confidence. Health-disease, normality-abnormality are unstable, possibly obsolete, terms.

The sense of the loss or absence of a living tradition is of course not unique to England. In 1918 Van Wyck Brooks expressed a representative sentiment about American cultural life: "We have no cultural economy, no abiding sense of spiritual values, no body of critical understanding . . . The present is void."[4] Interestingly enough, his touchstones for a criticism that reflects a living tradition are Thomas Carlyle in England and Jules Michelet in France. The American situation, for reasons peculiar to American history, is even more grave than that of Europe.

The difference between Arnold's time and our own, indeed between 1933 and our own moment, can be forcefully dramatized in the history of the term "center." Leavis refers to Arnold's "centre of intelligent and urbane spirit," and his own work is charged with judgments about the centrality or the absence of centrality of imaginative works. The fate of modernist literature has been a "decentering" of the imagination and intelligence—a deliberate loss of poise amidst the variety of experience, so that no point of view, no position is privileged. The current fashionable distinction between modernism and postmodernism is meant to rescue the classic moderns from this judgment. To be sure, there are distinctions to be made—for instance, between Joyce and Beckett—but they are not as radical as the one between Arnold and Eliot. As I try to show, the centrifugal element in Joyce's work, which makes for its affinity with postmodernism, remains powerful, despite the resistant, valuing, ordering impulse also to be found in the work.

In "The Function of Criticism at the Present Time" (1864), Arnold speaks of the profit for the spirit in the contrast that he draws between the hideousness of contemporary industrial life and the conventional eulogies of industrial civilization. Against Mr. Roebuck's prayer "that our unrivalled happiness will last," Arnold poses a child murder committed by a workhouse mother named Wragg.

> "And our unrivalled happiness"—what an element of grimness, baseness, and hideousness mixes with it and blurs it; the workhouse, the dismal Mapperly Hills—how dismal those who have seen them will remember—the gloom, the smoke, the cold, the strangled illegitimate child! "I ask you whether the world over or in past history, there is anything like it?" Perhaps not, one is inclined to answer; but at any rate, in that case, the world is very much to be pitied. And the final touch—short, bleak and inhuman: *Wragg is in custody*. The sex lost in the confusion of "our unrivalled happiness."[5]

If one wants a formal definition of criticism as Arnold and Leavis understand it, one might begin with "contrast." Contrast is the mode through which Arnold's irony manifests itself—and that irony pre-supposes a secure conviction about different and opposed realms of value. The conviction animates not only the critical essay but also the imaginative literature which criticism sustains, reflects, and under-stands. Implicit in Dickens's *Hard Times*, George Eliot's *Middle-march*, Lawrence's *Women in Love* are those contrasts which appear so vividly on the surface of the essays of Arnold and Leavis.[6]

It is a sure sign of the predicament of modern criticism that the moral sense of contrast has been severely weakened, if it has not com-pletely disappeared. It is certainly absent in contemporary avant-garde criticism (the French school and its American allies) which puts into question (the locution is French) the very nature of critical activ-ity in the normative sense. Jacques Derrida's *Glas*, for example, is a sustained exercise in what Geoffrey Hartman calls the crossing over of texts. The inherent instability of language, which modern imaginative literature reveals or betrays with a vengeance and which is as un-checked in Derrida's book as it is in *Finnegans Wake*, becomes the energizing principle of what purports to be criticism. Criticism in Der-rida is a montage of textures, a release of multiple meanings, a circus of the mind in motion, a kind of surreal protest against the constraints of moral judgment and systematic thinking. It becomes an intellectual simulacrum for modern life itself.

Derrida's term for what he is doing is deconstruction (cognate with decentering), an activity implicitly to be distinguished from demystifi-cation. Unlike demystification, deconstruction is an assault on stable hierarchical notions of reality. To demystify is to reduce *a* to *b* or to evaporate illusion *a* in favor of reality *b*. Deconstruction, on the other hand, ambiguously preserves everything and makes everything the object of suspicion. Nothing disappears, but nothing is stable. Thus in *Glas* Derrida places Hegel's *savoir absolu* against his letters, the effect of which is to show the personal roots of Hegel's system, but without subverting, that is, demystifying, the system. What is "established" is an equivocal view of Hegel, involving two juxtaposed elements of his life. Demystification, from the putatively unprivileged point of view of deconstruction, suffers from an old-fashioned assumption of the privileged point of view. To be sure, demystification has within it the deconstructivist possibility. The reality of the demystifier is always subject to suspicion as suspicion becomes the dominant attitude, one might almost say emotion.

The work of Roland Barthes similarly attempts to destabilize or to

show the inherent instability of what Barthes calls the "writerly" text.
Stability and unity are arbitrary functions of the reader's response.
The distinction between the "readerly" and the "writerly" text is paral-
leled by the distinction between the classic and the modern. The
classic text, in Barthes's view, is a readerly text in which values or
ideas are stabilized. Barthes's own performance as a practical critic of
Balzac's "classic" *Sarrasine* is to turn the text into an unstable modern
one characterized by a plurality of meaning. The "liberation" of the
text from its own constraints is vividly affirmed in a language un-
abashedly political.

> "Life" then, in the classic text, becomes a nauseating mixture of
> common opinions, a smothering layer of received ideas: in fact, it
> is in these cultural codes that what is outmoded in Balzac, the
> essence of what, in Balzac, cannot be (re)written, is concentrated.
> What is outmoded, of course, is not a defect in performance, a
> personal inability of the author to afford opportunities in his
> work for what will be modern, but rather a fatal condition of
> Replete Literature, mortally stalked by the army of stereotypes it
> contains. Thus, a critique of the references (the cultural codes)
> has never been tenable except through trickery, on the very limits
> of Replete Literature, where it is possible (but at the cost of what
> acrobatics and with what uncertainty) to criticize the stereotype
> (to vomit it up) without recourse to a new stereotype: that of
> irony. Perhaps this is what Flaubert did (we shall say it once
> again), particularly in *Bouvard et Pecuchet* where the two copy-
> ists of scholastic codes are themselves "represented" in an uncer-
> tain status, the author using no metalanguage (or a suspended
> metalanguage) in their regard. In fact, the cultural code occupies
> the same position as stupidity: how can stupidity be pinned down
> without declaring oneself intelligent? How can one code be supe-
> rior to another without abusively closing off the plurality of
> codes? Only writing, by assuming the largest possible plural in its
> own task, can oppose without appeal to force the imperialism of
> each language.[7]

Yet the effect of the liberation into plurality is to evoke the emptiness
of a game, not the richness of human possibility.

The distinction between game and human possibility may be gratui-
tously invidious from a structuralist point of view. But without the
distinction we are not able to perceive the transvaluation of values the
structuralists hope to achieve. The text is an "empty concept," an
"absence at the center" and at the circumference, which "opens up an

unbounded space for the play of signification" (Derrida). As Jonathan Culler remarks: "Given that there is no ultimate and absolute justification for any system or for the interpretation flowing from it [since there is neither center nor circumference], one tries to value the activity of interpretation itself, or the activity of theoretical elaboration, rather than any results which might be obtained."[8] It is difficult to see how the idea of seriousness itself is not threatened, in the way seriousness would be threatened if someone were to claim that life was no more than a game of chess, interesting only in the endless permutations and combinations by which its rules are enacted but without any ultimate and absolute justification. Why should one necessarily value interpretation, or, to use the subversive language of structuralism itself, why should interpreting have a privileged position? This is not to say that the problem of ultimate justification is not extremely difficult, if not insoluble. It is simply that the structuralist address to the problem is curiously, if not perversely, evasive. And it is evasive in the academic mode, for only the academic mind could assert, as Philippe Sollers asserts, that in "the final analysis we are nothing other than our system of reading and writing."[9] Our greatest books, *The Divine Comedy, King Lear, The Brothers Karamazov, Anna Karenina,* testify to the impoverishment of this view of the human project.

The works of Barthes and Derrida are fascinating examples of a powerful tendency in modernism. It is to be found, as I have already suggested, in *Finnegans Wake.* It is present in *The Waste Land,* in which, for example, the quotations from Dante, Spenser, and Marvell, among others, create a montage effect in relation to scenes from contemporary life. (Eliot's moral ambition was of course quite different from that of Derrida or Barthes: he was engaged in an effort to release the literary past from its temporal bondage and make it part of the simultaneous order which he called tradition. Or at least this is one possible interpretation of the effect of the quotations in *The Waste Land.*) What is remarkable and symptomatic about performances of the French critics is the displacement of this modernist aesthetic tendency to criticism itself. By radically weakening if not destroying the privileged point of view, modern literature has sanctioned for them the *de*moralization of criticism. Its evaluative function is now seen as an arbitrary exercise of taste. Interpretation has lost whatever certainty it had. Indeed, equivocation has been made virtually its first principle.

It is not simply the French school that argues for the equivocation and indeterminacy of meaning. Criticism inspired by Wittgenstein and J. L. Austin, for instance, confirms us in the conviction that we are dealing with a modern—or should I say modernist—phenomenon. Thus Stanley Fish insists on the irreducible, equivocal character of all readings. "In a sequence where a reader first structures the field he inhabits and then is asked to restructure it (by changing an assignment of speaker or realigning attitudes and positions) there is no question of priority among his structurings; no one of them, even if it is the last, has privilege; each is equally legitimate, each equally the proper object of analysis, because each is equally an event in his experience."[10] We are never enlightened about the assumption that all events in one's experience are equal in value. Fish is so intent on leveling the variety of experience that he seems unaware of the arbitrariness of the assumption. Or rather, the assumption is a modern dogma, to use Wayne Booth's useful phrase, which therefore requires no justification.

There is sufficient intelligent force in the modernist challenge to compel us to take it seriously, even if we are in an antagonistic relation to it. The impulse toward the moralistic censure of modernism in a critic like F. R. Leavis represents another kind of failure, a self-defeating unresponsiveness to and consequent incomprehension of modern reality.

In the chapters that follow, I try to understand the predicament of criticism not simply as a local issue for academic literary critics concerned with the logic of particular techniques but as the expression of contending spiritual views of experience as well. I found, for example, the religious background of modern literature absolutely essential to such an understanding. In trying to distinguish the Catholic and Protestant energies of modern literature, I have followed the suggestion of Carlyle and Arnold that literature is a branch of religion and revised Eliot's statement that a key to an understanding of most contemporary Anglo-Saxon literature is the decay of Protestantism.[11] Modern literature can be fruitfully viewed as a dialectic between the Protestant-inspired, largely English tradition from Carlyle to Lawrence and the Catholic-inspired literary modernism of Flaubert, Joyce, and Eliot. As I intend to show, Eliot's understanding of the decay of Protestantism inadvertently reveals his own decayed Catholicism. It is in the contentions between these traditions that I discover the relation between modernism and the critical spirit. Questions about the moral authority of literature and criticism often turn upon a prior question of what happens when the sacred disappears or is sublimated in the profane. In keeping with my effort to enlarge the territory of discussion, I have also addressed myself to analogous concerns in the other arts and in social philosophy.

1

Modernism and the Critical Spirit

HUMANIST CRITICISM, which has as its object the quality of life as well as works of art, no longer has authority. By "humanist criticism" I mean something richer and more significant than fault-finding literary journalism or the academic study of books, though it is possible for literary journalism and academic study to rise to the condition of humanist criticism. Matthew Arnold, F. R. Leavis, and Raymond Williams in the English tradition, Edmund Wilson and Lionel Trilling in the American, and Ortega y Gasset in the European are major instances, though they are by no means exhaustive, nor do they together express a single ideological point of view. The most impressive expression of humanist criticism occurs in nineteenth century England. The work of Carlyle, Ruskin, and Arnold has as its major theme the spiritual consequences of the new mechanical civilization and the French Revolution. It is a criticism inspired by a positive order of values, nourished by a moral understanding of the religious tradition and by a profound appreciation of the works of art and intellect of past and present, in Arnold's words, "the best that has been thought and known." Its principal expression is the essay, but it may express itself as a novel or poem. The authority implicit in such criticism has been beautifully stated by I. A. Richards:

> But it is not true that criticism is a luxury trade. The rearguard of Society cannot be extricated until the vanguard has gone further. Good-will and intelligence are still too little available. The critic, we have said, is as much concerned with the health of the mind as any doctor with the health of the body. To set up as a critic is to set up as a judge of values . . . For the arts are inevitably and quite

apart from any intentions of the artist an appraisal of existence. Matthew Arnold, when he said that poetry is a criticism of life, was saying something so obvious that it is constantly overlooked. The artist is concerned with the record and perpetuation of the experiences which seem to him most worth having . . . he is also the man who is most likely to have experiences of value to record. He is the point at which the growth of the mind shows itself.[1]

Some of our most gifted critics view the controlling impulse of criticism as an embarrassment to both the creative imagination and the life process. This view is implied in Susan Sontag's title *Against Interpretation*, which sees in the pattern-finding, moralizing habit of criticism an impediment to the unfolding of creative impulses. Her title may be a misnomer, for she is an incisive pattern finder herself. She is against the kind of judgment that would prevent her from being a celebrant of the works of art she discusses. The most remarkable instance of the impulse to deny or reject the act of criticism is Marshall McLuhan, who began his career as an authoritative cultural critic with a superbly witty dissection of the clichés of advertising culture in *The Mechanical Bride* (1951). It is costly to the spirit, he argues in that book, to hide oneself from the reality of mass culture by sticking one's head ostrichlike in the sand of the great books, costly not because mass culture is wonderful, but because any convincing declaration of a position for individuality and resistance presupposes a knowledge of the enemy. But McLuhan's fascination with technological culture flipped him to the adversary side. In his subsequent work there is no answering spiritual voice to the romance of science and technology. The marvelous practical energy that has produced computers, rockets, and space ships is all. The instances of Sontag and McLuhan (and there are many others) are not so much manifestations of an inspired progressivism as they are of the erosive force of an expanding reality. When the world becomes filled with the adversary, the places of resistance become fewer and smaller.

It is a mistake, however, to see the work of McLuhan or Sontag as a willful betrayal of the cause of criticism. If the fate of criticism is linked to that of literature, then we must look for analogues, if not causes, in the career of modern literature itself. We are certainly willing to link nineteenth century literature and criticism, and until recently criticism in the academy was inspired by the moral ideals of nineteenth century literature. Administrators and scientists in institutions of higher learning still turn to humanists for moral guidance on the assumption that the humanities are determined by the literary ideals of the nineteenth century. But contemporary humanists are more uncertain about moral realities than scientists, more plagued by a sense of ambiguity and ungovernable complexity. Those who turn to the humanities for "values," for moral guidance, are under an illusion about the nature of the humanities at the present time, an illusion that some humanists share.

The humanities are not the incarnation of an eternal spirit. They are a human and consequently historical creation—and in a specific sense. Humanism is in part an expression of contemporary literature. Its sense of the past is to a large extent mediated through the perceptions of contemporary literature. Tradition tends to be constituted by works of the past that nourish the contemporary imagination. I am uttering here the familiar wisdom of the modernist aesthetics enunciated in T. S. Eliot's essay "Tradition and the Individual Talent."

The humanities as an expression of the ethos of modern literature provide little more than an exacerbated sense of insecurity about the world. This is the lesson of modern literature, and if one institutionalizes this lesson in the university, one is getting not moral guidance but subversion. The value of modern literature (and I mean this without irony) is to introduce anxiety into the conscience of modern man. Moral anxiety is of course an essential part of spiritual progress. There can be neither growth nor conversion nor redemption without such anxiety. But the modern literary imagination at its best remains arrested in the state of moral anxiety, unable to conceive of a condition of being at once ethically responsible, spiritually fulfilled, and freed of anxiety. If it imagines the dissolution of anxiety, it does so at the price of moral sensitivity, as in the case of Camus's *The Stranger* or Gide's *The Immoralist* or Dostoevsky's *Notes from Underground*. The critical implication of modern literature is directed toward false confidence. Modern literature is not a source of confidence.

Dostoevsky's underground man violates every rule of moral and intellectual decorum in order to achieve a sense of individual vitality which will assure him that he is alive. He is never void of the moral sense; one might say that he is constantly suffering from it. But he regards the moral sense as a disease from which he is trying to purge himself. I am not rendering the story precisely in its own terms. The word "reason" is the adversary term in the idiom of the story. But reason is clearly the "moral reason" of Enlightenment philosophy, and the underground man for all his articulateness has only half-articulately, but unmistakably, pitted himself against ethical rationality in the manner of the immoralist. The underground man is pre-Nietzschean.

Gide's immoralist, who is post-Nietzschean, is hardly as rich in fictional reality as the underground man, but the ideological implications of his being are perhaps clearer. Michel, the hero of *The Immoralist*, gains his freedom and his health at the cost of his wife's life. The freedom proves illusory, and the sense of emptiness and directionlessness from which he speaks at the beginning and the end of the tale may conceal a sense of guilt. In any event, the terms of Michel's existence are such that he cannot at once be free and responsible to others.

In Camus's *The Stranger*, morality as perceived through the consciousness of the "hero" Meursault is seen as conventionality. The sense of horror at the callous and murderous behavior of Meursault is muted by the spiritual vacuity of society's values. Meursault's moral idiocy is made to seem attractive, even charismatic. It is not that Camus means to moralize on Meursault's behalf. He is rather trying to get us to suspend our conventionally ethical view of Meursault. The effect is to overcome a prejudice against him, not necessarily to create a prejudice for him.

This suspension of the ethical is precisely what is supposed to occur in our reading of the tales of Gide and Dostoevsky as well. Our view of the careers of these heroes or antiheroes is almost scientifically dispassionate. I should qualify this statement by noting that in the great novels that follow *Notes from Underground* the underground man is the demon within that the heroes (Raskolnikov, Stavrogin, Ivan) must overcome.

Modern literature deliberately refuses wisdom for truthtelling, the witnessing of chaos. Truthtelling, in this sense, depends upon the relaxation of the moral will. And the relaxation of the moral will is a heuristic for experiencing and seeing, but not for conduct. In becoming complicit with the vision, one is turning the heuristic into a guide for conduct—which when we think about the monstrosities contemplated by modern consciousness is a monumental absurdity.

Modern literature seems to be aware of its own loss of spiritual authority. In one sense, it does not criticize modern life so much as become part of it. For example, the ethos of modern artistic creation resembles the ethos of industry and technology. Innovation and novelty are primary values, which means that artistic creation like industrial production involves planned obsolescence, though ideas of uniqueness and quality still inform artistic creation, so that the analogy with industrial production is incomplete. It is not merely that one does not expect a style to last more than several years but also that the perishability of works of art is implied by the logic of such art. The sentiment about perishability is a candid confession that eternal values do not inhere in these works.[2]

The perishability of modern objects derives in part from their superficiality. The image has been flattened because the invisible spiritual reality to which it once referred seems no longer available to modern consciousness. The "new novelists" in France, for example, render the surface qualities of people and things without the least suggestion of anything below the surface. If a sense of a hidden reality emerges, it is because blatant superficiality becomes suspect, perhaps as an effort at concealment. The romantic idea that there are depths to the private life has been seriously undermined, if not destroyed, according to Natalie Sarraute, by the stupefying power of mass communication, which has made banality a major industry. Whether or not Mme. Sarraute has adduced the true cause of superficiality, the fact remains that an artist of her seriousness is in complicity with this view when she renders characters simply as bundles of reactions to situations—in a word, as tropisms.[3] Having lost permanence and depth, modern objects exist in an egalitarian space, which makes the critical capacity for discrimination and distinction irrelevant.

There is a paradox in the career of modern art as I describe it. The reduction of life to banality and the *uncritical* complacency with which it is accepted is the result of the hypertrophy of the critical faculty. The virtues of modernism are honesty and lucidity. All forms of mystification, aesthetic, religious and political, are the object of merciless, *critical* scrutiny.[4] "In an age of uncertainty," Eliot remarks in "The Frontiers of Criticism," "no explorable area can be forbidden ground."[5] But the effect of the scrutiny becomes uncritical at the point that it loses its basis in a conviction about values. And the point is reached in the unchecked drive to unmask all values for what they are—maskings of egoistic motives and power drives. It was Nietzsche, the modernist philosopher par excellence, who perceived the nihilist route of modernism and engaged simultaneously in the practice of unmasking and in a critique of the perniciousness of unmasking. He understood, too self-consciously alas, the need for illusions (values, pieties, beliefs) to sustain a life.

Descartes tried to free mind from the constraints of the body, that is, the irrational, in order to allow the mind to exercise its powers to the fullest. But his dualism unwittingly subverted those powers. The advantage of having mind rooted in and limited by the body is that it assures for the exercise of the rational or critical intellect a basis in conviction—or at least makes it possible. By the body I mean something richer than its physical component, though I do not want to minimize its importance: I mean the body in its emotional, passional, even spiritual aspect, on which D. H. Lawrence bestows the phrase "the greater life of the body." Without the body the mind cannot experience the world. Modernism is associated with the fate of science in the way in which it testifies to (without either sanctioning or condemning) the dissociation of mind from body and voice from persona. The result is a "critical" machine of extraordinary destructive power.

Beckett's work is a *locus classicus* for the consequences of the Cartesian split, which he presents comically and without moral animus. His characters are disembodied minds interminably turning every moment of experience into an endless exercise in scholasticism. It is an anxious scholasticism possessing neither a center nor a terminus. The mental energy of a Beckett character has been generated to no purpose. Its continuous triviality is redeemed for significance by the undeniable anguish of the voice. Godot is the anxious expectation of a terminus that never occurs.

Modernist virtues act as corrosives, subverting all tacit, unexamined acceptances and beliefs. The impulse to bring everything into the light, to rationalize the world, may represent a will to knowledge and mastery (an ambition of modernism), but it may also undermine deep, unquestioning commitment to institutions, activities, and people, the kind of commitment that sustains life. I think Baudelaire understood this in urging the importance of mystery. For him life had to be lived as problem and predicament, the significance of which was always to be partially concealed, so that society would discover in its activity a moral tension and spiritual awareness. It is as if this great modern poet is here an implicit critic of one major tendency of modernism. But his own formulations imply not a spontaneous relation to mystery, but a fabrication of it out of a need, a condition that implies a modern problem. It is from a sense of problem that John Henry Newman, Michael Polanyi, and Michael Oakeshott have engaged in an important critique of the nihilist tendency of modernism in its arrogant rationalist version of bringing everything into the light.[6] "Rationalist," I might add, in its *method* of reductive analysis (see Dostoevsky's underground man), not in its valuation of the life of reason.[7] They have argued in varying ways for the tacit element in knowledge and in the moral life. Reason, with its uninhibited questioning of everything, will create metaphysical anxiety and paralyze our critical faculty unless it is constrained from entering the precincts of our being from which our capacity for conduct, for affirmation, and for negation issue. These are the precincts of darkness and silence in which the absolute presuppositions of our being are to be found.

The young Marx understood very well the danger of an unrestrained criticism when he censured the "Critical Criticism" of the young Hegelians who "are not against love alone, but against everything living, everything which is immediate, every sensuous experience, any and every real experience."[8] In an eloquent passage, Marx defines the goal of true criticism:

> Criticism has plucked the imaginary flowers from the chains not so that man may bear chains without any imagination or comfort, but so that he may throw away the chains and pluck living flowers. The criticism of religion disillusions man so that he may think, act, and fashion his own reality as a disillusioned man comes to his senses so that he may revolve around himself as his real sun.[9]

Elsewhere Marx speaks of "the forming of the five senses [as] a labor of the entire history of the world down to the present."[10]

The positive unquestioned commitment to immediate sensuous experience is of course not the same as a commitment to moral or spiritual principles, but Marx is here sufficiently a man of the nineteenth century to resist the beginnings of the corrosive modernism that was to triumph in the twentieth century. Yet the resistance to the negative does not *define* Marx; as we shall see elsewhere, he makes his powerful contribution to it.[11]

The historical origins of the hubristic ambition of reason to bring everything into the light are, of course, in the Enlightenment. But in the Enlightenment the activity of demystification is limited by a constructive morality. Only when reason turns upon reason, as it does in the modern period, and the moral element in rationality is subjected to critique does reason become transformed into something diabolical, into irrationalism itself. Of course, the critical faculty, having burst the bonds of morality, cannot be constrained by fiat in the interest of morality or even of a sense of well-being. Once well-being becomes a censor of the critical faculty, it ceases to be well-being, for it becomes burdened with *dis*ease and guilt. However, if criticism is to recover its powers, it must rediscover its limitations, just as reason finds its strength when it acknowledges the transcendence and mystery of grace.

The triumph of modernism is the defeat of criticism.[12] The formula of triumph and defeat expresses the pure case, which one finds among the rare freaks and monstrosities of modernist literature. Indeed the greatest works of the modernist imagination exemplify a tension between the old and the new, between the modern and the antimodern.[13] One might define the classic modernist position as an attempt to strike a balance or maintain a tension between stable values and the claim of the new. Wyndham Lewis's attack upon the modern time-mind, in which subjects and objects lose integrity and security, rests on this view. Thus spatial form "offers men that illusion of security and repose necessary for human creativeness."[14] The time-mind is particularly congenial to modern life with its changefulness and fragmentation. The classic modernist position is to assault at once the Heraclitean flux and the nostalgia for a fixed past. It releases the adventurous element of the imagination in the hope of a new reordering of experience. The effort is to wrest a solid present from the flux of experience. Radical modernism (sometimes called postmodernism) has surrendered to the flux. Born in dialectical fashion as a criticism of modernity, humanism is rooted in moral values or pieties, which radical modernism with its profound passion for uncovering the amoral process of reality is bent on destroying. The complete triumph of modernism has been envisaged in dystopian nightmare, and it means the total destruction of the critical faculty. If neither the triumph nor the defeat is complete, there is nonetheless an extraordinary imbalance between the two impulses, an imbalance that has effectively demoralized the critical impulse.

My use of the term "humanist criticism" should not be associated with the versions of it provided by Irving Babbitt and Paul Elmer More, who gave it an unnecessary reactionary or repressive reputation. So hostile were they to modern literature that they could learn nothing from it. No vital criticism, however skeptical or ambivalent it may be about the claims of modernist literature, can afford to deny either the power or fascination or seriousness of its voices. A humanist criticism that is prematurely censorious, that does not permit itself a true knowledge of modernism, is doomed to sterility.

The critical spirit is the spirit of resistance, and "traditional" art has the critical spirit built into it. It is precisely because modernism has evacuated the critical spirit from art (that is, the moral element in the critical spirit) that there is an urgent need for a virile humanist criticism. What now passes for criticism is what I would call a mimetic criticism, which links itself to any particular exacerbation of art. Modern criticism has in effect become a nonresistant imitation of modern art—in spirit and in some cases (for example, Derrida) in form. To reassert the rights of criticism, the critic must cultivate his capacity for resistance without censuring the creative element in the modern imagination. The ideal is a dialectical relation between criticism and art.

I am trying to give an accurate characterization of the phenomenon of modernism, so as to reveal the falsity of certain moral expectations of modern literature. Modern literature is much like science in its ambition to describe impersonally its subject matter, the human spirit.[15] It is not concerned with, feels incapable of, providing wisdom about it. Oddly enough, the mode of ambiguity which the literary imagination cultivates and which seems to distinguish literature from science, with its predilection for univocal statement, serves to free our view of experience from particular moral commitments and biases. The suspension of disbelief resembles the scientific suspension of belief which prevents us from seeing the object as it really is. The various doctrines of aesthetic purism associated with the modernist movement are in great part directed against moral and religious interpretations of the literary process. They have an affinity, on occasion made explicit, with the scientific spirit. There is, in other words, a strong anti-humanist tendency in modern literature which makes the position of the contemporary humanist paradoxical to say the least. This situation has only to be compared with the natural affinity that existed in England between literature and humanist criticism in the nineteenth century, especially the criticism of Carlyle, Ruskin, and Arnold, which connected the act of true seeing with unambiguous moral doctrine.

THE EFFORT to make criticism scientific is an attempt to compensate it for its loss of moral power, and the compensation is seen as greater than its loss. Northrop Frye understands the present function of criticism as scientific rather than humanist—in the traditional sense of the term. It is not clear how important the scientific theme is in Frye's work. His model for literary study is evolutionary theory, though its provenance (whether Darwin or contemporary versions) is unclear. Frye does not establish his credentials in scientific theory. His own system tends to be taxonomic and inert—in a word archaic—from the scientific point of view. I think, however, that Frye's scientific attitude should be taken seriously as symptomatic of the present state of literary study. Since he is one of the commanding and influential critics of our time, it would be useful for our purposes to examine briefly his view of the critical function. In his book *The Critical Path* (1971), which is an account of literature in its social and historical context, Frye shows some understanding of the predicament of humanism. But like his colleague McLuhan, though from a different point of view, he does not regret the failure of humanist criticism. Indeed, he sees in the failure an opportunity for developing the only kind of criticism he values.

Frye's concern with historical context is somewhat anomalous, because his view of literature seems to imply that the critic ideally is engaged in a scientific study of a timeless activity. Frye's criticism reveals the permutations and combinations of mythic patterns within the literary tradition, but those permutations and combinations are logical possibilities of the imagination unfolded through, but largely unaffected by, time. "Myth," Frye tells us, "is the language of the present tense."[16] And yet such is Frye's ambition as a critic and theorist that he feels compelled to engage the phenomenon of historical time—that is, account for what is a nonphenomenon in terms of his own vision. What Frye does is reduce the "illusion" of historical change to myths of "concern" and "freedom," which in Vichian fashion recur with variations through history. The effect of this reduction is to distance us from the particular historical phenomenon so as to

make an active involvement with it—either through belief or disbelief
—very difficult, perhaps impossible or irrelevant.

Frye resists the implications of his position by plausibly claiming
that "beliefs may be held and examined at the same time."[17] It is true
that the kind of examination Frye is engaged in may reflect a desire to
hold on to values that are slipping away. The effect of trying to understand how and why men believed in the past may be an expression of
regret that conditions for belief no longer exist and even a wishfulness
that conditions for belief reestablish themselves. But the nature of
Frye's examination of belief is much too detached and impersonal to
persuade us that he is a believer concerned with the implication of his
actual beliefs or testing their validity in experience.

Frye concludes from the fact of the decline of the humanist ideal
that evaluation and discrimination are now neither possible nor desirable. The humanist ideal depends upon the existence of an elite, a
shared sense of values and norms. Since community and elite have for
all effective purposes disappeared, what remain are literary phenomena to be studied in the manner of a scientist.

> The mediating authority which provides the norms for judging
> and evaluating literature has gone, and consequently each judicial
> critic can speak only for himself, though a merciful provision of
> nature may conceal from him the extent of his self-exposure. He
> may try to believe that his norms and values still exist in some
> kind of Platonic heaven, but even if they did they would not carry
> much authority. Today each intellectual is, socially speaking, in
> the position of Archimedes in Syracuse, who could perhaps move
> the world if he were standing in a different position, but being
> where he is, is able to continue his work only so long as he is un-
> noticed by the murderous louts of Rome.[18]

In the terms of Frye's categories, "the critic *qua* critic is not himself
concerned but detached. His criteria are those of the myth of freedom
[for example, objectivity]."[19] The critic in his capacity as critic must
refuse himself the citizen's impulse to evaluate and discriminate
among poetical objects. His tolerance for all forms and versions of
poetry is in the interest of seeing every poem as part of the total poem
of the imagination. This comes close to a belief in poetry itself, but
such a relation to poetry can be characterized as belief only in the
sense in which one can speak of a belief in life itself. What is absent in
such tolerance is the exclusionary element of belief and commitment.
To believe one must reject as well as accept.

Involved in Frye's view is the historicist's conflation of history and morality. We are asked to accept the decline of the humanist ideal because it has occurred. If we feel that the decline is undesirable, we are nevertheless foolish to resist it, because history has more authority than the ideal. Frye can hardly be characterized as a historicist, but he is engaged in a bit of historicizing here. And the effect of this historicizing is to remove the problem of humanism from the area of will and choice. Frye makes us feel that we are dealing with inevitabilities. Despite my misgivings, I must admit that the tendency of my argument demands sympathy with his position. I said earlier that humanism to some extent is an expression of the state of modern literature with all its strengths and weaknesses. The prospect for a convincing critical humanism is not encouraged by an honest view of modern literature.

For all his modernist skepticism, Frye does not want to give up the humanist ideal altogether. Although Frye disparages views of culture that have "a definite image of a future and perhaps attainable society, for its tendency to purge" the tradition, he endorses the Arnoldian version of culture "which seeks to do away with classes."[20] In Frye's view, neither the present nor the future contains the possibility of such a society, but culture or the imagination is the place where such a society can be "realized" and enjoyed. "The imaginative element of works of art . . . lifts them clear of the bondage of history."[21] The statement raises some interesting unanswered questions. Doesn't Frye's attachment to the Arnoldian ideal imply some purging and selecting, since he must exclude works of literature that are recalcitrant to culture's vision of classlessness? Or if Frye means to encompass all serious works of imagination, what is the principle of conversion or transformation which elicits the classless character of a work from a hierarchical conception of life? And if the imagination lifts us clear of the bondage of history, what is the impact of culture on history and society where we live most of our lives? Frye's predicament is an interesting illustration of the ethical, spiritual element inherent in any vital relation to the literary tradition. He wants scientific detachment in a "discipline" which makes detachment impossible. He is the least narrow, the most humanistically inclined of those obsessed with a need for a literary discipline per se.

Perhaps my refusal to credit Frye's poetic ecumenicism as the expression of belief or concern will seem less arbitrary if we consider what the corpus of "belief" in Frye's system amounts to. It is at once nothing less than the whole literary tradition and something considerably less. For what Frye's system yields is literature demystified into archetypes. The archetypes are disembodied from the individual poems and fictions which contain them. Geoffrey Hartman makes the case incisively.

> The emphasis on demystification also helps with the curious flatness of archetypes as Frye conceives them. Archetypes are not hidden but almost too open—if we do not easily spot them it is because we expect the wrong kind of mystery. Frye does not practice depth criticism or depth psychology; in this he differs absolutely from Jung, and it is impossible to attach an occult or, simply, ontological virtue to the structures he derives from mythology.[22]

Frye's enterprise is a modernist one, in the sense in which I have defined modernism. If one can speak meaningfully of commitment or concern in Frye, it is not to literature but to the system-building which he envisages as the task of criticism. He does speak of an idea or spirit of literary culture, which is liberating and classless, but it is difficult to see what that is apart from the democratic community that any science creates.

Frye's view of criticism is, of course, un-Marxist,[23] except for the fact that both Frye and the Marxists wish to put literary study on a scientific basis. This means not only an exalting of criticism at the expense of literature but also a strong tendency to convert or reduce the literary work to categories other than those proposed by the work itself. "Criticism," the Marxist Terry Eagleton tells us, "is not a passage from text to reader. Its task is not to redouble [sic] the text's self-understanding, to collude with its object in a conspiracy of eloquence. Its task is to show the text as it cannot know itself, to manifest those conditions of its making (inscribed in its very letter) about which it is necessarily silent. It is not just that the text knows some things and not others; it is rather that its very self-knowledge is the construction of a self-oblivion. To achieve such a showing, criticism must break with its ideological pre-history, situating itself outside the space of the text on the alternative terrain of scientific knowledge."[24]

This is resistance to the text with a vengeance. It has a single task: demystification. To discover what the author intended ("the text's self-understanding") or what the text might teach us is to engage in an irrelevant pursuit. The text is an ignorant expression of a reality which it does not know, which it blindly tries to avoid. And yet Marx himself produced texts: what exempts the "true" critic from creating structures of "self-oblivion"? Who has not yearned for the kind of confidence in system exemplified by Marxist criticism—especially in the light of much unpersuasively descriptive and subjective criticism? But the Marxist view, even in its more sophisticated forms, verges on an intolerable condescension toward literature. One wants to know about the conditions of the making of a work of art but not necessarily at the expense of the work. As F. R. Leavis remarks, "Literature will yield to the sociologist, or anyone else, what it has to give only if it is approached as literature."[25]

The effort of literary structuralism (to the extent that one can generalize about such a diverse and inchoate movement) is to treat the linguistic structures of literary works with a view toward defining "the conditions of meaning of those works."[26] The scientific ambition of structuralism can be seen in its undermining the individuality of works and the elimination of the variables of personal and historical motives. The individuality and complexity of the work, its aesthetic and moral intentionality are irrelevant to the structural reality, which the critic can control for the purpose of scientific understanding.

Is there an alternative to the scientific view? No historical or moral law prevents a critic from taking "the position of Archimedes in Syracuse," to use Frye's figure. Is it possible to engage with confidence in the fruitful exercise of a moral criticism which will result in the "doubling" of the self-understanding of the critic-reader as well as of the text's self-understanding? To do so involves a set of convictions in the reader about life and art (as well as whatever literary training he may have) that are not to be gotten on the "terrain of scientific knowledge." One cannot predict whether the work of such a critic will have authority or not, but he may find that he exists in a larger fraternity than he thought. Certainly if he never spoke out he might never learn of the existence of the fraternity. And even if he discovers no such fraternity, he might want to declare himself on principle.

But the question remains, What is the substance of such an alternative? Lionel Trilling's essay "On the Teaching of Modern Literature" is moving and powerful in its implication of resistance, its refusal to be taken in by the destructive element.[27] But what we are left with in a positive sense is little more than ambivalence born of a subtle and intelligent instinct for moral and spiritual survival. I am not sure that

one can go much further at the present time. But I suspect the reason
for this is something to which I have already alluded—our continuing
experience of being intimidated by history. Paradoxically, it is the
authority of history (no longer rational in the Enlightenment sense)
which inhibits our access to the past as a source of values. The critic
feels he must take the past through the mediation of modern literature,
because modern literature has in some sense been validated by history. He feels that he cannot go directly to Augustine or Montaigne or
Pascal or beyond literature to life itself for wisdom, for if he does he
has no validating authority except the insufficiency of his own spiritual intuition.

/ I want to make a distinction between history and pastness because
the failure to do so leads to a gross misconception of the current cultural situation. Are we indeed suffering from the burden of the past as
Walter Jackson Bate, Northrop Frye, and Harold Bloom have claimed
in varying ways?[28] Or is it not rather the pressure of history under the
aegis of progressivism which has become oppressive in its demand for
the constant making of something new? It is not the past with its mul-
tifarious richness that crowds out the present-day artist, that makes
him experience himself as superfluous. It is rather that historical notions of uniqueness, radical changefulness, and difference have de-
flated the values of meditation, gradual development, even repetition.
So strong is the progressivist ethic in our cultural understanding that,
despite the demise of the Enlightenment idea of progress, literary history is imagined as a fierce evolutionary contest, a war against authority, a cannibalization of father figures. Antonin Artaud's modernist
mot d'ordre, "no more masterpieces," implies a culture without masters and fathers. The avant-garde destroys the preceding avant-garde.
It would not think of meditating upon the values of the past, developing, repeating them, though a real literary history might show that
these "conservative" acts have occurred, the manifestos to the contrary notwithstanding.[29]

A more conservative view of the "progress" of art need not devalue
the role of creative originality, which may turn out to be the unin-
tended deviation from a model or tradition that nourishes the originality, since the effect of repetition is never simply repetition. The originality may be the realization of a previously unperceived, undeveloped
potentiality of what exists. The conservative view of creative originality goes against the demand for a deliberate turning away from the

model, a willful insistence on the *sui generis*. One can—indeed should —be original after a genuine exhaustion of existing possibilities.

Contemporary avant-gardism has enforced the authority of history. Instead of creating a sense of freedom and alternative possibility, the avant-gardist legacy has generated an equivalent of conformism and classical constraint. Paradoxically, negative avant-gardist assertions that the novel is finished or that the narrative is no longer possible or that representation is "in" or "out" induce a kind of imitativeness, conformity, and fear of not being with it. Prejudices develop against the reading of certain books, against the seeing of certain pictures, and, conversely, for anything that has the aura or atmosphere or feel of novelty or historical inevitability. (If the avant-garde has the authority of history, it is gained through a certain organization of power in which publishers, galleries, patrons, the media, as well as artists play a role. It is useful to keep in mind the "collective" aspect of the avant-garde. For all the talk about originality and individuality, it is group action that makes a difference.)

The avant-gardist complaint about the burden of the past is somewhat anomalous in America, for some of its greatest artists and intellectuals (for example, Henry James) have experienced the absence of an American past as a burden. Whether the authority of the past is a burden or an opportunity, the fact is that until recently Americans have acted as if creation began with them. So that the avant-gardist attitude has seemed typical rather than adversarial. We have recently entered a period in which we have begun to suffer the fate that all nations suffer. The sense of limitless possibility which seems to have been an American birthright has begun to disappear in the face of harsh historical realities. Perhaps America's coming of age will have the effect of endowing her with a European consciousness of the past.

I am risking confusion by introducing another sense of history into the discussion, a sense which is opposed (though not diametrically) to the progressive conception of history. It is useful nevertheless to have before us this other sense of history, because it enables us to see the paradoxical and impoverishing antihistorical animus of progressive history. Briefly stated, history in the other sense provides a medium for experiencing the rich finiteness of one's being in relation to others, the cognate of society in which one discovers the freedoms and prohibitions that make civilized life possible. In contrast, the progressive view of history not only disvalues the past but also is impatient with the historical medium itself as a constraint on human freedom. The "progressive" conceives of history as a means to an end, which involves or tends to involve the negation of history itself. The end of history is the golden age, an age of perfection in which all the errors of history will be corrected, a time which will cancel time.

If the progressive conception of history limits our view of the possibilities contained in the past, it may be necessary to develop a historical perspective, which without being antiquarian increases the sense of alternative possibilities that reside in the past. In other words, the effect of a meditative history would not be to shrink the past but to enrich it for the present. To this the following caveat should be added: if one opens up history, there should be an insistence on the need for an appropriative relation to the past, a relation which is personal, finite, and selective. Otherwise, one is in the presence of a vast accumulation of inert documents.

THERE IS something to be learned about criticism from the vagaries of political radicalism, for political radicalism is critical of existing society from the point of view of an idea of a better society. And indeed, radicalism and humanism have much in common. Just as radicalism rejects exploitative materialism, humanism regards materialism as a degradation of humane values. In actual fact, however, radicalism and humanism are in opposition to each other, the sense of opposition being stronger on the radical side. Indeed, one favorite characterization of humanism by radicals is "bourgeois humanism," with its implication that humanism is exclusively the cultural expression of the bourgeois class or, more pejoratively, the culture that conceals the predatory reality of capitalism. But the basis for its critique of humanism is paradoxically its own affinity with bourgeois philosophy. Radicalism, particularly in its Marxist version, makes judgments from the point of view of progress. It sees humanism as culturally obsolescent, trying to resist the ineluctable march of history.

Radicalism, too, resists the march of history, when it is inimical to its purposes, but it conceals the resistance—often from itself as well as from others—by invoking a metaphysical conception of history, which it believes will emerge triumphant against the historical phenomena that seem to be against it. For example, fascism despite its horror becomes the *necessary* last stage of capitalism, the threshold of the new socialist society. The elevation of history to the position of supreme principle creates a need for a casuistry to justify morally abhorrent events. It is even possible to justify the bringing on of fascism in the interests of socialism. Or the enrichment of the working class, certainly a desirable condition, becomes inimical to the purposes of history because it weakens the revolutionary will of the working class.

Marxism has an a priori morality, which is not simply historical progress or the logic of history. In insisting that the morality be expressed in historicist form, however, it weakens its critical force. Humanism has not identified its character and fate with history, but in recent years it has not been able to resist very successfully the temptation to do so. To surrender to history would be the complete undoing of humanism.

Perhaps the most dramatic and instructive recent instance of the residual humanist capacity for resisting historicism is the case of Aleksandr Solzhenitsyn, who has affirmed values of justice and decency in a society which has declared them to be obsolete from a historical point of view.[30] The case of Solzhenitsyn is instructive because it shows that only when it feels itself to be irrelevant is humanism powerless in a totalitarian society. It is part of the reality of Russian literature that its humanism was the only dissident politics during the most authoritarian periods of Russian history.[31]

Humanism in a totalitarian society embodies the values of imagination, decency, and justice. If it cannot express those values directly because of censorship, it implies those values through the obliquity of fantasy. Abram Tertz (significantly a pseudonym) has argued in his essay on socialist realism that fantasy is the only realism possible in a totalitarian society, which adopts the idiom of realism to repress the truth about itself. But Solzhenitsyn through an act of incredible courage has shown that it is possible to rescue the idiom of realism from the oppressors. Solzhenitsyn's art is a counterdidacticism to the didacticism of the regime, distinguished only by its devotion to the truth. Both the fantastic route of Tertz and the realist route of Solzhenitsyn are paths of humanism.

Unlike Marxism, humanism may not be able to supply the basis for a new society. But if the new society fails to make a significant positive difference in the quality of life (or if the difference becomes nightmarish), humanist criticism becomes an absolutely necessary function. If the new society lacks the humility and honesty to admit its failures (which is generally the case), the effect of its victory is to destroy, among other things, humanist criticism—unless the Solzhenitsyns and the Tertzes are able to maintain their capacity for resistance.

The repressiveness of a free society is subtler than the obvious oppressiveness of an authoritarian society but, in the sentiment of artists and poets, perhaps more pernicious because more difficult to lay hold of. The ideology of art tends to stress the freedom and autonomy of the imagination from all moral as well as political dictation. If a work of art deals with morality, it either dissolves morality into an aesthetic solution or sees it as an inconclusive element in a dramatic situation. The politics of art is the politics of freedom. At least, this has been the case in free modern societies. But this freedom has tended to be illimitable and vague, so that humanism in its moral aspect and art may be at odds with each other. Art may regard humanism or culture[32] as bourgeois virtue, and humanism may mistrust the self-indulgence and moral irresponsibility and cruelty of art.

But art, for all its antibourgeois sentiment, has certain affinities with modern society: in its stress on innovation and novelty, in the insecurity of its standards. Art has become another item of consumption, which intimidates the person of discrimination. As with the objects of advertising, we are solicited to accept works of art on their own terms—without resistance. We are given a freedom of choice, but without principles of discrimination and the capacity for resistance such freedom is vacuous. It is here that humanism or culture has traditionally found its ground.

I have already indicated humanism's critical relation to political radicalism. Radicalism has a sense of justice and decency which it finds missing from actual society. But it also has its share of resentment and envy to the extent that it is an expression of the feeling of being deprived and excluded.[33] (The worst of it is the desire of the oppressed to become the oppressors.) Without rejecting the gains of democracy,[34] humanism can be a criticism of and corrective to the psychology of resentment, since it is nourished on a lucid poetic sense of the reality of human sentiment and attitude. Nowhere do we get a truer, more profound view of the motivation and human implication of the political life than in the great political novels such as *The Charterhouse of Parma, The Possessed, Nostromo.* Political radicalism is also deficient in its criticism of the quality of life. To the extent that it is born of deprivation, it expresses a desire to have what the possessors have. Political radicals cannot both want and criticize the quality of what they want in good faith. Moreover, those of the possessor class who guiltily reject their possessions are often not adequate critics of the quality of their possessions, because their rejection is wholesale. Humanism here again finds its ground.

Humanism, another term for criticism, may have as its target philistinism or art or radicalism not for the purpose of annihilation but for the reason that constructive discrimination is both possible and desirable. It has its own affinities with each of these targets in its moralizing, its sentiment about art, its critical attitude toward certain established values. Perhaps by "demystifying" the assumptions which have made the traditional functions of humanism seem obsolete (for example, the authority of history in deciding what is and what is not possible) we may learn to exercise them again.

2

English Social Criticism
and the
Spirit of Reformation

In one of his last essays Lionel Trilling argues that the ideal of a shaped self "has all but gone from a contemporary culture whose emphasis, paradoxically enough, is so much on self," because the act of shaping involves the closing out of "other options, other possibilities."[1] The act of shaping and limiting is not inimical to one's freedom, as the advocates of "liberation" would have us believe. The tradition that Trilling superbly exemplified during his entire career associates the very idea of shaping with moral freedom. The belief common to the work of Carlyle, Ruskin, and Arnold is that criticism (the great force of culture and education) has the moral or curative power to bring about benign change in the character and quality of individual and social life. The root of this belief does not lie in political ideology, but in the religious idea—that is, in a version of the religious idea of which literature is a natural expression. It is a version inspired by the long Protestant experience of England.

Neither Luther nor Calvin suggests the optimism implied by the belief in social change or moral progress. If the possibility of salvation is the measure of optimism about the spiritual life, the prospects in the pristine Protestant view are dim indeed. In the Calvinist view the will is completely depraved, the chasm between man and God is absolute; there is not even a *habitus*, as in the Catholic view, for the exercise of free will. And in Calvinism, which powerfully informed English Protestantism, the elect are precious few. In the Protestant view, the man-God relation is a one-to-one relation (albeit an infinitely disproportionate one) unmediated by corporate institutions. In a perspective in which man is completely depraved and God all-powerful, the sense of oppression and the absence of possibility must be overwhelming. But if the perspective changes, if the absence of mediation comes to be experienced primarily as a lessening of the distance between man and God, there develops a sense of possibility about the investment of the human will with divine energies.

English social criticism develops from Protestantism, but it represents a significant departure from its original inspiration. Protestantism would seem a less likely breeding ground for social criticism than Roman Catholicism. In the Roman Catholic view, countervailing religious and social institutions can mitigate the evil in human life, which has its origins in the heart of man. Protestant reactions against institutional abuses lead to a radical mistrust of institutional mediation between man and God and not to a belief in the capacity of man to remake himself or the world in which he lives, because the Protestant is committed in an even more virulent form than is the Catholic to the doctrine of irremediable original sin. Social criticism becomes possible with the advent of the Enlightenment and Romanticism, which sponsor the revival of prelapsarian man in the cultural consciousness. The revival of prelapsarian man focuses the moral imagination on the external circumstances which produced the corruption but which can be overcome through human effort. Paradoxically, Protestantism, with its view of an unmediated man-God relationship, may strengthen the belief in the power of the will to change the world. It may also qualify the Enlightenment belief in social progress with a residual skepticism about the benevolence of the human will. The greatest expression of the confluence between the Enlightenment and Romanticism, on the one hand, and Protestantism, on the other, is the work of Rousseau.

In Rousseau there is a decided imbalance between the Enlightenment and Protestant strains in favor of the belief in prelapsarian man. In the English tradition (represented by Carlyle, Ruskin, and Arnold), the tension between Enlightenment faith and Protestant skepticism is more visible. The English writers preserve Christianity's profound skepticism about the benevolence and efficacy of human will while accepting, though with a certain hesitation, the possibility created by Enlightenment thought of a prelapsarian man restored and a new society as the work not of a transcendent God but of man. The reformation of *every* self and the consequent reformation of society is a wholly modern post-Christian hope. The belief in the immanence of the best self in the world goes strongly against belief in original sin.

But the belief in a best self may be qualified, for example, by a disbelief in the possibility of ever actually attaining perfection. Ruskin's doctrine of the inevitable and even desirable imperfection of everything human is a doctrine of ceaseless striving toward an unreachable perfection. By combining faith in progress with a strong residual belief in original sin, Ruskin's doctrine of imperfection avoids the vanity inherent in the presumption that one has achieved perfection.

The belief that the will has the power to accomplish the conditions for salvation is heretical in the Christian view (both Catholic and Protestant), which asserts divine transcendence and hence would condemn any arrogation of divine power to human will. But the Protestant belief in an unmediated man-God relationship encourages a sentiment about the power of the will that leads to the ethos, if not the doctrine, of arrogation.

The time of the Reformation is an often conscious analogue for the nineteenth century in the mind of the English social critic. The ordeal of Luther that had its issue in a conversion is an analogue to Teufelsdrockh's personal crisis in Carlyle's *Sartor Resartus*, a seminal work in the rich body of English social criticism. Teufelsdrockh's despair is an expression of the spiritual element in his nature, which cannot be satisfied by a materialistic world. He is terribly alone, because the world is alien to him. He cannot accept the view of an "absentee God," the watchmaker God of deism, who set the mechanism going but is no longer needed. The condition of alienation and rejection Teufelsdrockh characterizes as The Everlasting No. It is the prolonged negation before the passage into the Center of Indifference, which is accompanied by the loss of fear and a consequent sense of communion with the spiritual vitality of the universe. At the heart of the Protestant conversion is the capacity for hearing the voice and seeing the light of God. The complete emergence from the crisis in *Sartor Resartus* is The Everlasting Yea which checks the self-inflationary excitement of discovering unmediated spirit. The self, confident in its new powers and yet impressed by its limitations, learns to perform the necessary tasks of the world. Carlyle attaches to the ethic of work the aura of divinity—and of aristocracy. And a principal aim of work is soul or character making. The human drama, Carlyle remarks at the conclusion of "Signs of the Times" (1829), is the slow "reformation" which "each begins and perfects on himself."

Only by ignoring or refusing to take seriously Carlyle's relation to the Protestant ethos can one read his work, as Philip Rosenberg[2] has

recently read it, as a thwarted effort of a man of the left to develop
and arouse revolutionary consciousness. Carlyle's antidemocratic criticism in *Chartism* is taken to be a leftist critique of the liberal tendency
in the movement. Carlyle's mistrust of the working class vote springs,
in Rosenberg's view, not from his contempt for the judgment and will
of the working class but from his disbelief in the effectiveness of the
vote, of the parliamentary system itself. Why then should Carlyle
have supported the Reform Bill of 1832 (which enfranchised the
middle class) and opposed the Reform Bill of 1867 (which enfranchised
the working class)? To attack the parliamentary system per se Carlyle
would have had to be suspicious of both bills. Rosenberg's political
view of Carlyle rests heavily on the populism of *The French Revolution*, on Carlyle's instinctive and knowledgeable compassion for the
suffering of the poor. That such compassion amounts to a leftist politics is highly doubtful. It assumes without argument that unlike Marx,
Carlyle lacked the social and cultural context for the development of
an activist ideology. Carlyle thought he had developed an activist ideology, though it differs from that of Rosenberg and Marx.

The appeal to men to change their hearts so that they can build an
effective social order is seen by Rosenberg as a failure at once personal
and cultural to create a program for changing the world. It is futile
and foolish, Rosenberg suggests, to expect a change of heart. But such
an expectation is precisely at the heart of Christianity and the belief in
conversion. How the experience of conversion can become conta-
giously social is of course an essential question from the political point
of view. The recent experiences of cultural revolution suggest that the
possibility of contagion is very real. Rosenberg's Marxism makes him
doubly insensitive to the power of religious ideas and to their secularized versions.

The Reformation, for Carlyle, is less a historical accident than a
prototype for recurrent renewals of the human spirit. "One often
hears it said that Protestantism introduced a new era, radically different from any the world had ever seen before: the era of 'private judgment,' as they call it." But "there is nothing generically new or peculiar
in the Reformation; it was a return to Truth and Reality in opposition
to Falsehood and Semblance, as all kinds of Improvement and genuine
Teaching are, and have been."[3] The principal virtues of the Carlylean
hero are his Protestant capacity for true seeing of reality and for
speaking and acting sincerely on the basis of this vision.

Carlyle's evocation of a medieval ideal, embodied in *Past and*

Present in the Abbey of St. Edmund, represents a Protestant perspective on the Catholic past.[4] Such a perspective appears less paradoxical if we think of Protestantism, as Ernst Troeltsch does, as prolonging the life of the middle ages. From one point of view, it delays the beginnings of "a free and secular civilization."[5] We miss the truth of Protestantism when we confuse the original Protestant inspiration with the fragmentation of institutional Protestantism into sects in its subsequent history. Herbert Luthy's characterization of the Reformation captures its original inspiration and suggests its prototypical aspects, of which, for example, Carlyle's own work is a perfect expression.

> By attributing to every man the vocation of a whole man, directly responsible before God and capable of hearing His voice, the Reformation smashed a social hierarchy much more than a hierarchy of spiritual values. We would be missing the point of the sermons on the dignity of labor and the castigation of idleness if we forgot their real target: the provocative luxury of the worldly prelates of the Church of the poor, and the dead weight of a monastic world which had become parasitic and depraved, far removed from its former role as center of civilization—not only of a spiritual and intellectual civilization, but of a material and technical one as well—in the vanguard of those ambitious projects for clearing and improving lands that had marked the activity of the communities of the first centuries after the barbarian invasions.[6]

The Reformation was dedicated to restoring the sense of wholeness to human life.

Ruskin's Gothicism is precisely an expression of this feeling for wholeness. Thus he can express his astonishment to a group of businessmen engaged in building a commercial exchange that "the churches and schools are almost always Gothic and the mansions and mills are never Gothic," and can ask in moral bewilderment what the meaning of this modern phenomenon is, for "when Gothic was invented, houses were Gothic as well as churches, and when the Italian style superseded the Gothic, churches were Italian as well as homes."[7] Ruskin assumes that the normal condition of human social life is unity inspired by religion. The "mountain brotherhood of Cathedral and Alp"[8] is one of Ruskin's most powerful images of the organic wholeness of life when it is healthy. The fragmentation of modern life is a symptom of the degeneration of the religious basis of life. One aim of the Reformation is the restoration of the Church Catholic.

The Protestantism of Carlyle and Ruskin is, I think, clear if not always self-evident, though it has its paradoxical moments in Carlyle's medievalizing and Ruskin's Gothicizing. But Arnold's relation to Protestantism is problematic and as a consequence more revealing of its "influence" on the literary imagination of nineteenth century England. Arnold's thought, with all its problems, is our immediate heritage in a way that the thought of Carlyle and Ruskin is not. We have inherited the problem of his extraordinary, some would say extravagant, claims for culture. His view of revolution, of political life generally, expresses something essential in the relation between the English literary mind and the political life.

To claim Arnold for the Protestant conscience is to make a paradoxical claim, for his work is filled with explicit and frequent anti-Protestant assertions. To be sure, much of Arnold's anti-Protestant animus is directed against contemporary institutional Protestantism.[9] But Arnold does not sharply separate Protestantism from its creators. He does not argue that the tradition represents a fundamental betrayal of the original inspiration.

The corruption to which Protestantism is liable consists in the incapacity to perceive spiritual states (man's fallen condition, the resurrection of Christ) as inward states. The heresy proceeds from the need to make the movement of the soul a physical drama in which visible material rewards and punishments necessarily occur. Arnold criticizes versions of this heresy in the religious and the social spheres. In the religious sphere, the object of scorn is the literalism of dogmatic Christianity, the attempt to give to what is essentially poetic and symbolic utterance a fixed "scientific" character. It is the inward meaning, not the putative circumstances of Jesus' resurrection, that is essential. The stress on the symbolic value of Christianity in Arnold and in other higher critics is not motivated by a desire to divert us from the vulnerability of Judaic and Christian texts as history but by a profound belief that the question of literal accuracy is a diversion from the intended meaning of the texts, which concerns the inner movement of the spiritual life.

Arnold characterizes the method of Jesus as "the preliminary labour of inwardness and sincerity in the conscience of each individual man,"[10] and goes on to say that "Protestantism drew it into the light and prominence again,"[11] but did not adequately develop the implications of its view of individual conscience as the basis of the spiritual

life. Luther "pushed the priest aside and brought the believer face to
face with his conscience again."[12] But he substituted for the priest and
the mass "the cardinal point in the Protestant system, justification by
faith." "The miracle of Jesus Christ's atoning sacrifice, satisfying
God's wrath, and taking off the curse from mankind, is the foundation
both of the mass and of the famous Lutheran tenet."[13] Like Catholicism, then, Protestantism in its Lutheran version renders the believer
passive in the presence of an external divine agency. Similarly, Calvinism, in its belief in predestined election, reduces the will to a nul-
lity, the grotesque effect of which is to eliminate the moral element
from religious life. Yet Protestantism has the advantage over Catholicism in that it "possesses in itself the means of deliverance"[14] by virtue
of its Pauline stress on inwardness.

The conception of the Bible and the Christian experience as an inward experience Arnold attributes to Paul and claims for it a fidelity
to the original texts, which Catholic and even Protestant versions of
dogmatic Christianity were subsequently to deny. (Arnold avoids the
arrogation of divine power to human will by defining God as the
"power, *not ourselves*, in which we live and move and have our being,"[15] but it is a power that for all practical purposes works within the
soul of man.) The literary mind with its feeling for symbol and metaphor has an instinctively right understanding of the texts that describe
religious event and experience. Both the making and the reading of
poetry create a habit of perception that redeems the Bible, indeed religious experience, from dogmatizing and literalism. This habit of
symbolic perception is the essential habit of the poetic imagination,
and in Arnold's view, its qualification as a vehicle for religious experience. The conflation of religion and poetry is the inevitable result of
Arnold's radical affirmation of inwardness.

> The future of poetry is immense, because in poetry, where it is
> worthy of its high destinies, our race, as time goes on, will find an
> ever surer and surer stay. There is not a creed which is not
> shaken, not an accredited dogma which is not shown to be ques-
> tionable, not a received tradition which does not threaten to dis-
> solve. Our religion has materialized itself in the fact, in the sup-
> posed fact; it has attached its emotion to the fact, and now the
> fact is failing it. But for poetry the idea is everything; the rest is a
> world of illusion, of divine illusion. Poetry attaches its emotion
> to the idea; the idea *is* the fact. The strongest part of our religion
> today is its unconscious poetry.[16]

The Protestant character of Arnold's social thought is, of course, less apparent than the Protestant character of his religious thought, but it is essential to understanding the motive of his social criticism. In attacking the Hebraism of the middle class (in *Culture and Anarchy*, 1869), he condemns the mindless adulation of the practical material energy of the Industrial Revolution as a diversion from the cultivation of the inner life. The view of industrial activity as Hebraism, the overly strenuous exercise of the practical will, is, of course, not based on any assumptions made fashionable by Max Weber and R. H. Tawney about the connection between religion and the rise of capitalism.[17] If Arnold could be said to have intuited such a connection, the basis for it was an intellectual sentiment about how the spiritual or inner life is corrupted when it is externalized. Like the dogmatism of institutional Christianity, the activity of industrial England represents a displacement of valuable human energy to unworthy corruptive objects.[18] Unlike Carlyle, who was concerned to imagine alternative materializations or externalizations of the spiritual life as a basis for a critique of mechanical civilization, Arnold's preoccupation with inwardness did not impel him to construct models of positive materializations. But it would be a mistake to see the pejorative idea of materialization in "The Study of Poetry" as including all externalization. In his acute awareness of the disjunction between the inner life (in its ideal form if not its actual condition) and the outer social and political life of man, Arnold was conscious of the need for a political and social life adequate to and expressive of the best self.

Arnold does not confine his criticism to the Industrial Revolution. His principal target in "The Function of Criticism at the Present Time" (1864) is the French Revolution. In that essay the revolutionary will is seen as an exemplification of the vicious presumption of the will generically to assert itself, to satisfy itself in the external practical sphere before it has achieved the condition of grace (the full and harmonious development of all human faculties) which would make its exertions valuable and desirable. Arnold's Protestantism is implicit and I think unmistakable in his excursus on Joseph Joubert's formula "Force till right is ready."

> (Force and right are the governors of this world; force till right is ready.) *Force till right is ready;* and till right is ready, force, the existing order of things, is justified, is the legitimate ruler. But right is something moral, and implies inward recognition, free

assent of the will; we are not ready for *right*—right, so far as we are concerned, *is not ready*—until we have attained this sense of seeing it and willing it. The way in which for us it may change and transform force, the existing order of things, and become, in its turn, the legitimate ruler of the world, should depend on the way in which, when our time comes, we see it and will it. Therefore for other people enamored of their own newly discerned right, to attempt to impose it upon us as ours, and violently to substitute their right for our force, is an act of tyranny, and to be resisted. It sets at naught the second great half of our maxim, *force till right is ready*. This was the grand error of the French Revolution; and its movement of ideas, by quitting the intellectual sphere and rushing furiously into the political sphere ran, indeed, a prodigious and memorable course, but produced no such intellectual fruit as the movement of ideas of the Renascence, and created, in opposition to itself, what I may call an *epoch of concentration.* [19]

Force, "the existing order of things," can be overcome, not through Jacobin precipitousness but through the preparation of the will for right action. But when is right ready, when is it prepared to act? The moment for true action is the confluence of will and grace—or willing and [true] seeing, as Arnold puts it. [20] The habit of activity when not governed by a relation to things as they are (a relation that presupposes a condition of grace) becomes spiritually impoverished and grotesque. It is interesting to note in this connection Arnold's quotation from Bishop Butler in *St. Paul and Protestantism* on the exercise of the will in relation to religious matters: "Men are impatient and for precipitating things." [21]

"The Function of Criticism at the Present Time" is a cautionary essay about the dangers of precipitous action, that is, the premature exercise of the will. In the figure of Edmund Burke, it offers a positive example of right action, an example that is supposed to make plausible Arnold's idea of revolution "by due course of law." [22] Arnold regarded himself as a political liberal and was unwilling to disown the ideas of the French Revolution. The failure of the revolution in Arnold's view was that it aborted the ripening of an order of ideas and hence "produced no such intellectual fruit as the movement of ideas of the Renascence." It is necessary to suppress the image of Burke as an antirationalist conservative to appreciate Arnold's appropriation of Burke to the liberal tradition. Arnold views Burke as living in a world remote from either English Liberalism or English Toryism, "the world of ideas." Burke's responsibility to ideas, to his own ideas, permitted him toward the end of his life to take a view of the French Revolution different from, though not contradictory to, the view that determined "his fierce struggle with the French Revolution." Within his own logic, or better, his own mode of thought, Burke had discovered the conditions which would give legitimacy to a genuinely revolutionary change. Arnold quotes from Burke's *Thoughts on French Affairs*.

> "If a great change is to be made in human affairs, the minds of men will be fitted to it; the general opinions and feelings will draw that way. Every fear, every hope will forward it; and then they who persist in opposing this mighty current in human affairs, will appear rather to resist the decrees of Providence itself, than the mere designs of men. They will not be resolute and firm, but perverse and obstinate."[23]

A revolution may create a new organic reality, which could only be opposed through a perverse rationalistic exercise of the will. Arnold characterizes this movement of Burke's thought as the "return of Burke upon himself," "one of the finest things in English literature, or indeed in any literature." Burke is for Arnold an example of the responsible exercise of political reason, which produces a revolution "by due course of law."

The motive for Arnold's admiration of Burke is clear enough: Arnold is here valuing intellectual integrity and honesty rare in political life. But Burke's (and Arnold's) position on the French Revolution requires some clarification. To regard the making of the revolution as an exercise in perversity but its consequences in the creation of a new society as morally and necessarily acceptable would seem to diminish the role of will to the level of political apathy, for in both cases what is valued is the absence of willing something new into existence. This cannot be what either Arnold or Burke intended. Arnold's attack on Calvinism (to shift back for the moment to the field of theology) is partly grounded in his view that the materialization of the idea of predestination makes the will to salvation for all practical purposes impotent.

What then is Arnold advocating? I think that an answer to this question depends on an understanding of the significance of the organic metaphor for society that one finds in Arnold and the other great social critics of the nineteenth century. Burke, Coleridge, Carlyle, and Ruskin provide us with the richest imagination of organic society.[24]

The aura that attaches to organic society in their writings derives, I think, from its acquisition of divine attributes. Society for Carlyle, for instance, is the medium and the object of worship. Paradoxically, the exaltation of society occurs at a moment when its historical condition is one of mechanistic alienation and abstraction.

It would seem a strange therapy to exalt society at a moment when actual society has been shattered into warring atoms, until we remember that the great English social critics are heirs of the Enlightenment and believers—though, as we shall see, equivocal believers—in progress. They see the ruins of religious orthodoxy wrought by Enlightenment rationalism as irreparable and they share the Enlightenment belief that society is the arena for man's moral and spiritual development. But their distinction and greatness lies in their resistance to the course of development that society has taken in the nineteenth century. They do not believe in the inevitability of the particular historical development which has determined the character of nineteenth century society. In utopian fashion they attempt to conceive an alternative society which externalizes "the best self," to use Arnold's phrase. In short, they wish to overcome the disjunction between man and society which they perceive to be the essential human condition at the present moment by conceiving society as expressive of individual life, when its faculties are in a state of harmony and health. Carlyle's writings, to be sure, leave the impression that the individual must lost his identity within an organic society. But the impression is misleading. Rather, Carlyle and the others wish to transcend the conception of individuality as separate from society, not by remaking the individual to conform to an abstract model of society but by remaking society to express the full moral and intellectual character of individual life. The idea of a real living organism is transferred to society, and the insistence on its naturalness is intended to dramatize its uncoercive character.

The ambiguity of change (is it repressive or liberating, progressive or reactionary?) is unresolvable. To change something is to act against the freedom of the given; the best self "tyrannizes" over the ordinary self. But to protect the freedom of the given may be to fix and petrify life. Beyond the dichotomies of repression and liberation, progress and reaction, is the question of what is desirable and valuable for a human life. This was the principal question for the social critics of the nineteenth century.

In *The Rise and Fall of the Man of Letters* John Gross suggests that Carlyle's organicist standard for judging society is the work of art.

> The analogy is dangerous, since social cohesion can never be as absolute as artistic unity; it will always be easy for those who dream of restoring an organic society to despair, and tempting for them to assume that a deliberately imposed uniformity will come to much the same thing in the end. A romantic is properly concerned with integrity—the integrity of a personality, the integrity of a poem. But politics is the art of rough, very rough approximations; and ever since Plato, the desire and pursuit of the whole has usually turned out, taken far enough and translated into political terms, to be a first-class recipe for totalitarianism.[25]

But the organic metaphor is at least as old as Aristotle, who conceived the whole of life (nature, politics, ethics, and art) as governed by laws of organic development. Art is not the source of the organic idea, nor is totalitarianism a necessary result of a belief in an organic society. Totalitarian societies may use the rhetoric of organicism to justify themselves, but their actual model is the machine.

The historical reality of the organic society has been a much debated issue. In Raymond Williams's *The Country and the City*, we have close to a magisterial effort to arbitrate claims for the reality of organic society at any given moment in the past several centuries of English history. Williams is clearly suspicious of sentimental falsifications of rural life and nature, and he marshals persuasive evidence against idealized versions of the organic society of any particular past. For example, rural capitalism may have "choked" a brook, may have caused the hollow cry of the bittern and the "unvaried lapwing cries," as in the following passage from Goldsmith's *The Deserted Village:*

> One only master grasps the whole domain,
> And half a tillage stints thy smiling plain,
> No more thy glassy brook reflects the day,
> But choked with sedges, works its weedy way;
> Along thy glades, a solitary guest,
> The hollow-sounding bittern guards its nest,
> Amidst thy desert walks the lapwing flies,
> And tires their echoes with unvaried cries.

But, Williams reminds us, such "destruction" was accompanied by an increased use and fertility of the land. Williams distinguishes between the "desert landscape" of the imaginative process and the productiveness of the social process, and sees the poet's lament as symptomatic of the "social condition" of the poet who is independent and honored in a pastoral economy as he is not in a society of wealth and fashion.

According to Williams, the totalizing rhetoric of Goldsmith and of the romantic poets (Blake, Wordsworth, and Shelley) is misleading, as when they isolate "humanity and community into the idea of culture."[26] It results in the reification of an abstraction.

> A necessary social criticism is then directed to the safer world of past: to a world of books and memoirs, in which the scholar can be professionally humane but in his own real world either insulated or indifferent. But also, and more important, this kind of critique of capitalism enfolds social values which, if they do become active, at once spring to the defence of certain kinds of order, certain social hierarchies and moral stabilities, which have a feudal ring but a more relevant and more dangerous contemporary application. Some of these "rural" virtues in twentieth-century intellectual movements leave the land to become the charter of explicit social reaction: in the defence of traditional property settlements, or in the offensive against democracy in the name of blood and soil.[27]

Williams is not content simply to demystify. He values the positive critical function of idealization, which he translates almost ritualistically into the phrase "structure of feeling." And yet he cannot give a lucid account of the value of idealization, because he does not allow sufficiently for the autonomy of the ideal. Whatever the source of the ideal, it can become by its presence a powerful dramatization of what is absent, a useful "fiction" for social change. The "organic society" remains viable as an idea, so long as it is not distorted, as it need not be, by nefarious political motives. This is not to say that the "organic society" may not be affected by its origins or that its abstractness does not become a problem when it is severed from its origins.[28] It is simply to argue against a polarization of possibilities which either grants complete autonomy to an idea or denies it any autonomous freedom. Williams himself tries to occupy the intermediate position I am suggesting, but the recent Marxizing tendency of his work seems to make the argument for autonomy more difficult for him to articulate. And yet the argument must be made: if not, where will the "historically liberating" ideas come from, to use Williams's phrase.

In a discussion of Marx's early work, *The German Ideology*, Kenneth Burke is most illuminating on the theme of idealization or mystification. Burke is suspicious of the Marxian passion for demystification because of its assumption that the ideals of a people at a given time are the simple abstractions that they become in historical retrospect. He argues that ideals should be regarded as a title of conditions, fully though tacitly understood by those committed to the ideals. For example, those committed to the god-term "honor" implicitly understood the "tangle of relationships (including a clear recognition of the material privileges and deprivations that went with a given structure)."[29] Burke is incisive in pointing out the misleading character of the term "mystification" insofar as it necessarily implies self-deception in the holders of ideals. However, the fact that the complex conditions of the simple title are only tacitly understood and therefore uncriticized justifies the activity of demystification. The risk of demystification is that the exposure of the invidiousness and corruption that may be concealed by the term evaporates the term as a possibility for future use.

The effect of a skeptical view of idealization is salutary, when the habit has been to see the ideal or idea in an *intellectual* historical vacuum—as has often been the case with Arnold. The habit is encouraged by Arnold himself in his failure, for example, to be sensitive to the problem of realizing his own abstract utopian idea (despite his remarkable Burkean sensitivity to the problem of realizing Jacobin ideas). Thus when he makes the state the expression of the best self, he legitimately incurs suspicion in answering the question, "How can you be certain that reason will be the only quality which will be embodied in it?" with an almost Jacobin insouciance, "you cannot be certain of it undoubtedly, if you never try to bring the thing about."[30] Arnold is willing to take the risk, not because he would suffer despotism gladly, but because he is enamored of the utopian possibility of "the action of the collective nation carry[ing] naturally great publicity, weight and force of example" in the interests of right reason. Arnold here betrays a profound inconsistency, one might say disingenuousness, in his conservatism, which is to present an ideological position in the guise of an organic traditionalism, a sort of Jacobinism with reactionary motives.

Arnold's evocation of the state as the administrator of culture (through the agency of the church) suggests the conservative tradition in Germany, in which the state is raised to the status of deity. My own view is that though Arnold's feeling for the state is conservative, expressive of an unreflective sentiment about law and order, it is an alien element in the logic of his view of culture, whose only coerciveness should exist in the persuasiveness of reason. The institution appropriate to culture is the school or the university, not the state.

One way of perceiving Arnold's confusion is by employing against it Ferdinand Tonnies's celebrated distinction between *Gemeinschaft* and *Gesellschaft*, which translates as community and society. *Gemeinschaft* is the organic community, the creation of the natural will and the source of all that is creative and formative in human activity ("akin to art"). *Gesellschaft* is society, the creation of the rational will and the source of man's commercial and political life. Setting aside the invidiousness of the distinction (Why can't commerce and politics be conceived as creative activities?), the value of the distinction is that it enables us to see that Arnold was conflating, if not confusing, considerations of natural community with those of society. Tonnies himself conceives the possibility of the "reconstruction of *gemeinschaft*, which would overcome the economic individualism of *gesellschaft*." Whether this reconstruction can be achieved by incorporating *gesellschaft* in a new way or by destroying it is unclear. Whatever the case may be, the regeneration of society according to the model of community (in Arnold's terms, the state according to that of the best self) is extremely problematical.

Arnold has no "theory" of social change (to use the contemporary idiom), only an evangelical hope. Like the other great social critics, he is projecting social or political externalizations of what he considers to be the best self. When he criticizes the behavior of a class, as he does extensively in *Culture and Anarchy* (he takes all classes to task), he is not led to see the behavior as *necessarily* exemplifying a law of social development or social conflict. His vantage point is moral and utopian. It is within the moral and rational powers of men to will the best self into existence, which of course means to externalize it in the social and public spheres. The emergence of the best self is not a predictable social phenomenon. Conversely, people do not have to act according to their class interest. They do have the capacity to transcend their ordinary class selves and be true to their best selves.

Arnold's utopianism, that is, his extrapolation of the good society from the best self, produces a contradiction in his treatment of class. In *Culture and Anarchy* Arnold makes his most powerful appeal to the best self of every member of all the classes (barbarians, philistines, populace) to rise to a condition of social understanding and harmony

"void of interest." The logic of such an appeal suggests a classless society rather than a harmony of classes, which Arnold seems character-
istically to advocate.[31] In his use of class, Arnold failed to realize that,
as Lionel Trilling puts it, "class is a category whose very essence is interest; take away the idea of special interest and in its usage in modern
society, 'class' ceases to have any meaning."[32] It is not possible to ask a
barbarian or philistine or member of the populace to act according to
his best self without at the same time asking him to "*un*class" himself.
Arnold's best self is theoretically universal and its environment is culture. But sometimes he seems to envisage a best aristocratic or best
middle class or best working class self, which may be the basis for his
thinking of society as a harmony of classes.[33] This equivocation in
Arnold between the idea of class harmony and the idea of classlessness
results from an unwillingness to allow the implications of his utopian
conception to disturb the fundamental economic relationships of
actual society. Arnold remains attached to the existing order of
property relationships.

Arnold avoids the perception of self-contradiction in his work because of the individualist basis of his social thinking, which, excepting
Marx, he shares with the other great social critics of the nineteenth
century. Though Carlyle, Arnold, and Ruskin see man as a social
creature, they do not, like Marx, deduce individual being from the
social matrix. Rather they project an ideal society from their sense of
individual life in a state of health.

The remaking of society presupposes the conversion of the self from
its condition of alienation and sickness to its "original" condition of
health. The myth of paradise and the fall is implicit in English social
criticism. There are no historical laws of social development independent of the spiritual life of the members of society. The dynamics
of group or class conflict become irrelevant to the drama being enacted by the individual in his externalization into society. The man-
God relation becomes the man-society relation in the nineteenth century.

The Protestant basis of their social thinking enables Arnold, Carlyle, and Ruskin to imagine alternative social realities. For example, in
appealing to a morality of heroic and self-sacrificing behavior, Ruskin
sets himself against the exponents of political economy, the dismal
science, which regards selfishness as at once necessary and desirable.
On the analogy of the expected heroic behavior of the soldier whose

primary imperative is to be willing to give his life for his country or of
the behavior of the ship's captain who "is bound to be the last man to
leave his ship in case of wreck," Ruskin expects the manufacturer, "in
any commercial crisis or distress . . . to take the suffering of it with his
men, and even to take more of it for himself than he allows his men
to feel."[34] The primary imperative of the merchant is to feed society,
not take profit. Ruskin can assert this morality without embarrassment, because his Protestant conscience empowers him to reject the
authority of history in its pernicious development in the nineteenth
century. Ruskin can speak and write as if the degenerative process implied by the rampant egotism of industrial life were reversible—and
reversible by an exercise of the moral will.

For Arnold the work of reformation will be done by a "saving remnant," analogous to the apostles that spread the gospel of Christ. The
"saving remnant" is the subject of "Numbers," an essay which can
easily be construed as an attack on democracy and a plea for elitism.
The Christian analogue, however, puts the idea of the "saving remnant" in a truer perspective. The "saving remnant" is the expression of
a perception to which the political distinctions of democracy and elitism are finally irrelevant. The work of the spirit (even, one might say,
in behalf of the democratic idea) is always the work of a heroic or
saintly few, willing to risk all for the sake of their idea. The "saving
remnant" is self-selectively recruited from all classes, though Arnold's
sociological intuition and his own class bias lead him, despite the severity of his strictures, to a belief that the future belongs to the philistines. In "A French Eton" Arnold envisages a redeemed society in
terms of a "cultured, ennobled, transformed middle class" and a
working class provided with "a practicable passage to . . . the joy and
beauty of life."[35]

The appeal to the Protestant conscience would be very difficult, and
probably inefficacious, if Protestantism did not have enormous prestige in England, its declining authority notwithstanding. Thus Arnold
doubts the pessimism of Bishop Butler about the supposedly dimin-
ished status of religion in English life in the following terms:

> One cannot but ask oneself, when one considers the steadiness of
> our country through the French Revolution, when one considers
> the power and prevalence of religion, even after every deduction
> has been made for what impairs its strength,—the power and
> prevalence, I say, of religion in our country at this hour,—one

cannot but ask oneself whether Butler was not overdesponding, whether he saw the real state of things, whether he did not attach overimportance to certain workings which he did see.[36]

In noting the critical response on the continent to *Literature and Dogma*, Arnold elicits the differences in attitude toward religion in nineteenth century England, France, and Italy and discovers that England alone has remained religious in its sentiment, notwithstanding the inroads of reason and the idea of progress. And Arnold attributes the survival of the sentiment in England to Protestantism.

> Liberal opinion tends, as we have seen, to treat religion and Christianity as identical; if one is unsound, so is the other. Especially, however, does liberal opinion show this tendency among the Latin nations, on whom Protestantism did not lay hold; and it shows most among those Latin nations on whom Protestantism laid hold least, such as Italy and Spain.[37]

Arnold's assertion of course does not prove "the power and prevalence" of religion in nineteenth century England. But it is, I think, very difficult to account for the persuasiveness of the idiom in which these social critics wrote without believing that an audience was prepared to receive what they had to say. Without the Protestant religion (the religion of Wesley and the evangelicals as well as high Anglicanism), no such audience would have existed. The "steadiness" of England through the revolution would not have been possible if the Protestant conscience (despite its corruptions) did not possess the principle of "self-correction and self-adjustment" which complements its powerful sentiment about human fallibility.

The great French historian Elie Halevy has argued that the evangelical movement imbued the elite of the working class with "at least an outward respect for the Christian social order"[38] that effectively undermined any impulse toward violent revolution. Moreover, the atheism of the Enlightenment philosophy embodied by the French Revolution profoundly offended English Protestants of all persuasions. "The modern Babylon was no longer Rome but Paris, Anti-Christ no longer the Pope, but Voltaire."[39] The threat that Napoleonic France posed to England no doubt helped consolidate national sentiment against the revolution. But the strength of this antirevolutionary attitude depended upon an effective reformism, which would lessen or eliminate the necessity for revolution. Halevy, for example, shows how William

Wilberforce's successful campaign against the slave trade was linked to his anti-Jacobinism. As a reformer, he had credit as an antirevolutionary.

THE BELIEF that self and world can be changed, which suffused English literature from Carlyle to Lawrence, is the expression of what might be called literary Protestantism[40]—literary, because it insists on the symbolic character of a religious event, not from a sense that religious authority per se is declining and that one must therefore rescue values that are threatened with extinction, but from a sentiment that the literary mind discloses the true power of Christianity. What the literary mind discloses is Christianity's perennial contemporaneity, its capacity to apply itself to new situations. The literary mind instinctively grasps that "the language of the Bible is fluid, passing and literary, not rigid, fixed and scientific."[41] It understands that judgment "in a fair mind . . . with fresh knowledge," is the result of a gracious and spontaneous relation to the subject and not the result of a "turmoil of controversial reasonings."[42] Reason that is the fruit of letters consists of "flexibility, perceptiveness and judgment,"[43] not the systematic intellect that produces rationalism. The flexibility, perceptiveness, and judgment of the literary mind has its counterpart in religious wisdom.

How convincing is this claim? In his essay on Arnold and Pater, T. S. Eliot argues that Arnold and Pater had reduced religion to morals and art respectively. Viewing the matter from an orthodox Anglican point of view, Eliot is unqualifiedly contemptuous of their alleged "reductiveness." Neither culture (as an embodiment of the moral life) nor art can give satisfaction to the religious appetite.

> "The power of Christianity has been in the immense emotion which it has excited," Arnold says, not realizing at all that this is a counsel to get all the emotional kick out of Christianity one can.
>
> The effect of Arnold's religious campaign is to divorce Religion from Thought.
>
> The total effect of Arnold's philosophy is to set up Culture in the place of Religion, and to leave Religion to be laid waste by the anarchy of feeling.[44]

Eliot's judgment of the alleged thoughtlessness of Arnold's religion and the unintelligible vagueness of his doctrine is unjust and reductive. Poetry and religion were for Arnold irreducible terms, involved in a mutually nourishing symbiotic relation. If we need a comprehensive term to express the relationship the term is "spiritual health." Arnold's concern was to find a remedy for what he called "this strange disease of modern life." It may be argued that health, even spiritual health, is a reductive term for religious life, for it converts questions of sin and virtue to matters of therapy. It is immensely difficult for a modern writer to avoid this, especially if religion is not in a flourishing state and if he does not have, as Eliot apparently had, a fully articulated dogmatic Christianity behind him. I would maintain, however, that there is a richness in therapeutic categories and sufficient analogical closeness to see the therapeutic as more illuminating than reductive. As the recent work of Philip Rieff and Erik Erikson has shown, the psychological element is close to the surface of the conviction of sin and the quest for salvation. Eliot's dogmatic posture prevents him from exercising the sympathy necessary for appreciating the strengths as well as the weaknesses of Arnold's position.

There are difficulties nevertheless in Arnold's view. Repelled by the literalizing of the religious "fact," Arnold failed to understand the power of the symbol at the historical moment when it was both fact and symbol—that is, symbolic without being fictive. Hell, purgatory, and paradise are "inventions" that reveal the real spiritual geography of the cosmos—in Dante's intention and in the understanding of his readers. Arnold betrays this failure of perception in his insistence on converting religious text, event, and experience into "significance." Carlyle, who shared with Arnold an acute understanding of the symbolic character of poetry as well as of real action and event, nevertheless insisted on the facticity of the symbol. He understood that faith depended upon nonallegorical conviction about the reality of the objects of belief.

> Hell, Purgatory, Paradise: these things were not fashioned as emblems; was there, in our Modern European Mind, any thought at all of their being emblems! Were they not indubitable awful facts; the whole heart of man taking them for practically true, all Nature everywhere confirming them? So it is always in these things. Men do not believe in Allegory. The future Critic, whatever his new thought may be, who considers this of Dante to have been all gotten up as an Allegory, will commit one sore mistake![45]

To insist on the figurative character of religious symbolism at the expense of its facticity is to weaken its authority by opening it to multiple interpretations and consequently to skepticism. The revulsion from the spiritually vacuous alternative of mechanical civilization produces an inordinate preoccupation with inwardness. This is the unsurmounted legacy of both Romanticism and Protestantism. In the preface to the collection of poems that contains "Empedocles on Etna" (1853), Arnold laments the modern condition in which suffering finds no release in action. The distinction of Greek tragedy in Arnold's view is the way the action of the play provides a cathartic discharge for the suffering of the hero and the spectator. The occasion for Arnold's remarks is the self-acknowledged failure of the poet of "Empedocles on Etna" to overcome the modern habit of conceiving inhibited, unexternalized suffering. Despite Arnold's subsequent effort, his imagination never found the releasing mechanism, and he remains very much the modern artist of the buried life.

To the extent that it affects the literary imagination, the continual dwelling on significance produces a kind of sentimentality. The happy ending of Victorian fiction is a case in point. The happy ending is not to be understood simply as an expression of nineteenth century optimism or as an attempt to please the middle class reader. It is a direct consequence of the secularization of the Christian imagination. The Christian appetite for salvation is strong in the novels of Dickens and George Eliot, for instance, but heaven has vanished from the landscape. So the only place for the saved soul in the Victorian imagination is a utopian space in the real world of daily life: a Bleak House or a Poyser farm in which those who live happily ever after insulate themselves from the hard facts of the real world. From the aesthetic point of view, the happy ending and the light-filled utopian space of, say, Bleak House is something of an embarrassment. It is false, a sort of infantile wish-fulfillment. Yet the happy ending is too deep in Victorian imagination to be so peremptorily dismissed. It expresses the need for literalism that is supposed, according to Arnold, to show the corruption of the religious imagination in the nineteenth century. The appetite for salvation is a desire for a real place where it may occur, and it presses writer and reader into a conspiracy to imagine such a place, though it has no existence in the world we know. Indeed, it would seem that the literalism of the orthodox Christian imagination has a distinct advantage over the literalism of the secularized Christian imagination. The orthodox view in *The Divine Comedy* enables Dante to view the actual world in a true light—as a vale of tears in which redemption is impossible. The seeing soul knows with the hard-headedness of the realist that salvation is not possible in this world. He is able to distinguish beatitude and wordly success. The two pursuits occur in distinctly different realms. No fulfillment on earth is comparable to a fulfillment in heaven. Arnold's "higher critical" conversion of religious fact into "moral significance" invites a confusion of earthly fulfillment and spiritual transcendence which culture is presumably combating.

One of the interesting incidental perceptions in Eliot's essay on Arnold and Pater is in Eliot's noting that Pater's aestheticism is in the line of Arnold, Ruskin, and Carlyle and not in the line of Flaubert and Baudelaire. Art, for an English aesthete, is never art for art's sake; it is, as Pater himself declared, a protest "against [the] predominance of machinery."[46] Art is not a condition of alienation but an instrument of social change. Arnold's appeal to the best self springs from a confidence in the poetic authority of religious experience and the religious authority of poetic experience. The feeling that the conversion of the inner man can possibly change the world and that literature can be an agency for such conversion is a phenomenon of modern English literature from Carlyle to Lawrence and it is a phenomenon peculiar to the Protestant temperament. In contrast, the sentiment about the social powerlessness of art is a fact in the cultural life of Catholic countries. One must turn to an Irish writer like Joyce, whose alienation from the English "community" urged him to French and European affinities, in order to find the condition of aesthetic alienation in English letters. Joyce's greatest admiration, appropriately enough, was for Flaubert.

Expressed as a virtue, the aesthetics of a Flaubert or a Baudelaire or a Joyce is a declaration of the purity of art, its freedom from contaminating moral and social concerns. As a vice, it is an expression of essential Catholic hopelessness about improving the world.[47] Joyce's celebration of the artistic imagination in *A Portrait of the Artist as a Young Man* implies escape from society and a merely personal liberation. But even the personal liberation of Stephen proves to be a delusion in *Ulysses*. This is not to say that Joyce has no feeling for the things of the world; his feeling for them is very powerful. Joyce, like Flaubert before him, is content, in D. H. Lawrence's words, "to make the perfect statement in a world of corruption . . . however corrupt the stuff of life may be." Unlike Lawrence, whose work has the inspiration of the social critical tradition of the nineteenth century, he does not envisage the act of imagination as involved in remaking the real world.[48] The triumphant modernism of Flaubert, Joyce, and Eliot,[49] among others, signals the failure of the critical spirit to prevail in our cultural life. Its passive nihilism is the despairing side of the contemporary sense of "liberation" that, in Trilling's words, "demands" a limitlessness in our personal perspective "analogous to the felt fluidity of the contemporary world." The paradoxical relationship between the sense of limitlessness and moral impotence is an old truth, which we may yet relearn.

3

The Reality of
Disillusion in T. S. Eliot

To ASSOCIATE Eliot with the anticritical tendency of modernism, as I intend to do, is paradoxical, if not perverse. After all, Eliot has been a major, perhaps *the* major critic of his time, and he has been explicitly engaged in social or cultural criticism. What then do I mean by making such an association?

One of the conditions of humanist criticism, as I understand it, is the implicit conviction that the critical act *shapes* as well as perceives its object. In order to have such conviction, criticism must be inspired by an order of values immanent, if not actual, in the world. The secularized Protestantism of Carlyle, Ruskin, and Arnold contains a dynamic principle of change counter to the mechanical principle that prevails in the world. Nothing in Eliot's social criticism persuades us that he is in possession of such a principle. To be sure, he laments the disappearance of a genuinely Christian society, and he is not utterly hopeless about its reappearance (as a Christian he would be committing the sin of despair if he were). But the disjunction between the idea of a Christian society and "the neutral society" which he claims is our present condition is so complete that whatever insights into the malaise of modern life he possesses seem unredeemed by a substantial sense of what a Christian society might mean for the modern world. In his criticism there is no dialectical interplay between Christianity and the modern world.

Eliot sporadically disavows any reversionary ambition. Medieval society is, he knows, irretrievable. But despite assertions that *seem* to envisage a Christianity responsive to the conditions of modern life, the actual imagination of the possibility of new supersessions is absent. Even the hope that Christianity "will probably continue to modify itself, as in the past, into something that can be believed in" is severely mitigated by the pessimistic view that "the majority live below the level of belief or doubt. It takes application and a kind of genius to believe anything, and to believe *anything* (I do *not* mean merely to believe in some 'religion') will probably become more and more difficult as time goes on."[1] Eliot explicitly rejects the alternative open to him of trying "to adapt Christian social ideals" to the modern world. He characterizes such an alternative as "a mere doctrine of expediency,"[2] and would seem to intend for Christianity a much more active role in shaping and determining social forms, rather than the passivity indicated by the term adaptation. Christianity remains for Eliot an institution ideally able to transform and save the world. Paradoxically, the actual imagination of Christianity as a transforming power is absent in the work of Eliot. William Chace's observation that "Eliot's political interests [one should characterize them as spiritual and moral as well] lay neither in disposing human energy toward the solution of social problems . . . nor in liberating human energy from social confines, but in showing how men failed to achieve a society in which certain religious values could be appreciated" seems exactly right.[3]

I have been arguing that our current malaise can be in part understood as paralysis resulting from an intimidation by "the logic of history." It might seem then that Eliot's insistence on a Christian idealism in defiance of secularism and rationalism is to be commended—an exceptional and salutary instance of criticism in the modern age. But the resistance to "the logic of history" should not entail an indifference to historical reality. It is one thing to hypostatize a historical tendency as an ironclad logic to which there is no choice but abject surrender. It is another thing to develop a healthy respect for genuine historical tendencies so as to discover in the interstices within and between these tendencies real and possible freedoms.

The man of principle can always score easy points against the compromiser. But "principle" may be a deceptive term, concealing rigidity of purpose, an unadventurous (dare I say cowardly?) aversion to the possibility of embodying the principle in real life—for embodiments always entail modifications of the principle. It is a delicate matter to decide between the integrity of genuine compromise (which may be involved in secularization, the necessary accommodation of spirit to the new forms of modern life) and trimming, but it will not do simply to make an automatic appeal to principle.

Eliot's sentiment about the past and tradition is ahistorical—he is unconcerned with the modern life of institutions he values. To advocate a Christian society one must acknowledge and examine the actual life of Christianity in the modern world. If a large portion of Christianity has been secularized, the insistence on a dogmatic Christianity as the religious basis of a society including Christians and non-Christians alike must seem quixotic, to say the least.

Eliot's idea of a Christian society is an abstraction. It is either an expression of nostalgia for a lost order or a ritualistic attachment to a dogma assumed to be true despite all the vicissitudes of history. The mere assumption of the existence of Christianity without a corresponding need to flesh it out anew gives an impression of spiritual aridity, as commentators have noted. The loss of faith is simply judged, not understood.

The sentiment of resignation, verging on hopelessness, which is never fully admitted, is, as I have already remarked, a characteristic of the modern Catholic imagination. Of course, Eliot's heritage and temperament (which he reminds us in his essay on Goethe is Calvinist and Puritan respectively) suggests that one must qualify Eliot's affiliation with the Catholic imagination, so as to understand how it differs, for example, from that of Joyce and Flaubert.[4] He does not take a profane pleasure in the beauty of the world. The propensity toward blasphemy, so strong in Joyce, is absent from Eliot. His severely moralizing habit, which would make for solemnity if it were not for a superb self-irony akin to Christian humility, links him with the great Victorians.

It would be a distortion to separate Eliot radically from the tradition of English social criticism of the nineteenth century. The lines of connection, the affinities, even the oppositions suggest that Eliot belongs in an important way to the company of Arnold and Ruskin. Despite sharp strictures on Arnold's conception of culture, Eliot's view of culture is a response to that of Arnold. His Christian view of capitalist profitmongering as an unwholesome basis for a healthy and valuable civilization explicitly recalls Ruskin. Even his hostility to liberal democracy and his feudal preference for a class society turn out under more careful scrutiny to be somewhat equivocal. At least Eliot evolved to a qualified appreciation of the claims of democracy and even of liberalism (the target he often designated for attack), and his criticism after World War II, to the extent that it can be taken seriously, is meant to effect changes within democracy. Eliot may be to the right of Arnold, but there are affinities between them in the discriminations of their critique of contemporary liberalism.

Even so, a significant gulf divides them, which a preoccupying empirical concern with particulars might overlook. Eliot's "Catholicism" is a decisive characteristic of his thought and art, and it shapes his criticism, particularly his social criticism, in a way that essentially distinguishes it from the English social critics of the nineteenth century (not excepting Newman) and associates it, paradoxically, with the modernism that Eliot at once helped create and which, morally, he condemned.

Indeed, for Eliot Protestantism, and in particular what he calls decayed Protestantism, is anathema. The symptoms are already in the secularism of Arnold, who (in Eliot's view) surrenders Christianity to culture. The decay of Protestantism means for Eliot the loss of the sense of original sin and signifies the disappearance of moral struggle—which in turn makes for human unreality. Ironically, the evidence of moral fatigue and exhaustion is very strong in Eliot. One is reminded of Ezra Pound's acerbic and funny remark that Eliot became the supreme critic by disguising himself as a corpse. What we get more often than not in Eliot's criticism, as well as in his poetry, is inert melancholy and resigned acceptance of moral disarray and human ineffectuality. The sense of struggle is much stronger in the decayed Protestantism of Carlyle, Ruskin, and Arnold than it is in the decayed Catholicism of Eliot. One might remark here a certain bad faith in Eliot. He complains about the secularism of decayed Protestantism with its unbelief, but he tolerates, indeed values, Charles Maurras's "Catholicism," which is also without faith in God. It is possible to do a study of the effects of decayed Catholicism by beginning with Maurras and concluding with Eliot. Eliot's introduction to *The Intimate Journals of Baudelaire* provides a striking instance. It need hardly be pointed out that it is decadence, a perversion of the intention of the doctrine, to regard "the possibility of damnation as an immense relief in the world of electoral reform," and to assert "that damnation itself is an immediate form of salvation—of salvation from the ennui of modern life, because it at last gives some significance to living."[5] One could easily substitute "excitement" for "significance."

Eliot's strenuous hostility to the secularization of Christian thought (exemplified by Arnold) manifests itself in his mistrust of secular reform and secular reformers.

> Fr. Demant is concerned with the reform of this situation, in a secular society; and with the right position of the Church in a secular society. But unless I have misunderstood him, he appears to me to take this secularization for granted. Assuming that our present society is neutral rather than non-Christian, I am concerned with inquiring what it might be like if it took the Christian direction.[6]

Thus he characterizes the "secular reformer" as someone who for the most part conceives "the evils of the world as something external to himself," and seems to echo the nineteenth century complaint against the belief that "there is nothing to alter but machinery." Unlike the nineteenth century critic, however, he is unable to conceive a secular ambition which locates evil in the heart of man and wishes to convert the individual as the basis of social reform. This inability to see society as a medium for the spiritual life shows itself in the subtle non sequitur of the following passage.

> We are all dissatisfied with the way in which the world is conducted: some believe that it is a misconduct in which we all have some complicity; some believe that if we trust ourselves entirely to politics, sociology or economics we shall only shuffle from one makeshift to another. And here is the perpetual message of the Church: to affirm, to teach and to apply true theology. We cannot be satisfied to be Christians at our devotions and merely secular reformers all the rest of the week, for there is one question that we need to ask ourselves every day and about whatever business. The Church has perpetually to answer this question: to what purpose were we born? What is the end of Man?[7]

Why is the week necessarily divided between Sunday devotions and secular reform? The classic Protestant complaint about typical churchgoing concerns the split between devotions and "business as usual." The person who issues from the church with a desire to change the world during the week may be seen as acting out a life of spiritual integrity. The questions, To what purpose were we born? and What is the end of Man? may be answered in terms of man's social fate, Eliot to the contrary notwithstanding.

Spiritual fulfillment and worldly success are conceived (in *Murder*

in the Cathedral, for instance) in diametric opposition to each other.
Eliot does not envisage the nonascetic possibility that one can hold the
view that the spirit can continue to live in the world though materialist
values degrade life. Without this view of the spiritual life, social reform is an irrelevance. Society for Eliot is no more than a scaffolding
for the man-God relation. Social life itself contains no spiritual gratifications. Medieval society (Eliot's implicit ideal) at best implies an
order of temporal satisfactions, which Eliot himself seems unable to
imagine. His Christian society is the obverse of a sense of futility
about the spiritual possibilities of modern society. The terms are in a
kind of static tension—in which Christianity serves to remind man of
the essential joylessness and gracelessness of his social existence. Contemporary society is a "neutral society." "The great majority of people
are neither [Christians nor non-Christians], but are living in a no
man's land."[8]

To feel, on the one hand, the impotence of the modern and to be
committed, on the other, to a religious ideal which has already been
realized both institutionally and doctrinally in a dead past is to be continually tempted by despair. For it is not simply that the ideal is so far
beyond the modern experience; it is rather that it is a finished ideal,
related to modern experience only through contrast and irony. How
is this ideal to penetrate the modern world and become a dynamic
principle within it? It is not enough to concede the difficulty of such
penetration. The very conditions for penetration seem to be absent.
Moreover, the realized quality of the ideal is a kind of intimidating
presence, an unachievable other, which only intensifies the modern
feeling of ineffectuality. Arnold's Christianity (and that of Carlyle)
had, in its time at least, the advantage of an inchoate dynamism: it is
an aspect, not an alien transcendent principle, of the actual life of
nineteenth century man with all its ambiguous possibilities.

In the light of the ineffectuality, indeed one might say deliberate
ineffectuality, of Eliot's Christianity (his inactivism is profound and
consistent), his strictures against humanism, like his strictures against
Protestantism, are misconceived. "It is doubtful," Eliot writes,
"whether civilization can endure without religion, and religion without a church."[9] Humanism is a "parasitical" doctrine, "merely the state
of mind of a few persons in a few places at a few times." If humanism
has virtue for Eliot, it is for the reason that it promulgates order
against anarchy. Eliot does not credit humanism with sensitivity to

questions of justice and equity, to the uses and abuses of power. In Eliot's view, humanism is at best no more than a classicism. Moreover, it lacks universal appeal. But it is probable, the humanist can reply, that it is more difficult to restore a universal church than to spread humanism to the people. The university in a democratic society, one of the principal institutions of humanism, has an active diffusive power at least as effective as the contemporary church and perhaps more inventive and more inspiring in its "message."

This is a serious criticism to make of Eliot, because of the Catholic and universalist bias of his thought and vision. His criticism has as its target all individualistic and sectarian tendencies in modern thought and expression. But his universalism is itself a form of sectarianism in the light of modern experience. For by addressing the Christian reader exclusively and by dividing the world between Christian and non-Christian or pagan, he is ignoring those who are not accurately described by either category and he is assuming for the contemporary Christian a universality which is simply presumption. That modern society can be seen as failing according to standards provided by medieval Christianity is at once indisputable and by now uninteresting. What Eliot's hostility to secularism prevents him from appreciating is the significance (and virtues) of secularization—the survival of religious values in secular (desacralized) form. The consequence is a view of history as a perplexing chaos.

> After such knowledge, what forgiveness? Think now
> History has many cunning passages, contrived corridors
> And issues, deceives with whispering ambitions,
> Guides us by vanities. Think now
> She gives when our attention is distracted
> And what she gives, gives with such supple confusions
> That the giving famishes the craving. Gives too late
> What's not believed in, or if still believed,
> In memory only, reconsidered passion.
>   ("Gerontion," lines 34-42)

Eliot's wholesale repudiation of modern society has the effect of making the critical function of high culture irrelevant. However distressing contemporary society may have seemed to the nineteenth century critics, it remained the arena for the spiritual life and consequently susceptible to high cultural criticism. The hope of the apostles of culture was that culture would overcome its minority status.

Arnold was not exaggerating when he characterized the social effect of his work in the following terms.

> We have not won our political battles, we have not carried our main points, we have not stopped our adversaries in advance, we have not marched victoriously with the modern world; but we have told silently upon the mind of the country, we have prepared currents of feeling which sap our adversaries' position when it seems gained, we have kept up our communications with the future.[10]

Eliot, on the other hand, has no such ambition for culture. Like Leavis, he insists on and values its minority status. Unlike Leavis, he does not believe that the minority can or should exercise a powerful social influence.

High culture, for Eliot, is in a congenial relation to popular culture, which he views as the legitimate creation and possession of the lower classes. The nourishment which popular culture provides to high culture is reciprocated by high culture's respect for the self-sufficient integrity of popular culture. In the perspective of the alliance of high and popular culture, mass culture is the corrupt, *incorrigible* work of middle class industrial civilization, satirized, for example, in "Choruses from 'The Rock.' "

The work of Raymond Williams and Richard Hoggart derives from the perception of the congeniality of popular culture and high culture. For them as for Eliot, mass culture represents the commercialization of popular culture, whereas high culture is enriched by it. Hugh Kenner speaks somewhere of the refining of popular art in its appropriation by high art, but refinement may be too weak a term, suggesting attenuation rather than the energizing activity of popular culture. Eliot differs from most of the English social critics (from Arnold to Williams and Hoggart) in the absence of sympathy he shows for the irreversible characteristics of modern life: secularism, industrialism, democracy. These are middle class achievements with which even the most severe critics of mass culture try to come to terms.

Moreover, he sees high culture as powerless to make any real difference in the life of the modern world. It exists for an elite, parasitically nourishing itself on popular culture.[11] It may use the debris of modern life as texture for its art, but it refuses to see the possibility of meaningfulness in modern life, indeed in life itself. The critical function is weakened precisely in its unwillingness to engage and discriminate among elements within the general culture. The privileged minority encloses itself within its own environment in order to evaluate its products. Criticism develops its power exclusively in relation to the arts: it is directed toward the making of discriminations within the scope of high art and high culture. The specialism of the New Criticism is the next logical step. As a critical force vis-à-vis society, high culture becomes irrelevant—though paradoxically Eliot remains a social critic.

ELIOT'S VIEW of poetry as intransitive (as distinguished from a criticism of life) has its source not in aestheticism with its cult of purity but in an implicit analogy with Christian transcendence. Eliot's poetry incarnates the frozen dialectic between Christianity and the modern world that Eliot presents discursively in his essays. The impotence of the modern is the "subject matter" of the poetry. Eliot's poetry in its aesthetic organization as well as its content reveals the attitudes that create the paralytically conservative tension of his social and political criticism: the sense of the total ineffectuality and vacuity of the modern world, on the one hand, and the devotion to an impossible-to-achieve timeless order, on the other hand.

> The river's tent is broken: the last fingers of leaf
> Clutch and sink into the wet bank. The wind
> Crosses the brown land, unheard. The nymphs are departed.
> Sweet Thames, run softly, till I end my song.
> The river bears no empty bottles, sandwich papers,
> Silk handkerchiefs, cardboard boxes, cigarette ends
> Or other testimony of summer nights. The nymphs are departed.
> And their friends, the loitering heirs of city directors;
> Departed, have left no addresses.
> By the waters of the Leman I sat down and wept . . .
> Sweet Thames, run softly, for I speak not loud or long.
> But at my back in a cold blast I hear
> The rattle of the bones, and chuckle spread from ear to ear.
> (*The Waste Land*, lines 173-186)

The lines shuttle between time present and time past, between the contemporary scene of empty bottles, sandwich papers, cigarette ends (for the moment vanished, though evoked by the poet), and Spenser's sweet soft-flowing Thames and Marvell's cold, blasting time. The shuttle expresses a nostalgia which is overcome by the sense that

under the aspect of eternity, the difference between past and present is
of no importance. The past embodied in the lines of Spenser has no
resistant power.[12] One has only to compare the following lines from
Arnold's "The Scholar-Gypsy" to see how Eliot deliberately undermines the contrast between past and present.

> O born in days when wits were fresh
>   and clear
> And life ran gayly as the sparkling
>   Thames;
> Before this strange disease of modern life
> With its sick hurry, its divided aims,
> Its heads o'ertaxed, its palsied
>   heart, was rife—
> Fly hence, our contact fear!
>
> (lines 201-206)

Marvell's line only confirms the corrosive power of time, which Eliot
enforces by fusing it with a grotesque cynical image of modernity.

> But at my back in a cold blast I hear
> The rattle of bones, and chuckle spread from ear to ear.

This is the modern condition, which is at once a historical moment
and an expression of the eternally fallen human condition. Eliot's
vision is simultaneously time-bound and timeless.

The juxtaposition of past and present in *The Waste Land* has a
cubistlike effect. The analogy is in the relation between background
and foreground that we find in cubist paintings. The cubist painter
violates the requirements of illusionism by bringing objects traditionally in the background up to the picture plane, so that he can maintain
the ambiguous illusion that the object is simultaneously foreground
and background. The effect is a fluidity of appearances rather than a
fixity of forms in space that we find in illusionist painting. The instability of appearances relates to the inescapable subjectivity of vision.
That the object world is firm and solid is a metaphysical assumption
very difficult to maintain in the disillusioned modern consciousness.
The failure of the past (in Eliot's poem) to differentiate itself from the
present, to represent an Other from which the squalors of the modern
world can be seen and felt is symptomatic of the radical estrangement
of modern consciousness from the possibility of transcendence. Eliot
demurred from the view that *The Waste Land* was an expression of
disillusion. He preferred to have it read as a record of modern man's

illusion of disillusion, implying that for Eliot transcendence remains a possibility.

There is, to be sure, a distinct aesthetic pleasure produced by the poem related to but not identical with its meaning. The impressions of montage, of the fusing of incongruent elements, of the striking of notes that are dissonant have a richness and excitement that run counter to the mood of despair or of disillusion which informs the poem. I am, of course, aware of a view which virtually constitutes an orthodoxy, that the "bitterness and desolation are superficial aspects of his poetry." Rejecting the claim that "Eliot confesses his impotence to release the healing waters," I. A. Richards, for example, approves the testimony of readers that Eliot's poem in its realization of the plight of a whole generation makes it possible for them "to find the saving passion."[13] Richards's view is inextricably bound up not only with the need to establish Eliot as the major poet of the period but also with the very terms in which the modernist claims for all poetry are to be made. Eliot's affirmation is sounded through "the music of ideas." "Music" overcomes the referentiality of the poem, encloses it upon itself. Richards's idea of the poem as a place or occasion for finding the saving passion implies, I think, a mistaken conflation of poetry and Christianity. Eliot intended the poem as poem without a particular audience, a poem that "declares" itself as the essence of poetry. Though Richards apparently reads *The Waste Land* as an aesthetic object, he understands the activity of art as offering an experience comparable to that of salvation. I am willing to allow the positive excitement of all great poetry. But one simply wills away an important aspect of the experience of the poem by denying "its bitterness and desolation."

The doctrine that links Eliot's poetry and his religious and social thought is expressed through his famous phrase "dissociation of sensibility." According to Eliot, the dissociation of sensibility occurred in the seventeenth century, the century which witnessed the breakdown of the medieval synthesis, Eliot's Golden Age. The phrase occurs in an essay on metaphysical poetry in which the social implications are only implicit. Yet a little reflection on what Eliot is arguing should make one implication clear—that modern poetry has as its task the overcoming, or the attempt to overcome, the dissociation that took place after the vogue of metaphysical poetry. This task can be accomplished only if the collateral task of reestablishing a Christian order modeled

on the medieval synthesis is also accomplished. Eliot does not share
the aesthetic faith in the salvational powers of art implied by Richards's view. He succeeded as a poet, not as a social thinker. He managed to revive the associated sensibility of the metaphysicals in his
poetry (a certain kind of fusion of thought and feeling), though he did
not begin to restore Christianity to the modern world. On one level,
the comparison is unfair and absurd. As a poet Eliot had only his creative imagination to worry over, while as a social thinker he would
have had to master the whole society. But the comparison suggests an
important distinction that Eliot makes in *After Strange Gods* between
tradition and orthodoxy—between, that is, unconscious and conscious forces. For the genuine poet there is no orthodoxy, only tradition, to which in his self-discipline he "instinctively" adheres. The
shared imaginative conviction of poets through the ages is largely tacit
or unconscious. There is none of the often self-defeating proselytizing
for an orthodoxy that necessarily characterizes the social and political
life.

Eliot's success as a poet should not be confused with the possibility
of salvation. For Eliot the church—and the church alone—is in tension
with human failure and evil. But in the modern world the resources of
redemption represented by the church seem poor indeed against the
weight of so much negative vision and Eliot knows this. In "Choruses
from 'The Rock' " Eliot distinguishes the modern age as a time in
which men have turned from God not as in other ages to other gods,
but to no god at all, and he wonders whether man has abandoned the
church or the church has abandoned man. The modern age is a radical
version of man's fallen condition.

The sense of an unredeemable temporal order pervades Eliot's
work. The "doctrine" is asserted in *Four Quartets*.

> Time present and time past
> Are both perhaps present in time future
> And time future contained in time past
> If all time is eternally present
> All time is unredeemable.
>
>   ("Burnt Norton," I, lines 1-5)
>
> In my beginning is my end. In succession
> Houses rise and fall, crumble, are extended,
> Are removed, destroyed, restored, or in their place
> Is an open field, or a factory, or a by-pass.

Old stone to new building, old timber to new fires,
Old fires to ashes, and ashes to the earth.
                    ("East Coker," I, lines 1-6)

One is reminded of Leopold Bloom's Vichian meditation on the filling
and emptying of cities in *Ulysses.*

> Cityful passing away, other cityful coming, passing away too:
> other coming on, passing on. Houses, lines of houses, streets,
> miles of pavements, piled up bricks, stones. Changing hands.
> This owner, that landlord never dies they say. Others step into
> his shoes when he gets his notice to quit. And so they buy the
> place up with gold. Swindle in it somewhere. Piled up in cities,
> worn away age after age. Pyramids in sand. Build on bread and
> onions. Slaves. Chinese wall. Babylon. Big stones left. Round
> towers. Rest rubble, sprawling suburbs, jerry-built, Kernan's
> mushroom houses, built of breeze. Shelter for the night.[14]

One may plausibly object to a negative (or for that matter positive)
interpretation of the Vichian process as an arbitrary interruption of it.
Since beginning and ending continually follow upon one another, one
cannot say simply from the evidence of the process itself whether affirmation or negation is taking place. But there is tone, cadence, and
statement.

What might have been is an abstraction
Remaining a perpetual possibility
Only in a world of speculation.
What might have been and what has been
Point to one end, which is always present.
                    ("Burnt Norton," I, lines 6-10)

The negativity comes through the cadence and tone of the verse:
the sense of the futile inevitability of the process. Even in the apparently positive statement "Only through time time is conquered" we
have the repudiation of the world of time which is the world of Vichian process. It may not be fair to offer the statements of a character in
one of Eliot's plays as an expression of Eliot's negativity, but again the
statement and cadence remind us of Eliot's lyric verse. Here is Harry's
self-description in *The Family Reunion:*

                    . . . I am the old house
With the noxious smell and the sorrow before morning,
In which all past is present, all degradation is unredeemable.[15]

In stressing the negativism of Eliot's attitude in his poetry I am
countering the still dominant view of Eliot as invisible poet, maker of
an impersonal art. This view can be found in exemplary fashion in
Allen Tate, who, following Eliot, attempts to disentangle what he
understands as confusion in the minds of many readers between Eliot's
putative despair in "The Fire Sermon" (in *The Waste Land*) and the
objective irony in the scene. "For the seduction scene shows, not what
man is, but what *for a moment* he thinks he is."

> The meal is ended, she is bored and tired,
> Endeavors to engage her in caresses
> Which still are unreproved, if undesired.
> Flushed and decided, he assaults her at once;
> Exploring hands encounter no defence;
> His vanity requires no response,
> And makes a welcome of indifference.
> (And I Tiresias have foresuffered all
> Enacted on this same divan or bed;
> I who have sat by Thebes below the wall
> And walked among the lowest of the dead.)
> (*The Waste Land*, lines 236-246)

According to Tate, "the clerk stands for the secularization of the religious and qualitative values in the modern world. And the meaning of
the contrast between Tiresias and the clerk is not disillusion, but
irony."[16] The effect of the distinction is to protect Eliot against the
charge that he is committing the sin of despair. Moreover, the insight
of the poet into the blind vanity of the clerk is a saving virtue. "But for
the grace of God," says the poet in effect, "there go I." "The Fire Sermon" can be regarded as an exemplum of Eliot's entire achievement or
at least an aspect of it, so that Tate's view of it can be generalized to
mean that Eliot's imagination is ironic, not despairing, and that the
irony is a defense against despair.

I do not think that Tate has fairly read the implications of Eliot's irony. Why is the moral failure of the seducer simply man's momentary
self-image, and not his reality or a significant aspect of it? For don't we
feel that we are in the presence of contemporary man and that how he
thinks of himself is in part at least what he is? And why should we
exempt the poet from participation in the condition which he is
describing? An insight need not transform a man into a superior being.
Irony provides a contrast, but it is not necessarily transforming—as
I argue in the chapter on Flaubert. Indeed Eliot would clearly wish

to avoid the "pretension" scorned in *The Family Reunion* "to be the uncommon exception to the universal bondage."[17] Tiresias's irony expresses a gulf between spiritual perception and ordinary life that betrays the impotence of spirit as much as it does the squalor of the quotidian.

The self-impoverishing split between spirit and the world is schematically presented in Eliot's play, *The Cocktail Party*. When Sir Henry Harcourt-Reilly, the psychiatrist-priest of the play, offers Edward, the protagonist of the drama, the two paths of deliverance from his anguish, we can be confident that there are no other paths in the mind of the dramatist. However limited Reilly may be, nothing in the play qualifies his authority at this particular moment. Much has already been made of this moment by critics. Lionel Trilling, for example, has pointed to Eliot's deficiency in his imagination of the life of the common routine. The pain, the ethical discipline, even the possibility of joy and glory in ordinary life are absent. The lives of ordinary people are habit-ridden and consequently spiritually unfree. Trilling locates the origins of this deficiency in Tolstoy, another religious type, who was obsessed with the terrible squalor of ordinary life.[18] Of course, such a view of the life of common routine is to be expected from an imagination that conceives of salvation (not simply deliverance from pain) as involving the suffering of martyrdom and communion with God. Salvation is transhumanization through the intensification of suffering: the spiritual effect of this is what certain critics have characterized as Manichaeanism, a split, in Denis Donoghue's words, between "the life of the common routine and the way of beatitude."[19] The Manichaeanism is not simply characteristic of *The Cocktail Party*, but is a governing principle of Eliot's imagination. And it is a feature of this principle that it refuses to allow the spiritual idea to fertilize the practical life, because it fears that spirit will be compromised and corrupted in the process. If the common life is unredeemable and the lonely pursuit of salvation is as absurdly quixotic as that of Celia, the ascetic martyr in *The Cocktail Party*, possible only to a handful and certainly not the way for a whole society, Eliot's wisdom about a Christian society must be extremely dubious. The nihilism from which his Christian defenders like Allen Tate are trying to save him by displacing attention from Eliot's despair to objective irony in the work remains resistantly there.

There is a mitigation of the Manichaeanism in Eliot's development in the plays. In *The Confidential Clerk*, for example, the deflation of romantic expectations in one's vocation as well as in love means the acceptance of the second rate, not disillusion. Sir Charles can collect objects instead of being a first-rate potter, Colby can enjoy his less-than-distinguished piano playing. What makes the acceptance of human imperfection possible is the religious dimension to which the characters aspire and which they do not realize. But the mitigation is not to be confused with any real sense of human fulfillment.

Eliot, of course, is not alone in his incapacity either imaginatively to redeem ordinary life or to conceive of a convincing transcendent otherness, though he is particularly vulnerable to suspicions of bad faith because of his confident religious conviction. As William Chace remarks, Conrad, Mann, Camus, as well as Eliot, "All proceed to explore the greater horror underlying the horror of the surface [of human life] and none seems capable of figuring forth the world of illumination, rationality and Dantesque splendor of which their own Infernos are the antithesis."[20] Indeed, the exploration of the horror becomes a compulsion, which may even become invested with the feeling of liberation. Lawrence's imagination of a life of extreme self-disintegrative sensation is charged with such feeling. Read, for instance, the passage in *Women in Love* in which Birkin responds to and recoils from the African figurine. It is at once an opportunity and a menace to the self. (In Lawrence, there is a countervailing illumination and splendor in which life is affirmed, though there is nothing like the Dantean reconstitution after the descent into the abyss. The abyss in Lawrence remains a permanent threat at least as formidable as the promise of wholeness and radiance.) This "fragmentary Danteism" is part of the definition of the modern.

Eliot, to be sure, is at war with this "fragmentary Danteism." The question is: how effective is he? Eliot's principal aesthetic weapon is his classicism, which he ranked with his Anglo-Catholicism and royalism as tenets of his faith. He is a "classical" critic in upholding the virtues of the vernacular, the language in its normative aspect spoken by the community. (Eliot's lucidity as a critic is a perfect exemplification of it.) A certain mistrust runs through his comments about Shakespeare, for instance, as if Shakespeare's magnificently willful way with language (a willfulness permitted by the rich and various susceptibilities of the English language itself, particularly at the historical moment in which Shakespeare wrote) were the expression of an individual (divisive? alienated?) inner voice[21] and not the common orthodox wisdom of the ages. Virgil and Dante are for Eliot the supreme classics who impersonally, self-effacingly realized in a way never to be surpassed the resources of Latin and Italian respectively. Eliot makes the doctrine of the impersonality of art seem as if it were an inevitable condition of all good art. In a sense it is, but the particular force it has for Eliot cannot be understood unless one understands its connection with the communal ethic implied by Eliot's classicist advocacy of the vernacular and the Christian "cult" of humility. Personality and personal emotion are divisive and alienating (in communal terms); they are tainted by the cardinal sin of pride (in religious terms). Eliot's aesthetic has extra-aesthetic motives.

For Eliot the supreme modern instance of classicism is unfortuitously the Catholic Joyce. Both Catholicism and classicism impose the demand of orthodoxy. Thus despite his personal repudiation of Catholicism, Joyce never disfigures the Catholic idea in his presentation of it. For instance, in the opening chapter of *Ulysses*, the Englishman Haines asks Stephen doubtingly: "You're a believer, are you? . . . in the narrow sense of the word. Creation from nothing and miracles and a personal God." Stephen responds with the precision of a carefully trained Jesuit: "There's only one sense of the word, it seems to me." This is Stephen's scrupulously orthodox understanding of ideas and words. Which does not keep him from diabolically declaring ("with grim displeasure") "You behold in me a horrible example of free thought." Yet shortly afterward, Stephen perceives an analogy between his thoughts and "the slow growth and change of rite and dogma."[22]

Eliot's affirmation of classical virtues diverts us from exploring the deformation and distortion of his own vision. A truly classical view would not divest the life of common routine of all meaning. Leavis's often extravagant claims for Lawrence's centrality and normality make sense if we keep in mind that Eliot hovers in the background. Leavis is trying to associate the sentiment about the fullness and richness of the common life with centrality and normality against Eliot's predilection for austerity and ascesis. It is interesting to note that in *After Strange Gods*, Eliot, taking the position of health and centrality, diagnosed Lawrence as "sick," only to admit later that when he wrote the book he himself was sick.

Eliot is protected from "nihilism" by an instinctive commitment to the formal powers of art—its simultaneous capacities for order and variety. Eliot was, of course, no aesthete. When he responds favorably to writers in the aesthetic tradition—for example, Baudelaire and Joyce—it is their complex and orthodox relation to Christian idea and sentiment, not their cult of art, which interests him. Indeed, for most of his career he was in ideological combat with aestheticism as one of the false surrogates for religious experience that constantly menaces the modern world. But the principle of vitality in Eliot remains a version of aestheticism, which links him with Flaubert and Joyce. The simultaneous order of great works of art constitutes the tradition in Eliot's view. It is enacted in *The Waste Land*, in which the Eliotic vision incorporates Dante, Chaucer, Spenser, Marvell, among others. The effect of this order is to free literature from historical contingencies. The "freedom" of literature is an ambiguous condition: it can intensify our despair with actual life.

A strong view of the spiritual impotence of modern man conjoined with a strong belief in a dogmatic Christianity (undisturbed in its dogma by the vicissitudes of history) produces a pessimism of the will. This pessimism of the will undermines the positive aspect of critical activity. Man's fallen condition, not the possibility of redemption, receives the emphasis. So there is a false play of opposition between the modern and the Christian in Eliot, for both his modernity and his Christianity are characterized by inertia and ineffectuality. The anomaly of Eliot's originality is his discovery of the aesthetics of modern ineffectuality. Paradoxically, this discovery is the most effectual principle of his art. And it is a paradox that his immense prestige as a critic has contributed to the undoing of criticism.

I acknowledge the one-sidedness of my treatment of Eliot, a poet and literary critic whom I greatly admire. Indeed, even as a cultural critic he is not without a constructive side—as in his valuation of popular culture and ethnic variety. But the one-sidedness is necessary, I believe, to put in perspective a tendency in Eliot which a more "balanced" view would probably blur. How important this tendency is in Eliot (relative to whatever else he may have accomplished) is a matter for debate, but I think it beyond dispute that the effect of this tendency was to undermine the social ambition of criticism.

4

The Organic Society of F. R. Leavis

THE HUMANIST criticism of the nineteenth century persists in the work of F. R. Leavis. As critic and teacher for over forty years and as editor of *Scrutiny*, Leavis has been the modern embodiment of this critical tradition. His work provides an excellent measure of its present strengths and weaknesses. Against increasing skepticism about the legitimacy of high culture, Leavis has passionately argued that at stake in the defense of what he calls the great tradition is not simply English as a discipline but the creative spirit itself.

In Leavis's work, description, analysis, and interpretation serve the principal function of criticism as he understands it: the judicial function. Leavis is always concerned to locate the vitality or its absence in a work of imagination. And in his discussion of poetry, it is striking how often the standard for judgment is the rhythm or syntax of speech. Donne, for example, gets high marks from Leavis, because his poetry embodies living speech.

> I wonder by my troth, what thou and I
> Did, till we loved? Were we not weaned till then?
> But suck'd on country pleasures, childishly?
> Or snorted we in the seven sleepers den?
> 'Twas so; But this, all pleasures fancies bee.
> If ever any beauty I did see,
> Which I desir'd, and got, 'twas but a dream of thee.

And when Leavis sets about discriminating the verse of Milton, the contrast is between what he hears as stilted and what he hears as live speech. Thus he contrasts what he calls the hollowness of Milton's "Grand Style":

> And all amid them stood the Tree of Life
> High eminent, blooming Ambrosial Fruit
> Of Vegetable Gold

with the "Shakespearian-life" of these lines from *Comus*:

> And set to work millions of spinning Worms
> That in their green shops weave the smooth-hair'd silk.

Magisterially, he refuses "to try and argue with any one who contended that 'Vegetable Gold' exemplified the same kind of fusion as green shops.' " The territory of impossible argument has always been inordinately large in Leavis. But he leaves no doubt about his values.

> The extreme and consistent remoteness of Milton's medium from any English that was ever spoken is an immediately relevant consideration. It became, of course, habitual to him; but habituation could not sensitize a medium so cut from speech—speech that belongs to the emotional and sensory texture of actual living and is in resonance with the nervous system; it could only confirm an impoverishment of sensibility. In any case the Grand Style barred Milton from essential expressive resources of English that he once commanded.[1]

I am less interested in the justice of his particular discrimination here than I am in the assumptions that lie behind his appeal to speech. What Leavis says of speech in Shakespeare and Donne holds for the language of the novels of Jane Austen, George Eliot, and D. H. Lawrence. The living speech of great poets and novelists is the revelation of the interconnectedness of people within a living community or what Burke, Coleridge, Carlyle, indeed virtually every significant writer since the eighteenth century understood as the organic society.[2]

Has there ever been an organic society? Can the term "organic" adequately describe a whole society? I am not sure that one can give a convincing answer to these questions. Yet the organic society has been at the very least a powerful myth and its power depends on some kind of corresponding reality. The principal "documentary" sources of Leavis's conception of the organic society are two books, *Change in the Village* and *The Wheelwright's Shop*, descriptions of rural life immediately before the full emergence of the Industrial Revolution by a contemporary observer and participant, George Bourne. These two books virtually constitute the subject matter of *Culture and Environment*, which Leavis wrote in 1933 in collaboration with Denys

Thompson. However skeptical one may be of "the organic society" as a characterization of a whole society or of the fierce moral advocacy that attaches to it, it is hard to deny the authenticity and force of Bourne's descriptions.

> So he [Turner] knows, or thinks he knows why certain late-bearing apple trees have fruit only every year, and what effect of the potato crop is caused by dressing our sandy soil with chalk or lime; so he watches the new mole-runs or puzzles to make out what birds they can be that peck the ripening peas out of the pods, or estimates the yield of oats to the acre by counting the sheaves that he stacks, or examines the lawn to see what kind of grass are thriving. About all such matters his talk is the talk of an experienced man habitually interested in his subject, and yet it is never obtrusive. The remarks fall from him casually; you feel, too, that while he is telling you something that he noticed yesterday or years ago his eyes are alert to seize any new detail that may seem worthy of attention . . .[3]

> A good wheelwright knew by art but not by reason the proportion to keep between spoke and felloes; and so too a good smith knew how tight a two-and-a-half inch tyre should be made for a five foot wheel and how tight for a four foot, and so on. He felt it, in his bones. It was perception with him.
>
> The lore was a tangled network of country prejudices, whose reasons were known in some respects here, in others there, and so on. In farmyard, in tap-room, at market, the details were discussed over and over again; they were gathered together for remembrance in village workshops; carters, smiths, farmers, wheelmakers, in thousands handed on each his own little bit of understanding, passing it to his own son or to the wheelwrights of the day, linking up the centuries. But for the most part the details were but dimly understood: the whole body of knowledge was a mystery, a piece of folk knowledge, residing in the folk collectively, but never wholly in any individual. "However much a man know," old Bettesworth used to say, "there's sure to be somebody as knows more." And that is characteristic especially of all folk knowledge.[4]

The very tacitness of folk knowledge presupposes an unproblematic community, for the need for explicitness and conceptualization arises only when community has an uncertain existence.[5] Bourne contrasts the paradoxical mystery and certainty of folk knowledge with the knowledge of the new industrialism, which is uncertain and requires articulation. "In watching Cook put a wheel together I was watching practically the skill of England, the experience of ages; but to watch the bevelling and subsequent putting on of a wide tyre was to watch only a makeshift operation lately hit upon in my own little shop." The sentence is crucial for Leavis, who as a critic and teacher is naturally interested in the way in which knowledge is transmitted from generation to generation. The model for transmission implicit in Bourne's account is the master-apprentice relation. In the act of watching Cook, Bourne himself is simulating the wise passiveness of the apprentice who silently and confidently imbibes "the skill of England."[6] Bourne is affirming a relationship against a background of change that will entail the disappearance of the relationship. Leavis, writing sixty years later with the knowledge and experience of the Industrial Revolution, looks toward Bourne as offering a viable model for the cultural life.

How is this possible? Though the organic society may have disappeared as a system of social and economic relations, it has not vanished completely. What was true of the mechanical arts is still true of literature. Literature, the quintessential expression of language, continues to retain the structure and character of organic society.[7] Indeed the organic society becomes the principal metaphor for literature. It is present when Leavis cites Logan Pearsall Smith, who remarks that "the strength and subtlety of English idiom derives from an agricultural way of life,"[8] and in his awareness of the paradox of claiming for words a power of spiritual silence, of inarticulate knowingness: "language is not merely a matter of words—or words are more than they seem to be."[9] And again the organic society reveals itself in the view of poetry as doing and being rather than meaning.[10] Poetry is the equivalent, if not the identity, of a living community—a condition that makes consciousness paradoxical. Like his hero D. H. Lawrence, he wants at the same time more and less consciousness—that is, more concrete consciousness and less abstract consciousness—for only then can literature realize and express values, a "process necessary to any organic growth and experience." What is remarkable about this view is that what Leavis calls the collaborative activity of literature is not simply a representation of the organic society but the very society itself. *Faute de mieux* literature becomes in the modern world the medium in which the most spiritually developed natures live.

For all of Leavis's directness and explicitness, his theoretical position must be constructed from scattered remarks throughout his numerous essays as well as from extended descriptions of, say, the organic society in which the implications for literature and literary study are not fully worked out. This is because of Leavis's antitheoretic bias, which stems from his hostility to abstract consciousness. And yet Leavis has wanted and needed theoretical support (not simply historical models) against the various forces antagonistic to the creative literary tradition as he understands it: technological civilization, Americanization, behaviorism, analytical philosophy. It is only recently that Leavis has found philosophical support for his sense of English as a discipline —in particular in the work of Michael Polanyi and Polanyi's disciple Marjorie Grene.[11] Both philosophers continually stress the prerational community of assumption, often tacitly held, that inspires all genuinely vital thinking. Every discourse, according to Polanyi, rests upon unarticulable presuppositions that give a personal though not irrational character to the discourse.

How do we understand the role of originality—I was about to say creative originality—in this communal enterprise? Is it necessarily the case that the mastery imbibed by the apprentice becomes originality? One is reminded of E. H. Gombrich's discussion of the artisanal ideal of the Sienese painters of the fourteenth century whose goal was the perfect imitation of the masters, a goal he distinguishes from the ambition of Florentine artists who inaugurated the modern cult of originality.[12] One might say with justice that no matter the intention, there is no such thing as perfect imitation, so that the artisan apprentice is always making his version of the master's model. But this is a far cry from the expectation of radical originality, which in the modern view is the justification of art. On the artisanal model, Leavis in effect keeps creativity and originality sufficiently apart so that he can think of the literary tradition as a communal effort, a sharing of imaginative energies rather than a series of progressive innovations.

The organic society is an antiprogressive model, not simply because it belongs to an earlier time, but also because organicism with its seasonal aspect conceives of change through renewal, the recovery of existing or preexisting vitalities. Edmund Burke speaks of the organic society as "a condition of unchangeable constancy, moving on through the varied tenour of perpetual decay, fall, renovation and progression."[13] Yet it is irrelevant to dismiss Leavis's attachment to a model of creative relationship derived from the past as an expression of reactionary nostalgia, as J. H. Plumb does, for example, in *The Death of the Past*:

There are shifts of power from time to time in the governing class
of any nation, and those who lose tend to romanticize the past in
order to compensate themselves for what they no longer enjoy,
often at the same time denouncing the decadence, the corruption
of the times in which they have to live.[14]

And Plumb offers us as an instance Leavis, "whose picture of nineteenth-century England is as totally unrealistic as it must be emotion-
ally satisfying."[15]

Apart from its inaccuracy in representing Leavis's view of the nineteenth century, this easy dismissal of Leavis rests on an artificially
neat separation between past and present. There is a more interesting
distinction to be made between a living past that informs and animates
the present and an inert and discrete past which the present cannot recover. The living past plays an indispensable role in every present exercise of choice. Leavis puts the difference very well in one of his
American lectures.

> I have used the phrase "cultural tradition" rather than Snow's
> "traditional culture," because this last suggests something quite
> different from what I mean. It suggests something belonging to
> the past, a reservoir of alleged wisdom, an established habit, an
> unadventurousness in the face of life and change. Let me, as
> against that, extend briefly the quotation I've permitted myself
> from my Richmond lecture. Having in comment on Snow's claim
> regarding the "scientific edifice of the physical world," pointed
> to the "prior human achievement of collaborative creation . . .
> the creation of the human world, including language," I go on:
> "It is one we cannot rest on as something done in the past. It lives
> in the living creative response to change in the present." A little
> further on, insisting on the antithesis to what "traditional" usu-
> ally suggests, I put it in this way, and the formulation gives me
> what I need now: "for the sake of our humanity—our humanness
> —for the sake of a human future, we must do, with intelligent
> resolution and with faith, all we can to maintain the full life in the
> present—and life is growth—of our transmitted culture."[16]

Indeed, the failure to make this distinction yields the ideological
confusion that often inheres in the use of terms like progressive, conservative, reactionary. To mistrust the idea of progress is not necessarily evidence of an attachment to conservative or reactionary ideas.
It is one thing to advocate a return to a social order of the past (one

might even add, to a discredited social order); it is quite another thing to want to hold on to certain values of that social order or, better, to loosen these values from their original historical context and re-embody or recreate them in the present. Thus Leavis warns against the danger of a reactionary view when he endorses the following passage from Eliot's *After Strange Gods*: "The danger is . . . to aim to return to some previous condition which we imagine as having been capable of preservation in perpetuity, instead of aiming to stimulate the life which produced that condition in its time."[17] This is not to say that Leavis may not confuse the living past with an inert unrecoverable past, but the argument must be made beyond the facile dichotomies of progress and reaction. To be content with anything less is to prematurely short-circuit the fundamental question of a possible critique of actual culture. Leavis is not a critic of alienation like Jean-Paul Sartre and Herbert Marcuse, but he shares with them a radical dissatisfaction with the present, and the question becomes what gives one critique persuasiveness or even legitimacy, whereas another seems to be deprived of it. This is not a question for those who doubt the continuing validity of the critical enterprise and see the life of the mind simply as an affirming immanence in the excitements of modern change.

There is an ambiguity in Leavis's view of the organic society. On the one hand, he suggests that what is real for literature may be an unrealized ideal for society. On the other hand, the organic society is conceived as an ideal for literature itself, which in Leavis's view is threatened by the same corruption one discovers in society. And the source of the corruption is the evacuation of the sacred, or in Leavis's term vitality, from the ordinary world of time and space.

Leavis's work is most interesting and most problematic when he conceives of literature and society as threatened by the same corruptive forces. Against those forces he invokes the theme of vitality, of *present* life. Whether or not he is a reactionary, he is certainly not an antiquarian. His strenuous espousal of the study of English literature is accompanied by a resistance to the "once familiar case for making the Classics—Greek and Latin literature—the staple of humane education." Leavis, our contemporary, states unequivocally that "English . . . has its reality and life (if at all) in the present."[18] What Leavis means by life in an honorific sense can be grasped through instances. For example, his ambivalent view of Eliot is finally explained by his disappointment that Eliot, genius that he is, is incapable of sacralizing the physical world. The disappointment is keenly reflected in his treatment of the following passage from "Burnt Norton."

> Words move, music moves
> Only in time; but that which is only living
> Can only die. Words, after speech, reach
> Into the silence. Only by the form, the pattern,
> Can words or music reach
> The stillness, as a Chinese jar still
> Moves perpetually in its stillness.
>
> (V, lines 1-7)

>   The detail of the pattern is movement,
> As in the figure of the ten stairs
> Desire itself is movement
> Not in itself desirable;
> Love is itself unmoving,
> Only the cause and end of movement,
> Timeless, and undesiring
> Except in the aspect of time
> Caught in the form of limitation
> Between un-being and being.
> Sudden in a shaft of sunlight
> Even while the dust moves
> There rises the hidden laughter
> Of children in the foliage
> Quick now, here, now, always—
> Ridiculous the waste sad time
> Stretching before and after.
>
> (V, lines 23-39)

Leavis remarks, "What compels my 'no' is the assumed antithesis between the 'now' and time—for 'time' here, the waste, sad and ridiculous (what belongs to it 'can only die') represents that which is 'only living.' It is an antithesis unmistakably meant as a dismissing judgment passed on the world of time and on life that involves time, being necessarily lived in it."[19]

The adversary Eliotic term is "eternity" with its implication of permanence and fixity. Leavis's Protestantism, akin to D. H. Lawrence's, moves him to search for spirit as an immanence in the world of time. Leavis elaborates his objection to Eliot's eternity:

> The evocation that Eliot presents as a gleam and resonance of the transcendent is actually an evocation of life—the life that is

merely living. All the evocations he depends on to precipitate what may pass for a concrete apprehension—something to be taken as the convincing upshot of his complex and insistent *procedé*—are similarly evocations of life. It couldn't have been otherwise: Eliot in assuming that it can be is a victim of self-deception implicit in his undertaking—to which no undivided man could have lent himself.[20]

It may be a question to some readers of *Four Quartets* whether Eliot is as self-deceived as Leavis makes him out to be. Isn't Eliot seizing upon what Joyce calls epiphanies, arrested moments in time pregnant with transcendental significance? But Leavis is quite right to note Eliot's revulsion from process and change—and he may be right, if a bit prim in a psychotherapeutic way, in attributing this revulsion to emotional and spiritual insecurity, to an incapacity for an adult facing of reality.

Eliot's aversion to the world of time bears directly on his conception of tradition and the individual talent. For Eliot tradition is paradoxically ahistorical, a simultaneous order of monumental works altered at any moment by the introduction of new work, but free of the pressure of real historical life. Moreover, Eliot's tradition is an abstraction in which individual talent has lost all personality and become a mere catalyst. To say this, of course, is to characterize Eliot's critical doctrine, not his poetic achievement. Leavis makes an invidious comparison between the authentic presence of a living tradition in Lawrence's and Eliot's classicist view of tradition which (according to Leavis) is meant "to absolve the artist from responsibility toward life."[21] Like Lawrence, Leavis conceives tradition in the world of human time and in a physical and social space.

For Leavis the present moment is without life, because it has cut itself off from what is alive in the tradition. There is an acknowledgment of "the despair or vacuous unease, characteristic of the civilized world which comes of profound human needs and capacities that the civilization denies and thwarts, seeming—paralyzingly—to have eliminated in its triumph all possibility of resurgence."[22] ("Seeming" is crucial here, for Leavis refuses to acknowledge the impossibility of resurgence.) Much of modern literature is an incarnation of the malaise. Modern life is not merely the subject of modernist literature, it is in some sense its source for style and form. Fragmentation, deliberate incoherence, the absence of organic development (marked by a beginning, middle, and end) are converted from mere negatives to aesthetic values. Thus Joyce, or Leavis's version of Joyce, is anathema, and to the extent that Eliot "cultivates" the fragment and the still life, he is the object of severe censure.

Leavis's increasing ambivalence toward Eliot has corresponded with the strengthening of his early conviction that Lawrence is the supreme genius of the modern period. And the ambivalence is emblematic of a hostility toward the modern element in modern literature. Lawrence, unlike Eliot and Joyce, continually sacralizes, or rather discovers the sacred, in ordinary life. Eliot deplores the absence of the sacred, but is incapable of imagining it within the world of common routine. The work of Flaubert, Joyce, and Beckett, to name the greatest modernist writers of fiction, is nourished by the clichés of everyday life and by a parodistic relation to classical literature. Indeed, "parody" does not quite do as a characterization, for the luxurious exercise in parody or pastiche becomes virtually an end in itself and we are carried beyond satire to something close to acceptance, if not affirmation. Our satiric sense of Gerty MacDowell's lower class Bovarisme (in the Nausicaa episode in *Ulysses*) is overcome by a supersaturation of detail in which we achieve an empathic intimacy with her suffering and her perceptions. Joyce and Beckett are supreme examples of the process which passes through Flaubertian self-hatred to a grimly gay self-acceptance, but there are countless instances in contemporary fiction of the comic, desacralizing, profaning imagination. Indeed, some contemporary critics argue that the vitality of serious contemporary fiction (a vitality Leavis finds depressing) depends on its refusal to be pious and portentous about the high literary past. Profanity is the order of the day. Leavis is incapable of facing the possibility that the vitality of contemporary literature may depend upon the nihilism or negativism that he deplores, because he may then be compelled to take up a moral position outside of literature and become a critic of the literary mode.[23] Though his conception of literature is remote from any narrow aesthetic formalism—literature for Leavis is charged with moral and social themes[24]—his conception of literature as *the* sacred milieu leaves him without resources when literature becomes profane.

Vitality or living speech is not an easy standard to invoke against modernist profanity. If the cadence of living speech—living, that is, in the present not in the past—is an essential condition of vital literature, the clichés of everyday life belong to the literature. By definition clichés are empty of spiritual reality, like dogmatic vestiges of once powerful theological truths. Yet the obsessive imaginations of cliché-ridden minds that one finds in the work of, say, Joyce and Flaubert releases a sense of life of an almost demonic energy. Donald Barthelme, a latter-day master of the cliché, has a writer-character in one of his fictions admit that "I limit myself to what people say, and thinking what pamby it is, what they say. My nourishment is refined from the circles of the mind in motion."[25] Leavis does not find nourishment in this kind of energy (his response to Joyce and Flaubert are the touchstones here) because he detests the inorganic environment that sustains it. Unfortunately, the living environment that he values is fast disappearing, being now little more than a vestige in the English provinces. The vivid speech of Lawrence's coal miner is becoming a rarity and can no longer be expected to be a staple of modern fiction.

Leavis's preference for rural life is a limitation in a critic who must deal with the literature of the city. I suspect that his long blindness to the greatness of Dickens, only recently corrected, is a symptom of this limitation. One motive of Leavis's "discovery" of Dickens may be the belated recognition that the city has an organic life of its own.[26] The London that emerges in a Dickens narrative, in *Bleak House*, for example, is a complex articulation of families, individuals, institutions. Dickens's plot discloses the coherence of the living body of the city, overcoming the initial impression of randomness and discreteness. But what of the inorganic, the synthetic, the artificial—the debris of urban life one finds in Joyce, for instance? Leavis's antiurbanism provides no illumination.

By vitality Leavis means an order of experience usually characterized by the terms positive, creative, moral, healing, affirming. It is interesting to observe his response to a vitality which is negative. Though his response can encompass the ambiguity, it is clear that his predisposition is to resolve it to a negative judgment. Jonathan Swift provides an instructive occasion.

> Swift's negative horror at its most disturbing, becomes one with his disgust-obsession: he cannot bear to be reminded that under the skin there is blood, mess and entrails; and the skin itself, as we know from Gulliver, must not be seen from too close. Hypertrophy of the sense of uncleanness, of the instinct of repulsion, is not uncommon; nor is its association with what accompanies it in Swift . . .
>
> We have, then, in his writings probably the most remarkable expression of negative feelings and attitudes that literature can

offer—the spectacle of creative powers (the paradoxical description seems right) exhibited consistently in negation and rejection.[27]

The negative judgment is implied in the medical view of the "disgust
obsession." We are dealing with an illness. But is the diagnosis accurate? Is it Gulliver or Swift who cannot bear to be reminded that there
is blood, mess, and entrails or that the skin must not be seen from too
close? Or is it Leavis who cannot bear to be reminded by Swift? Indeed, Swift's awareness of blood, mess, and entrails is nothing less
than heroic. That he cannot convert his perception of sordid reality
into Rabelaisian delight may be the mark of Swift's moral intolerance
of life. But it is not clear that anyone (Leavis included) would be able
to tolerate Swift's vision if he had the capacity to share it.[28]

Leavis's medical view masks an intolerance which impoverishes his
criticism. An adversary intelligence or imagination is too often regarded as sick or stupid or vile. Little effort is made to understand
why such bêtes noires as technological civilization, behaviorism, and
Americanization are such powerful tendencies in modern life. To be
sure, Leavis tries to represent the stupidity or turpitude as culturally
significant. Thus C. P. Snow, or alternately Lord Robbins, is a por-
tent, but Leavis's insistence on the representative character of these
men does not make them less mystifying. There is a motiveless malig-
nity in modern life, incarnated in Snow, for example, which Leavis
believes can be surmounted, but which he can encounter only with a
moral indignation verging on incredulity. His view of the adversary
often has the appearance of paranoia. His condemnation of the egotism of others seems to be immodestly asserted to his own advantage.
He could have profited from the following sentence that he quotes
from a letter of Gerard Manley Hopkins: "A man who is deeply in
earnest is not very eager to assert his earnestness, as they say when a
man is really certain he no longer disputes but is indifferent."[29]

He affirms the virtues of centrality and normality, but his own great
tradition is idiosyncratic, particularly in its exclusions. Jane Austen,
George Eliot, Henry James, Joseph Conrad, and D. H. Lawrence are
unquestionably very great novelists. But the Leavis tradition miraculously begins in the nineteenth century. Where are Richardson and
Fielding? Dickens was until recently only a great entertainer, except in
the comparatively slight *Hard Times*. Leavis has revised his estimate
of Dickens and now even invokes Shakespeare in relation to him—
though, as John Gross justly points out, without any admission of

error. (Leavis seems constitutionally incapable of admitting a mistake.) Less vulnerable are the exclusions of Thackeray, Charlotte Brontë, and Thomas Hardy, but Leavis's canonical sense of greatness can be unnecessarily dismissive.[30] A writer like Joyce cannot be assimilated to what is essentially an English and organicist tradition. (James and Conrad are perhaps not so easily confined to that tradition either.) But then one might acknowledge the possibility of an alternative tradition: for example, Flaubert—Joyce—Beckett. Leavis's great tradition permits no alternatives.

His Manichaean opacity to the evil Other is the price he has paid for his uncompromising conscience and his secure conviction. He will simply not resign himself to the inevitable, he will not concede that the destructive process is irreversible. But the conscience and the conviction require what Leavis does not provide—a corresponding insight into the social process which would accomplish the kind of change (or restoration) that he desires.

The closest we get to an understanding of how or why the cultural decline occurred is in *Fiction and the Reading Public* (1932), by Q. D. Leavis, his wife and collaborator. Mrs. Leavis sees the plight of modern culture in the decline, which began in the eighteenth century, of an intelligent, extensive, if not mass, reading public. The decline was the paradoxical result of an increased general literacy fed by a corruptive journalism, most notably exemplified by Lord Northcliffe. By providing an "easy read" for masses of people, modern journalism undermined the taste for serious books. The literary counterpart of tabloid journalism has been the best seller.[31]

Mrs. Leavis's much debated argument is a version of cultural elitism that encompasses a kind of social radicalism, for it was characteristic of the premodern taste of the yeoman or working class of rural England to seek its literary and spiritual pleasures in Defoe, Bunyan, and Milton. The reconciliation of high culture and popular culture in the work of Raymond Williams and Richard Hoggart is already implicit in Mrs. Leavis's book. What is common to both high culture and popular culture on this view is "the puritan conscience" that "gave the mind a certain positive inclination which there seems every reason for supposing made more than amends for the absence of formal education."[32] The adversary then becomes mass culture (not to be confused with popular culture) which proliferates intellectually enervating and anaesthetizing sensations through the technological media.[33]

What this view fails to account for—indeed, could not account for in 1932—is the apparent complicity of a portion of the educated class, and of creative artists themselves, with the array of forces antagonistic to what the Leavises regard as the creative spirit. It is not simply C. P. Snow who proposes a problem (with which Leavis deals explicitly), it is Marshall McLuhan and Hugh Kenner (with whom he is not concerned), who represent in various ways a welcoming incarnation of modern technological life into the spirit of art and poetry. More than easy sensationalism and catering to the worst instincts of the masses is involved. And Leavis has made no effort to understand what he hates and fears.

His flaws and limitations are partly temperamental, but they can be found in varying degrees in any modern critic who insists that the business of criticism is not simply a value-neutral taxonomy of modes and genres or an unjudging avant-gardist celebration of every "creative" novelty or an exercise in demystification, whether it be the Marxizing of *Pilgrim's Progress* or the Freudianizing of Dickens. (Leavis is committed to seeing the object as in itself it really is.) The prospect of Leavis composing and defending his tradition remains a model, albeit a seriously imperfect one, of what any judicial critic must do. The making of the tradition is a making of a community which joins poet not only to poet but to reader and critic as well. The tradition presupposes the necessity of making judgments of value. The community excludes as well as includes. Though it emphasizes the communal aspect of literary creation and study, the stress on the irreducibly personal element is a salutary assertion against the doctrines of impersonality and objectivity one finds in the work of Eliot and Frye, for example. Leavis's conception of literature as a community with the attributes of organic life implies a symbiosis between art and life that modern literary theory and practical criticism often deny in an exclusive attention to the internal history of literature.

But the sense of serious limitation persists. Unless the communal ethic, valuable as it is, is under sufficient constraint, it becomes an oppression to the individual talent, or, through a kind of xenophobia, the community resists exchanges with the talents of other communities. One form of the xenophobia is Leavis's essential confinement to the English tradition which results from his stress on language. Even American English tends to be regarded as a foreign language with its own literary tradition—though exceptions are made for Hawthorne's *Scarlet Letter*, for example.[34] Leavis's failure as a critic on his own terms is his unwillingness or inability to engage the adversary or the Other (whoever or whatever it may be) in a dialectical—or should I say communal—exchange. The failure is manifest in the fact that despite his organicist ideal his own criticism shows little growth and development. One must concede the failure at the same time one acknowledges Leavis's still valuable presence in modern criticism.

5

A Postscript to
the Higher Criticism:
The Case of Philip Rieff

THE MODERN crisis in intellectual authority and confidence has no easy solution. It cannot be solved by moralistic fervor or by an exercise in irony directed against "liberationist" attitudes and ideas. The "conservative" reaction against modern nihilism has its symptomatic character.

Philip Rieff is a social philosopher, the most conservative of the troika that philosophize in the therapeutic mode. Like Herbert Marcuse and Norman O. Brown, Rieff's intellectual conscience has been largely formed by Freud, but he is also influenced by the critical tradition that springs from Matthew Arnold and is thus particularly relevant to the condition I am trying to define. If Rieff's thought has a more conservative appearance than that of Marcuse and Brown, of the three his spirit is the most genuinely critical. He encounters the tradition and the apocalypse with an extraordinary combination of commitment to human survival and skepticism about all final solutions. If he has adopted the prophetic mode in *Fellow Teachers*,[1] his extended denunciation of the prophets of the apocalypse, it is because he has felt the need for making the strongest statement possible against the barbarian threat to the critical intelligence. The book is a kind of Arnoldian revival in the therapeutic mode, at once symptom and diagnosis—a timely exercise in prophecy verging on obsolescence.

Rieff's second book, *The Triumph of the Therapeutic*,[2] is a continuation of the argument made at the conclusion of his first book, *Freud: The Mind of the Moralist*.[3] There Rieff argued that the modern age had witnessed the emergence of a new kind of spiritual personality from the ruins of religious orthodoxy. This personality Rieff designates as Psychological Man.[4] Rieff understands the psychological not simply as the adjective form of a discipline for studying the psyche; he sees it in the modern world as a mode of spiritual or pseudospiritual activity. Rieff's argument evokes the Nietzschean vision of the death of God and his acceptance of the death, like Nietzsche's, is tough-minded. This is because Rieff's view is mediated by the Freudian passion to disabuse mankind of its illusions.

Yet for all his admiration for Freud, Rieff is unwilling to identify himself with Freud's analytic amoralism. Rieff places Freud in the "democratic" tradition of modernism, which in its commitment to the variety of experience refuses to discriminate among experiences. He concedes Freud's vestigial attachment to a hierarchical conception of life, to notions of high and low, better and worse, but the analytic pressure of Freud's thought is to dissolve any and all idealisms which depend upon such discriminations. The effect of value-free psychoanalysis is not merely egalitarianism but atomism as well. "Being analytic, the [Freudian] movement can never become communal."[5] The analytic is corrosive because it disintegrates, separates, engenders an alienating self-consciousness. Adhesion or affiliation is impelled by some emotional or spiritual force that transcends the analytic. The analytic carries the freight of reason, but it is reason in its disintegrative aspect, not to be confused with the life of reason according to classical stoicism or to the Enlightenment.

Because he knows that men cannot live by analysis alone Rieff is responsive to men of lesser genius in the field of the therapeutic: Jung, Wilhelm Reich, and D. H. Lawrence. In all these men, Rieff finds not only intellectual failure, but also radical deficiencies of character. They do not compare with Freud as thinkers or as persons, but they have performed indispensable roles in modern cultural history by virtue of their refusal to be epigones. What they understood, each in his own way, was the need for a post-Christian, postanalytic faith that will incorporate the gains of analysis and make communal, indeed human, life possible.

> It may be said that Jung's faith in faith cannot compete intellectually with the brilliant specificity of Freudian analysis. On the other hand, the aim of psychoanalysis may be too modest even to maintain its original strength . . . In the last analysis, a leap of faith might be necessary, if the patient is to be free to choose— and to choose because his knowledge, being personal, compels

him thus. The hardest thing to learn is not how to choose but rather how to acquire that passionate knowledge which will permit us again to be chosen. In this sense, Jung represents the uncertain and confused renewal of an effort toward personal knowledge that is also, at the same time, faith.[6]

Rieff measures the capacity of a culture to survive "by the power of its institutions to bind and loose men in the conduct of their affairs with reasons which sink so deep into the self that they become commonly and implicitly understood—with that understanding of which explicit belief and precise knowledge of externals would show outwardly like the tip of the iceberg." Rieff's thought already has a tradition behind it, the "conservative" tradition of Edmund Burke, Thomas Carlyle, John Henry Newman, Michael Polanyi, and Michael Oakeshott, with its sentiment about the prerational and unspoken depths of our being when we are in a state of health. Freud's place in this tradition manifests itself, paradoxically, not in an animus against rationalism (Freud, after all, was perhaps the greatest of modern rationalists), but in his "attack on the moralizing function of modern culture [or religion]." Rieff cites Freud's view that religious questions induce the very symptoms they seek to cure. "The moment a man questions the meaning and value of life, he is sick, since objectively neither has any existence."[7] In Rieff such a statement comes to mark the limits of the rationalist position. "Meaning" and "value" do not disappear. They are implicit in a state of health. To bring them to the surface as the objects of philosophical or social inquiry is symptomatic of personal and social illness. One of the earliest expressions of this view can be found in Carlyle, for whom unconsciousness is not as in Freud a condition to be overcome, but the desirable balance between body and soul. Jung, Lawrence, Reich, and even Rieff represent a return to this view through the formidable experience of Freudian rationalism.

Freud opens a path to a transcendence of rationalism (without endorsing it). His rationalism compels him to assert the possibility and desirability of an unillusioned life, but his postulation of an unconscious, the result both of intuition and of the logical requirements of his system, leads him to value those moments in a person's life when all questions cease. There is at the core of life irreducible mystery and silence, which the problem- or puzzle-solving rational intellect cannot, indeed should not, reach. Thus Freud's own work testifies to the limitations of his analytic ethic, and yet he is unable, and unwilling, to move beyond it.

Freud assimilates religion to "the dissociation of sensibility" that defines man's alienation from himself. It is not the loss of religion, in Freud's view, that has devastated man's psychic life, but the loss of innocence of which religion itself is an expression. Freud shares with Marx a revulsion from what they both regard as the illusory and misleading character of religion. In that sense, they are true sons of the Enlightenment with its corrosive sense of all religious pretensions. Freud, however, does appropriate the higher critical habit of reading psychological significance into Biblical texts—as he does, for example, in his version of the Moses story.

I would make, however, an anomalous, some might think perverse, claim for the antirationalism of Freud's hostility to religion. If religion is a mode of explanation or understanding of the "meaning" and "value" of the universe, it can be seen as a kind of reasoning about the universe, which Freud diagnosed as symptomatic of illness. The condition of health to which men ought to strive is an Edenic ideal of spontaneous consciousness, which of course can never be perfectly achieved. I am suggesting, in other words, that there is a ground that Freud treads, but which is hardly acknowledged in his work, of which perhaps he was only barely conscious, that he shares with his adversaries Lawrence, Reich, and Jung.

What Freud did not consider was the possibility that for many religions, god-terms designated precisely that area of existence which gives a person a sense of well-being beyond reason, philosophy, even language. Certainly the condition of mystery and unconsciousness that Lawrence celebrates is at once religious and free of the quest for "meaning" and "value" that Freud deplores. It is this ill-defined ground that Rieff is tracking through Freud and beyond. Accepting the putative "fact" that religion is dead (or defunct), Rieff revives the discussion of the importance of god-terms in a manner which links the post-Freudian concern with faith with the higher criticism of the nineteenth century.

The great achievement of the higher critics was to trace a path between the Scylla of dogmatic literalism and the Charybdis of rational disbelief by altering our expectations of the veridical character of the Bible. If the Bible were not read as literal history—a view held by rationalists and dogmatists alike—but as an exercise of the symbolic imagination, the Bible would remain part of the permanent spiritual experience of mankind. Indeed, as I have already shown, the habit of reading the Bible literally is heretical (in the higher critical view), pro-

ceeding as it does from a perverse need to make the movement of the
soul a physical drama in which visible material rewards and punishments necessarily occur. As Matthew Arnold argued in one of his several roles as critic, it is the inward meaning, not the putative material
circumstances, of Jesus' resurrection that represents the real intention
of the New Testament. Rieff (as do I) comes to the higher criticism not
through Protestantism but through an analogous Judaism or Jewishness which searches out the spiritual law in things.

The effect of Arnold's performance as a higher critic is to poeticize
religion and to sacralize poetry, as we can see in the famous passage
about the future of poetry, which I cite again.

> The future of poetry is immense, because in poetry, where it is
> worthy of its high destinies, our race, as time goes on, will find an
> ever surer and surer stay. There is not a creed which is not
> shaken, not an accredited dogma which is not shown to be ques-
> tionable, not a received tradition which does not threaten to dis-
> solve. Our religion has materialized itself in the fact, in the sup-
> posed fact; it has attached its emotion to the fact, and now the
> fact is failing it. But for poetry the idea is everything; the rest is a
> world of illusion, of divine illusion. Poetry attaches its emotion
> to the idea; the idea *is* the fact. The strongest part of our religion
> today is its unconscious poetry.[8]

Rieff offers a comparable view when he speaks of the loss of authority of the traditional objects of faith in the idiom of the therapeutic.

> The therapy of all therapies is not to attach oneself exclusively to
> any particular therapy, so that no illusion may survive of some
> end beyond an intensely private sense of well-being to be gener-
> ated in the living of life itself. That a sense of well-being has be-
> come the end, rather than a by-product of striving after some
> communal end, announces a fundamental change of focus in the
> entire cast of our culture—toward a human condition about
> which there will be nothing further to say in terms of the old style
> of despair and hope.[9]

Rieff's link with Arnold consists in their shared view of the necessary provisionality of all symbolism, that is, externalizations of the
material life. For Arnold, the materialization in "the supposed fact" of
dogma results in the death of the spirit. Spiritual fullness consists in
the ultimate freedom of the idea from any particular materialization.
The spiritual consequences, from Rieff's point of view, of *not* attach-

ing oneself exclusively to any particular therapy is equivocal, carrying us into a region beyond hope and despair.

Rieff knows, as Arnold and Lawrence knew before him, that we have come to the end of belief in a fixed religious or moral organization of psychic life—though we may not have lost our religious appetite. D. H. Lawrence states the case in the idiom of Christianity. "Never did God or Jesus say there was one straight way of salvation, for ever and ever. On the contrary, Jesus plainly indicated the changing of the way. And what is more, He indicated the only means to the finding of the right way."[10] The right way varies according to the shifting dialectic of our psyches in which dominant needs change from time to time. Any attempt to fix the self inside a dogma kills the spirit.

Northrop Frye refers to a comparable phenomenon when he characterizes "intellectual idolatry" as "the recurrent tendency in religion to replace the object of its worship with its present understanding and forms of approach to that object." Frye's instances, curiously enough, are Coleridge, who "tried to make criticism a natural theology," and Arnold, who "tried to reduce religion to an objectified cultural myth."[11] Frye's charge against Arnold is misconceived, for the very principle of culture is the provisionality of all symbolic representations of permanent values. If the idea is everything, as Arnold claims, then every narrative or lyric expression of it has an only heuristic or provisional status for the spiritual imagination. To be sure, Arnold does not ever suggest that the Bible or Shakespeare or Milton will become obsolescent. But his "theory" does not preclude the possibility. Arnold's view does not encourage an aesthetic veneration for the art object itself, since the actual physical structure of the object has a contingent or provisional status. Arnold's view of literature as symbolic of religious or spiritual experience, with its strong suggestion of the provisionality of all symbolic structures, would seem to modify, if not contradict, his ritualistic insistence that the task of criticism is to see the object as in itself it really is. In any case, we may apply this higher critical view to the experience of literature itself in order to understand not only the need for preferences and discriminations but also the fact that preferences and discriminations are subject to historical changes.

The capacity of a reader of literature to accept the contradictions of the literary tradition (Tolstoy vs. Dostoevsky, Joyce vs. Lawrence, Whitman vs. Eliot) without necessarily experiencing a sense of incoherence may be explained by the dialectic of what Rieff calls control and release. The oppositions correspond to a variety of intellect, temperament, and sensibility, not only in mankind as a whole, but within each of us as well. Some of our most valuable critics insist on making choices, often radical choices between possible objects of admiration or worship. Among writers they may choose between Whitman and Eliot or between Joyce and Lawrence. Their choices may have a fanatical element in them, a tendency toward unfairness. Nevertheless, the performance of these critics is a signal warning against the danger of blandness. The moral implication of our shifting psychic dialectic is that we must allow the dominating need, whatever it may be at any period in our lives—whether an individual life or the life of our culture—to find expression. In Lawrence's high-flown, god-laden language, a person must obey the presiding gods or demons in one's soul. Discrimination, preference, subordination are fundamental human energies. The danger is in the petrification of any particular subordination and discrimination—the attempt to fix forever a canon or a tradition. The opposite danger, exemplified by Frye's own work, is that the "commitment" to the "autonomy of culture" is so undiscriminating that the human need for particular affirmations and rejections is undervalued—at least at the level of serious critical response. It is hard to see how one can be an interesting participant in, or critic of, the cultural life if one chooses to be Olympian in one's acceptances.

If the Therapeutic According to Rieff is in the tradition of the higher criticism, it is an advance upon, or a regression from, its original inspiration. Rieff does not derive his values from the detritus of Christian pieties as Arnold does, but rather from a psychological study of man, from the therapeutic conclusions about what constitutes man's well-being. Arnold believes as a matter of faith that the Biblical tradition contains *permanent* values in symbolic form. In Rieff these values have to be judged according to a psychological standard. The difference in procedure is important, for Rieff's freedom from commitment to the religious tradition increases the sense of provisionality of all symbolism. It undermines the claim for permanence of the values themselves. In contrast, Arnold's view rests on the *données* of the culture, though he is critical of some of these manifestations. Rieff is at a moment in the history of culture when the validity of culture itself has come into question even for him. Though he winds up by affirming culture, the affirmation is by no means a foregone conclusion nor is there much hope connected with the affirmation.

The increase in the sense of provisionality creates, paradoxically, an anxiety to discover adequate externalizations of the inner life. The inwardness that Arnold cherished is the nemesis that haunts Rieff's work. It is as if the higher critical demolition of all diminishing and corrupting materializations of the spirit had accomplished its task only too well, and we are left with a dangerous preoccupation with our "well-being," our inwardness—the therapeutic category that must be escaped for it to be reinstated.

Rieff's sensitivity to the need for adequate externalizations of inner life is not matched by his imagination or understanding of them. For example, the aesthetic realm, in Rieff's view, is "bracketed and raised above the ordinary workaday world, yet related to that world as revelation is related to that which is revealed—superior and saving."[12] Again, "the work of art becomes that *wholly other*, present and yet inviolate, by means of which the cultivated may escape, for the time of this relation, their self-isolation." This is the language of the romantic ambition for art, which Rieff unaccountably displaces to modern art. In an extended passage he claims utopia for the modern artistic imagination.

> The modern artist, too, has had the role of a spiritual preceptor thrust upon him. And, indeed, because modern artists move in the direction of release, there is a religious pretension inherent in the work of the moderns, reacting as they do to a situation in which nature has been taken out of their purview by science and technology. They have deliberately created alternative realities to those put in jeopardy by science. The inherent interest of modern art is not chiefly in experimenting with the representation of some microscopic reality, or in some correspondence with a presumed macrocosm, but, more importantly, in the production of a picture that would suggest, within its frame, the multiple and alternative realities through which the modern may enliven an existence divorced from both nature and faith. The artist represents what we are trying to become, the shape we are trying to take in our effort to escape the pressures of timeworn inwardness while also escaping the bondage of new internalities. It is for his professional effort at unfixed externalizations, valid first to his own psychological economy, that the modern artist has been handed a spiritual preceptorship. By exploring the range of presentable realities, quite apart from the "natural" or the "socially accept-

able," the modern artist has broken his vocational connection
with moral demand systems, beginning with that of the middle
classes. In achieving an impersonality no less impressive than that
achieved by modern science, painting, in particular, augured the
emancipation from the classical moral demand system, rejecting
the *person* as an object of aesthetic interest and concentrating on
the self-fulfilling function of the work of art itself. Thus the art
work has become, in a strict sense, a therapeutic mode.[13]

This is eloquent but much too facile. Rieff presents, it seems to me,
an ideal prototype of the artist, composed of elements of the nineteenth and twentieth centuries. "The modern artist" who has broken
with the "moral demand system" can already be found in the nineteenth century Bohemian. Moral revolution, especially in its nihilist
forms, is primarily a twentieth century (post-World War I) phenomenon. On the other hand, the imagination of "multiple and alternative"
realities is essentially an expression of nineteenth century utopianism.
The literary imagination of the nineteenth century, particularly in
England and America, is characterized by its remarkable confidence in
the moral capacities of men. In contrast, if the contemporary artist
imagines alternative realities, he is probably engaged in an exercise in
negative or downward transcendence, for these realities are versions
of hell. Rieff's conclusion that the achievement of impersonality in art
has produced an emancipation from the classical moral demand system is accurate only if the word emancipation is neutralized of whatever positive connotation it might have.[14]

The inability of art, even in its utopian aspect, to provide an adequate cultural therapy (which is not to deny it any therapeutic value)
is implicit in a distinction Rieff makes between Luther and Lawrence,
between the religious politician and the religious artist.

When Luther saw what violence his liberation of the inner man
from his inwardness had let loose, he hedged in remorse against
the consequences of his own position. The later Luther became
far more the institutional Catholic than the revolutionary Protestant. Lawrence, however, polemical enthusiast for the same liberation, but without that experience of organizational responsibility which is thrust like an object lesson upon every revolutionary,
rejects all hedgings. Welcoming as he did the imminent end of a
culture created out of the divine ordering word (*logos*), he is not
appalled by the "scream of violence," which to him expresses not
death but the birth, in "pain and splendor," of true individuality.[15]

But if Lawrence is to be faulted for lacking organizational responsibility (the natural condition of the artist), Luther should be offered as
an instance of the compromise and domestication of spirit when it
assumes the burdens of institutional life. If institutions cannot suffer
the irresponsibility of art, art may have to stand forever clear of the
tendency of institutions to domesticate and emasculate their original
spiritual inspiration. In either case, the externalization proves to be an
inadequate therapy. Neither art nor social institutions seem capable
of achieving the necessary balance between the inner and the outer. I
suspect that part of the meaning of Rieff's conception of the provisionality of all externalizations of the spirit is his sense of their inadequacy, though sometimes he writes as if he were taking the ideal intention of the therapy as its reality. Indeed, this sense of inadequacy,
one might call it his antiutopian strain, is what distinguishes him from
his adversaries in the therapeutic mode: Herbert Marcuse and Norman
O. Brown.

It is precisely the uncertain spiritual character of Psychological Man
that makes Rieff's ambivalent view of the therapeutic. To paraphrase
Sir Philip Sidney, Rieff intends neither to affirm nor to deny the therapeutic. Or rather he sees the therapeutic ambiguously as the necessary
wave of the future and as the possible source of nihilism. *Fellow
Teachers* is his own effort at a leap of faith, one which goes counter to
the destructive tendency of modern life and is not simply an exacerbated version of it.

It is anomalous to characterize Reiff's thought as a leap of faith, because his work is filled with annunciations of the irreversible end of
the religious life as we know it, the life controlled by divinely sanctioned interdictions, in which remissions are always generated out of
interdictions. Until recently, liberation meant a freedom which involves a new system of interdiction. Freedom entails the recognition
of necessity, however differently the new necessity may be conceived
from the old one. Now liberation is the shibboleth of a culture of remission, implying as it does a repudiation of all interdictions. The
failure of all interdictions does not necessarily mean that the need for
interdiction has disappeared. It is simply that submission to interdiction depends upon a belief in a particular model. Against the need for
interdictions, which constitute the basis for shaping a self, is the infinite diversity of possible selves or roles which clamor for attention.

Since Rieff does not enjoy a proleptic vision of a spontaneously

ordered culture of remission like Marcuse or Brown, what then does a
leap of faith entail? An answer to this question cannot produce a coherent result, because Rieff is mired in the contradictions of the age.
For him the institution that externalizes—or should externalize—the
life of spirit is the university. In *Fellow Teachers*, Rieff celebrates the
priesthood of intellect, an inescapable "confusion" of categories, because he believes it represents "a surer stay" against the corrosions of
modern life than any of the apocalyptic proposals for a Dionysian
reconstruction of the ego, which have yet to prove that they have a
semblance of a notion of how one gets beyond the act of demolition.
That itself is a contradiction, for it means that Rieff implicitly identifies the university with the church. Though Rieff is obviously opposed
to the recent counterculture, his own counterapocalypticism implies an
expectation of the university that suggests the events of the late sixties
are irreversible. The fact that Rieff's priesthood of intellect performs a
religious function as well as an intellectual one—or rather the intellectual life is conceived as satisfying a religious appetite—would seem
to compromise the argument for the disinterestedness and objectivity
of the university.

Yet Rieff's equivocation cannot be easily dismissed. What a number
of teachers discovered during the late sixties was an appetite for
authority among students that underlay their rebelliousness. They
wanted, unconsciously no doubt, not vertiginous freedom but a sense
of direction. Any teacher alert to his own experience during this period could cite many instances.

The classic examination of the relations between the intellectual life
and the spiritual life, between university and church, is John Henry
Newman's *The Idea of a University*, where one finds a similar equivocation. In *The Idea of a University*, Newman is careful to distinguish
knowledge from faith. The aim of knowledge is to produce a cultivated man, a gentleman. Knowledge yields neither grace nor virtue.
The distinction is essential to Newman's argument, for he is interested
in justifying not only the university but also by implication the
church. At the same time there is an ambiguity in his language that
suggests that knowledge is not simply *sui generis*, that it reaches or at
least has aspirations to the condition of spirituality.

> That perfection of the Intellect, which is the result of Education,
> and its beau ideal, to be imparted to individuals in their respec-
> tive measures, is the clear, calm, accurate vision and comprehen-

sion of all things, as far as the finite mind can embrace them, each in its place, and with its own characteristics upon it. It is almost prophetic from its knowledge of history; it is almost heart-searching from its knowledge of human nature; it has almost supernatural charity from its freedom from littleness and prejudice; it has almost the beauty and harmony of heavenly contemplation, so intimate is it with the eternal order of things and the music of the spheres.[16]

It is *almost* prophetic, *almost* the repose of faith, though earlier he had stressed the illusoriness of the resemblance between knowledge and virtue.

Knowledge is one thing, virtue is another; good sense is not conscience, refinement is not humility, nor is largeness and justness of view faith. Philosophy, however enlightened, however profound, gives no command over the passions, no influential motives, no vivifying principles. Liberal Education makes not the Christian, not the Catholic, but the gentleman.[17]

Newman equivocates between quantitative and qualitative conceptions of the difference between knowledge and virtue. From the point of view of logical consistency, *The Idea of a University* is not, as Pater claimed, the perfect handling of a theory.

But the equivocation represents a profound, though not fully mastered, intuition about the nature of education and in particular a liberal education. Knowledge is not quite the word that Newman wants. He does not or should not want it because it implies an incremental conception of learning, it is the sign of utilitarian fact-gathering. Learning for Newman is more truly conveyed by words like shaping, changing, ordering, enlarging, terms akin to the operation of grace. Education is a moral power in the way that it works upon the mind and character and shapes one's vision of life. It is for this reason that "knowledge" is legitimately an end in itself. Newman is claiming for knowledge and the university, its institutional home, more than he believes he is claiming, a fact which is the source of its power and its classic status. Raymond Williams is puzzled why Newman did not fix on the word culture as Matthew Arnold did. The reason is that Arnold wanted a conception of intellectual formation that included the spiritual and moral powers. Culture is an aggrandizing term, whereas knowledge, for all its deficiencies, is a more modest word, which allows for the kind of distinction Newman wanted to make. It is, to be sure, a distinction he had difficulty sustaining. Rieff's phrase "the priesthood of intellect," in all its ambiguity, is implicit in Newman's *The Idea of a University*. It is, in Arnoldian terms, the apostleship of culture.[18]

Those for whom science is a calling tend to view such a claim for the authority of the teacher as pernicious mystification. Max Weber's "Science as a Vocation" is a superb definition of the "authority" of the scientist as teacher, which consists in no more than the body of knowledge he possesses and the degree of rational conceptualization of it. The contemporary idea of "expertise" is, of course, derived from Weber, though it is interesting that Weber's view, or should we say vision, of the life of reason is suffused with the language of moral integrity. Weber recoils from the vision of "thousands of professors," attempting to be "petty prophets in their lecture rooms" and it is difficult not to sympathize with him. But Weber ignores the limits of the disinterestedness of the life of reason: for instance, its ideological refusal to acknowledge even the possibility of miracle and revelation. More important, it ignores the *charismatic* freight, to use a word reinvented by Weber, that the life of reason has traditionally borne. One has only to invoke the name of Socrates to remind oneself how closely reason has been tied to the moral life. The severing of the two that occurs in the following passage in "Science as a Vocation" simply overrides the inescapable continuities that exist between reasoning and valuing, continuities that inhere in the enterprise of teaching.

> One can only demand of the teacher that he have the intellectual integrity to see that it is one thing to state facts, to determine mathematical or logical relations or the internal structure of cultural values, while it is another thing to answer questions of the value of culture and its individual contents and the question of how one should act in the cultural community and in political associations. These are quite heterogeneous problems. If he asks further why he should not deal with both types of problems in the lectureroom, the answer is: because the prophet and the demagogue do not belong on the same platform.[19]

If Weber's division of function were allowed to prevail, there would be neither speculation nor teaching in the humanities. In criticizing Weber, I am, of course, lifting his argument out of the immediate historical context in which he wrote. The essay was written in 1919, the year immediately following the defeat of Germany in World War I. The threat from demagogues and false prophets was real. I need in-

voke only 1933 to remind one of the realized dangers. Weber's po-
lemic may have been a necessary one, but the Weberian argument survives among contemporary social scientists and is vulnerable in the
present context.

Rieff wants a return of intellectual authority to the university—
which is not simply a matter of erudition or even conceptual capacity.
Authority involves character, and character entails priestly wisdom
about the interdictions and freedoms of the cultural life. Rieff is claiming nothing less: so the vatic mode he shares with his adversary Norman O. Brown is not gratuitous. And yet—or because of this—Rieff is
a symptomatic writer perhaps more than a diagnostician. The interdictory thrusts itself forward in too strident a manner. As a corrective,
it pushes us too far in the opposite direction. Because Rieff understandably wishes to set boundaries to nihilistic criticism, he feels he
has to make the interdictory the unexamined absolute presupposition
of his argument. At its worst, Rieff's manner suggests a thwarted authoritarianism which runs counter to the doctrine of self-limitation.
At its best it is an assertion of individuality in a culture that is predom-
inantly remissive; it seeks to rectify the balances between interdiction
and remission.

Such is the level of discourse in America today that an argument for
an interdictory, as opposed to a remissive, culture is bound to be received with mistrust or indifference. The setting of limits seems like an
archaic exercise in conservatism. It suggests repression in both the
psychological and the political sense. What does it indeed mean to argue at the present time for an interdictory culture? Is this simply a
mindless "conservative" reflex to the dangers of liberation, or is it a
necessary response to the new "freedoms" at play in the cultural life?
Is it an effort to paralyze genuine progress, or is it a dialectical test for
the claims of progress, a test in which progress may continue?

Nietzsche spoke of the adventure of immoralism as an experiment,
and he meant experiment seriously. Not everyone is to perform the experiment and one must await results. We have already gone through a
rich experience of immoralism and should be able to judge the experience. It is not necessary for us to be automatically heuristic in our
suspension of the ethical, which would in effect turn the heuristic into
an end itself. This is not the same as wanting to end experiment. It is
rather the repetition of the same experiment that no longer seems necessary. The point of experiment should be not to destroy all interdic-

tion or, put differently, the very idea of authority, but rather to discover what interdictions are and are not necessary for a human life.

Rieff shares with his adversaries a desire for an integrated life. But whereas Norman O. Brown conceives of integration as a mode of incorporating all possibilities (the total release from repression means for Brown the realization of all possibilities), Rieff sees chaotic impossibility. The rebellion against repression has produced self-hatred and self-destructiveness, not a richer and fuller selfhood. Rieff's insight into the self-destructive character of the release from repression is profound.

The polarized choice between interdiction and remission, liberation and repression, distorts the ambiguity of the situation, which is beautifully exemplified in an episode in Doris Lessing's *The Golden Notebook*. In the novel, the writer-heroine complains about the teleological character of story, the ineluctable way in which a sequence of events moves toward some foreordained conclusion.[20] Events are not interesting in and of themselves, but as they contribute to an end, a purpose—for instance, the events of a love relationship are seen as anticipations of its dissolution. The heroine is thinking of her fiction in particular and of modern fiction in general; if she were thinking of Victorian fiction the anticipations would be, of course, of a happy marriage. The immediate experience, the present moment for its own sake, is of no consequence, a view, incidentally, which denies or ignores the possibility that an event gains interest and intensity from its significant participation in a chain of other events. The heroine's complaint is not aesthetic or even philosophical, it is moral. For her a story in its classic, teleological form is a relatively firm ironclad sequence of events, which robs the events themselves of their intrinsic interest and intensity and which excludes other events. The heroine of Doris Lessing's novel commits herself to adventure, which for her is not lived along the classic line of teleological narrative. Adventure continually risks chaos. To be adventurous is to refuse to be dominated by the fear of chaos, because such fear means impoverishing self-limitation, the incapacity to commit oneself to the variety and intensity of experience. This at least is the ideology of liberated consciousness. But Doris Lessing is a sufficiently searching and honest novelist not to accept, or rather not to allow her heroine to accept, the ideology on its face value. This is what the adventure means or comes to feel like.

And yet I was thinking: This quality, this intellectual, "I wanted to see what was going to happen, I want to see what will happen next," is something loose in the air, it is in so many people one meets, it is in me. It is part of what we all are. It is the other face of: it doesn't matter.[21]

We are given the other face of liberation. Note the determinist atmosphere of the statement. What is going to happen occurs apart from the will. The detachment, the absence of committed feeling, suggests that the adventurer must immunize himself against the experience in order to engage in it. This perception reverses the claims of the adventurer, for the commitment to liberation has its own teleologic. Doris Lessing's mode is finally dialectical and exploratory. Her novel does not turn into an ideological tract or liberationist homily, but it does assert a complex truth about efforts to achieve individual freedom: it is an exercise of the moral intelligence.

For all the distortion and excess in Rieff's work, it deserves serious attention, for he has made a valiant attempt to rectify an imbalance in our cultural life. Rieff's call for interdictions and limitation belongs to a small stream, rather, a trickle (compared to the flood of liberationist literature being written) of critical works which set themselves against the dominant strain of what might be called apocalyptic egoism, a native American product with imperialist tendencies. Quentin Anderson's *The Imperial Self* (1970), for example, is a long complaint that the American self, imagined by Emerson and Whitman, gobbles up the world: it has no respect for historical or "spatial" limitation. One of the ways in which the imperial self proclaims itself is through the autonomy of the work of art. The work is self-governing, insubordinate, owing allegiance to no one and to nothing but itself—like the idealized modern individual. Anderson's critical vantage point is the nineteenth century European with his steady view of rank, station, role—in short, human limitation. Anderson remarks the irony of his enterprise.

I have all along been aware of the irony implicit in my enterprise; my contemporaries show a strong impulse to step out of time and the constraints of associated life; I have been complaining that Emerson was their predecessor (ancestor is impossible in this context)—in the process I am enacting the role of the time-bound nineteenth-century European.[22]

The imperial egoism described by Anderson presupposes a faith in the limitless power and benevolence of the impulsive self. Even those "imperialists" who allow a certain aggressiveness and cruelty to personal expression regard the self as essentially benevolent, because they implicitly value the particular self over the objects of its aggression. What is good for the valuable self is good for the world. Given the disastrous historical manifestations of this view, it has become morally insupportable. Moreover, imperial egoism has become democratized. Which means that the demonic self, free of all moral inhibitions, acting out an aesthetic destiny, has experience more often than not of disintegration and impotence rather than of strength and fulfillment. Indeed even for artists, heroes, and saints, the doctrine of imperial egoism may be insupportable, the moral of *Death in Venice* for example.

Anderson provides a valuable perspective on American culture, but it suffers from negativism, from his inability or unwillingness to get "beyond the irony implicit in his enterprise." What is needed is a more sympathetic, though critical, understanding of the conditions which have made for imperial egoism. Emerson, after all, did not wilfully create the self. It was implicit in American experience, which I think is one implication of Anderson's remark about ancestry.[23] History, or in my term the past, for Anderson is a moral or spiritual category like Original Sin: it is chastening, humbling to be a historical creature. But to want to be ahistorical may be an irresistible historical phenomenon to which moral scorn is an impertinence. The American imagination self-consciously, but perhaps necessarily, defined itself against the constraints felt by the European imagination. It did not have the experience of the necessity of being time-bound or role-bound or space-bound.[24] And if the absence of this experience might prove in the long run a case of innocence, the sense of freedom at the moment was genuine. It cannot be a matter of simple conspiracy that major figures as temperamentally different from one another as Emerson, Whitman, and James should enjoy this sense of freedom. Moreover, it is not at all clear that the long-run view has refuted nineteenth century America's sense of possibility, at least not on the terms of the time-bound European. The twentieth century European no longer feels time-bound in the nineteenth century sense, having been caught by the American influence. It is by no means an easy or perhaps even possible matter to bind the self to a nineteenth or pre-nineteenth century European sense of space and time, even with the disappearance of a sense of limitless possibility.

Unless one has a real vision of alternative possibility (by no means an easy achievement), one can do little more than engage in elegiac statement and the profession of irony. One can begin to argue for the moral power of the past or of history (in Anderson's sense) only if one begins to see it not exclusively under the aspect of limitation.

Rieff's argument in *Fellow Teachers* suffers from a similar negativism. In arguing for a need for a "science of limits," he denounces the spirit of liberation in a wholesale way that seriously undermines the quality of his insight. His own sense of a healthy culture as a balance of interdictory and remissive energies (indeed, interdictions generate remissions) would seem to make it imperative that he sort out what is valuable and destructive in the exercises of liberation. For example, to decriminalize marihuana is one thing, to foster an atmosphere in which drug-taking is a symbol of freedom is another. Rieff's manner is a self-contradictory imitation of his adversaries. He is the Norman Mailer of interdictions, engaged in histrionic performance rather than careful reflection. That he should feel the need for such a performance is itself a cultural symptom. Perhaps he feels he cannot be heard or listened to above the din—unless, that is, he raises his voice to apocalyptic decibels. Is there perhaps a demonic need in Rieff to achieve the status of guru—or, in the idiom of Mailer, to counterrevolutionize American consciousness?

To compare Rieff to Mailer is, among other things, to suggest Rieff's deficiency as a sociologist. Rieff's call for a reinstating of interdiction is connected with no apparent social economic need apart from what he perceives to be the social psychological necessity for a regulated life: the alternative, according to Rieff, is misery. But Rieff's analysis needs to be linked to a substantial sense of the development of technological civilization. Without the analysis, his discussion has the disabilities of abstract moralizing.

A sociological account might take as its model Weber's classic analysis of *The Protestant Ethic and the Rise of Capitalism*. In that book Weber shows how the interdictions of Christianity, sporadically applied to ordinary people and more fully applied to monastic orders in Catholic countries, systematically penetrated the mundane activities of the whole society in Calvinist dominated countries. This puritanism supported the growth of industrial capitalism by instilling in the new class of factory workers habits of punctuality, regularity, and temperance. The development of new interdictions related to an organizational need of society. The break with the moral demand system of the middle class that Rieff asserts to be one of the characteristics of the Bohemian artist spread to the rest of the population at the moment that the productive capacity of technological civilization became so great that the need for punctuality, regularity, and temperance was attenuated. Rieff's moralistic fervor prevents him from making an adequate response to the social and economic realities that support a remissive culture.

Though Rieff's extreme rhetoric makes him sound as if he were interested in developing a rational system of interdictions for the whole of society as Calvin and his followers did in the early period of bourgeois civilization, there is little corresponding to such an intention in the concrete philosophical elaborations of Rieff's work. It is interesting to note that such a systematic, all-encompassing intention can also be found in the work of Rieff's adversaries, Marcuse and Brown, and there too the systematic "rationalizing" impulse manifests itself more through rhetoric than through the concrete elaborations and prescriptions one finds in earlier system builders. Of course, the substance of the doctrines of Marcuse and Brown, with their commitment to spontaneity and passional expressiveness, would seem to run counter to a systematic unfolding of a prescriptive conduct. The reason for this is that the revolutionary change of consciousness which they advocate cannot be achieved by a simple *laisser-aller*. New interdictions are needed to establish the higher spontaneity. Marcuse and Brown as well as Rieff confront us, though in significantly different ways, with the coercive challenge of new interdictions in a remissive culture.

Given the history of repressive societies, it is necessary for a contemporary advocate of new interdictions to show the humane character of the society he wishes to see realized. Historically, interdictory cultures have been motivated by envy, fear, invidiousness. One apparent difference between interdictory and remissive cultures is the authoritarianism which presumably inheres in an interdictory culture. In contrast, remissive cultures assume the capacity for freedom and self-governance of each person. But if most adults as well as children need authority in order to govern themselves as well as form themselves, then a remissive culture may be ultimately a delusion. Authoritarianism will manifest itself in countless unregulated ways in a remissive culture. The value of an interdictory culture is that it is conscious of the authoritarian or authoritative elements in the cultural life. It prescribes its limits as well as its prerogatives and in the long run may be more humane than a remissive culture. Though interdictions entail punishment, they need not be motivated by envy, fear, or invidiousness.

In Rieff the argument for a rational interdictory culture occurs in a mood of futility. For all his moralist urgency, Rieff is ultimately an elegist. The death of God is a fact to be accepted, but with regret. Until god-terms are reinvented there can be no hope. Even moral humanism cannot be sustained without the sanction of god-terms.[25] This is tantamount to saying that the instinct for self-preservation requires divine sanction. Modern cultural history would seem to give support to this view. But does it prove it? By acting out what he calls "the logic of secularization," Rieff places himself in an intolerable dilemma. Psychological Man is the result of an irreversible desacralization, but man cannot survive without god-terms. It is very hard to see the alternative to nihilism and moral suicide. One must subvert the logic of secularization in order to find a way out.

The threat of nihilism may not be in the death of God but in the historical authority that gives this putative fact so much cultural power. Smerdyakov does not kill his father because God is dead, but because he has accepted the authority of Ivan Karamazov's (and Dostoevsky's) postulate that if God does not exist, everything is permitted. The English have been less apocalyptic than the Russians, or for that matter than continental Europeans, about the consequences of the death of God. Thus the social or moral instinct, for George Eliot, survives the extinction of God and immortality perhaps because Protestantism (God or no God) remains so residually strong. A system of interdictions is an expression of a need for survival, not simply a tablet handed down from Mount Sinai. Or to reconcile the two possibilities, the tablet from Sinai is the imagination's response to the need to survive. I am not saying that the instinct for survival is strong enough to withstand "the logic of secularization." Without belief or a sense of purpose or a feeling of the rightness of things the instinct for survival has been known to disappear or disintegrate. In his confusion and uncertainty, Rieff may be hoping against hope that the destructive logic of secularization can be aborted by a sense of purpose that is at once atheistic and spiritual, so that the god-terms remain, confirming Proudhon's original sense of the "inescapability of religious language." Not exactly a gratifying situation, but there seems to be no other alternative at the present time.

6

The Formalist Avant-Garde
and the Autonomy
of Aesthetic Values

MODERN ART is an unreliable "spiritual preceptor," to use Philip Rieff's phrase,[1] partly because of its ascetic character, which expresses itself as "formalism." As I understand it, formalism is an attempt to make order in a world that is resistantly disorderly, an effort that entails severe renunciations. The desire for order is a permanent human motive as profound as the need for freedom and variety. Formalism, however, is a peculiarly modern satisfaction of this desire because of its implicit sensitivity to modern disorder. Any account of modernism that stresses its centrifugal side as mine does has an obligation to account for its impulses toward order. What I hope to show is that the manner in which it conceives of order is symptomatic of the modern condition of fragmentation and consequently powerless to redeem it. Formalism is a term common to both art (or certain kinds of art) and criticism. Criticism may impose formalist categories on art or it may attend to the formalism that art has self-consciously or even half-consciously internalized.

One expression of the impulse toward order is the restriction of the field of discourse. Thus, for example, in *The Anatomy of Criticism*, Northrop Frye rules off-limits any criticism that is not based exclusively on the literary medium, thereby purifying literary discussion of extraneous moral, religious, and political concerns. Though Frye rejects the New Critical claim for the intrinsic value or interest of the individual work, he is very much in the line of New Criticism in postulating a specifically literary medium, which determines the properties of literary study. Needless to say, this formalist tendency is not confined to literature. Indeed, modern abstract painting would seem to

provide an especially powerful example of modernist formalism, because it is a nonverbal art and hence naturally less accommodating to
explicit moral and philosophical concerns than literature. In a passage
cited in the previous chapter, Rieff notes that painting in particular
achieved an impersonality, one might add, a formalism, no less impressive than that achieved by science, which "augured the emancipation from the classical moral demand system, rejecting the *person* as
an object of aesthetic interest and concentrating on the self-fulfilling
function of the work of art itself."

What I would like to consider is an unusually lucid and provocative
statement of the ideology of formalism by the art critic Clement
Greenberg. His essay "Modernist Painting" is an attempt to express
the critical logic of the masterpieces of modernist art. For Greenberg
the history of modern art is not the empirical reality of its total production but its rationality implicit in the sequence of artistic events
that the critic uncovers. Greenberg mutes the historical aspect of the
sequence in order to dramatize its rationality. The aura given to history in the nineteenth century tended to mystify history. Greenberg
wants to keep his subject hard and rational—virtually scientific. The
intellectual motive of this view of modern art cannot be grasped unless
we appreciate its profound debt to the Enlightenment conception of
history. The modern artist, like the Enlightenment philosophe, conceives of sequences in historical time as increasingly rational and
hence progressive.

Greenberg himself acknowledges the origins of modernism in the
Enlightenment, but he is interested in making a distinction. "The Enlightenment criticized from the outside, the way criticism in its more
accepted sense does; Modernism criticizes from the inside, through the
procedures themselves of that which is being criticized." In Greenberg's view, modernism derives its inspiration from the Kantian conception of criticism. "I identify Modernism with the intensification, almost with the exacerbation, of this self-critical tendency that began
with the philosopher Kant. Because he himself was the first to criticize
the means itself of criticism, I conceive of Kant as the first real Modernist."[2] The distinction is an essential one for Greenberg's view of
modern art, but before we pursue it we should keep in mind the common theme of both the Enlightenment and modernism. The goal of
criticism is the achievement of perfect rationality.

The self-critical effort of art has as its goal the elimination "from the

effects of each art any and every effect that might conceivably be borrowed from or by the medium of any other art."[3] The impurity of effects is irrationality, and purity is the rationality of art. The use of the
term "aesthetic" from a formalist point of view is problematic because
it covers what literature, music, and art have in common and the formalist imperative is toward separation and purification. Painting, for
example, is not to be confused with literature—or sculpture and architecture, for that matter.

In the case of painting, what had been conceived by the old masters
as the limitations of the medium, which they tried to overcome
through realistic illusionism, is perceived by modernist painters as the
very essence of painting—the flat surface, the shape of the support,
the properties of pigment. The history of modern art then is a series of
attempts to solve problems created by the limitations of the medium,
which are also the opportunities for solutions. The variety of modern
art is in the ways in which the artist presents his visual solutions
within the admitted constraints of two dimensionality, the shape of
the support, and the pigment. Greenberg argues that the critical, problem-solving activity is within the artistic process itself and not simply
the formulation of the critic who is trying to rationalize the process.
Nevertheless, he does not want to gainsay the received view of the
artist as working through a kind of instinct, if not inspiration. So the
self-critical activity of art itself occurs in a "spontaneous and sublimi-
nal way."[4] A conception of criticism which is spontaneous and sub-
liminal is paradoxical, to say the least.

The increasing self-consciousness about the medium and the realization of the virtues of the particular medium is the tendency of modernism in all formal social activities. We find it in literature and music as
well as in painting. This tendency is self-critical in the sense that the
laws of the medium in which the artist works provide the basis for a
criticism of his achievement. There is no imposition of or appeal to
standards from the outside. It should be noted that Greenberg, like
Frye and unlike the New Critics, does not see the individual work as
having its own constitution. He is concerned with the properties of the
medium. Since those properties are in the process of a progressive exploration and realization, the business of both artist and critic is art
history—or a certain understanding of art history.

Greenberg's view is a version of classicism, which has always been
concerned with a defense of the inviolable integrity of genres and

forms. Irving Babbitt's *New Laokoon,* for example, is largely a complaint against the synaesthetic, or in Babbitt's word hyperaesthetic, effects of romantic and modern art. "Word painting," "programme music," "color audition" are symptoms of a pathology in which the sensing apparatus itself becomes diseased. Babbitt's censorious classicism leads him to a hostility to the one genre with a natural appetite for incorporating incongruous elements. Of the novel, Babbitt writes:

> The novel is the one *genre* that the neo-classicists had not regulated, partly, no doubt, because they had not thought it worth the trouble. It had no formal laws and limits, and so was admirably adapted as Rousseau showed in the "Nouvelle Heloise," to free emotional expansion. The novel is not only the least purposeful of the literary forms, the one that lends itself most naturally to all the meanders of feeling, to a vast overflow of "soul" in the romantic sense, but it also admits most readily a photographic realism without selection. The triumph of the novel has been, if not the triumph of formlessness over form, at least the triumph of diffuseness over concentration. Friedrich Schlegel was right from his own point of view in exalting the novel as a sort of confusion of all the other literary forms, the visible embodiment of that chaos of human nature of which he dreamed.[5]

Babbitt's hostility to modern art and literature (despite his having been T. S. Eliot's mentor) is well-known, so it may seem perverse to attempt to link the reactionary aesthetic of Babbitt with the unequivocal modernism of Greenberg. But the link does exist and it helps us see the ascetic basis of formalism. Both Babbitt and Greenberg want to purify art of its vital elements. The difference between Greenberg and Babbitt is, however, an important one. Greenberg's classicism is futuristic, the medium having not yet realized its essential character. Babbitt's classicism is nostalgic, an evocation of its perfect expression in the work of the ancient Greeks.

The effect of Greenberg's progressive, problem-solving view of modern art is to destroy the popular stereotype of the avant-garde as a generator of the historical discontinuities, a self-starter, within a field of infinitely possible beginnings. "Modernist art [in its progressive development] belongs to the same historical and cultural tendency as modern science,"[6] which again recalls Rieff's comparison between painting and science. Greenberg wishes to purify avant-garde vocabulary of its "liberationist" or catastrophic idiom. The avant-garde for Greenberg is always the next step in a problem-solving series. Something like a new beginning may lie at the origins of modernism itself, that is, the break from realistic illusionism to "medium self-consciousness," though even there the case is not clear.

If we are to take a critical view of Greenberg's theory, we must distinguish between his theory that the history of art constitutes a particular progressive sequence of solutions to problems thrown up by the medium and his view of what the constraints of the medium are. For example, one may quarrel with the particular sequence that Greenberg proposes (a sequence, let us say, that begins with Manet and eventuates in Pollock, Louis, Olitzki, Noland, and Stella) without upsetting his claim that modern art history progressively realizes and articulates the conditions, which is to say the virtues, of the medium.

Greenberg's criticism has a strong judicial or evaluative element. Michael Fried, Greenberg's most able disciple, is justified in objecting to Hilton Kramer's *unargued* dismissal of Greenberg as a historical determinist. "The impersonal process of history appears in the guise of an inner artistic logic."[7] Fried is right in pointing out that Greenberg presents the history of art as the result of individual decisions and not as the effect of an impersonal process.[8]

The artistic logic, according to Greenberg, expresses itself through the historical process. Greenberg is unlike Harold Rosenberg, who appears to take the view that a virtually impersonal historical process determines the course of art. Rosenberg ambivalently accepts the process as inevitable and regards many of its results as contemptible. History, for Greenberg, has no authority by itself. Greenberg's open view is that history is to be trusted, only because the art that has been enacted and survived is intrinsically valuable. Greenberg never argues that history is critical as a matter of definition, or that what is successful is to be valued because it is successful. What matters is the artistic medium, which reveals itself through history.

This attitude enables Greenberg to assume a rationalist, one is almost tempted to say moralist, position with respect to values. He can make value judgments, because he has standards within the art medium on which to base his judgments. Contrary to the view of Greenberg as a historical determinist, I would argue that Greenberg's modernist tradition is similar to Eliot's tradition in its attenuation, if not evaporation, of the historical sense. The series of problem-solutions, like Eliot's simultaneous order of monumental achievements, inhabits a logical space in which the contingencies of time are largely irrelevant.

In using the problem-solving model, Greenberg cannot avoid the suspicion that the new masters are superior to the old masters. For Eliot
the new revision of a tradition does *not* imply the progress entailed by
problem-solving. Eliot allows for the supreme greatness of Dante and
Shakespeare and the superiority of Donne to the modern masters at
the same time that a creative revision of the tradition is always possible by a modern master.

One important practical result of the problem-solving sequence that
Greenberg sets up is the exclusion of certain kinds of art from the
tradition, for example surrealism. Such exclusions, when they are not
simply a matter of good and bad work, immediately provoke a
question about the adequacy of the values implied by the medium.[9]
Can the medium itself supply an adequate set of values from which
one can make judgments about the authority of individual works of
art? If such values are merely derived from the medium, they would
tend to be the minimal conditions for a work of art, the conditions all
works of art share irrespective of their individualities. Such minimal
conditions might be particularly interesting to the artist himself, who
must be concerned with his craft. But they would not be the source of
his freedom or individuality; neither would they be very interesting to
most spectators, certainly not of absorbing interest.[10]

I am, of course, treading on dangerous ground. The spectator, innocent of the history of art, may defend his innocence by protesting the
opacity of the work of art. But I think the issue goes deeper than the
familiar estrangement between artist and philistine. Greenberg's doctrine implies the opacity of the work of art to all spectators except the
ideal spectator, the artist himself or the critic who is able to embody
the values of the artist. Art is turned in upon itself, it is not an exercise
in communication, for communication implies the fragility, the provisionality of the barriers that separate artist and spectator, art and experience.[11]

Moreover Greenberg's vision of art history as a whole becomes severely reductive. The old masters, we are told, having mistaken the
limitations of the medium as negative factors, dissemble the medium,
"using art to conceal art."[12] The principal means of dissembling is of
course realistic illusionism which tries to overcome the flatness of the
canvas. But then all the problems conceived by the old masters (perspective, illusionism, expressiveness) become irrelevancies from
Greenberg's point of view. They are masters despite themselves—that

is, only if we reread and revise their work in the modernist perspective. Given the process of purification and minimalization, the losses incurred in our "reading" of the old masters must be considerable. The revisionary readings may be necessary for certain working modern artists, but it is not at all clear why they are necessary for the spectator, or even for all artists.

As I have already noted, Greenberg understands the process of purification as a critical exercise, engendered by the Enlightenment, to which all formal social activities were subject. Only religion seems to Greenberg exempt from the exercise, since it was not a task that the Enlightenment took seriously. Greenberg shows here an ignorance of the significance of the higher criticism in the nineteenth century, which tried precisely to discover the essential character of religious experience. Men like Arnold and Ernest Renan attempted to uncover the quintessential movements of the soul that religious dogma expresses and conceals. Religious dogma, in this view, is comparable to subject matter in art. It must be reduced to or transformed into the sui generis substance of religious experience itself. The effect of the reduction is to identify religion with literature. Religion, like literature, becomes a symbolic activity expressive of the movement of the spirit. Now such a situation is quite different from the one that Greenberg describes. The effect of such "purification" becomes the translation of one thing into another.

Such translation occurs in the nineteenth century in the attempt of poetry to purify itself of its ideological dross in order to discover its essential character. "De La Musique avant toute chose," Paul Verlaine declares in a celebrated poem, which then proceeds to demonstrate the case. The dross Verlaine dismisses as "littérature." Verlaine's claim is expanded by Pater, who asserts that all arts aspire to the condition of music. The motive for such a translation may be the effort to overcome the referential aspect of the art. Music is the art par excellence which refers to itself. Analogously the disintegration of the narrative into a new kind of musical orchestration of prose in the early twentieth century may be seen as an effort to destroy or overcome the referential aspect of fiction. Of course, it can be argued that in destroying narrative, one diminishes the possibilities of the medium of fiction. Another motive for the attraction to music as the quintessential art, related to its nonreferential character, is its transcendental suggestiveness. It is the art of the spheres, the language of divine harmony. The

appetite for religious transcendence remains strong despite a default-
ing religious orthodoxy.

There is an ambiguity in the ambition of art to be autonomous
which complicates the idea of aesthetic purity. Autonomy means,
among other things, that a work of art is itself and not to be confused
with anything else. For example, art is not religion. But the ambition
of art suggests that autonomy contains or masks the idea of transcendence. The work of art is invested with a special quality to which we
are tempted to give the word transcendence. Freed of any servile function, art becomes the godhead. It requires no justification beyond itself; it is its own reason for being. Art or form is implicitly burdened
with values and intensities which are perhaps beyond the capacity of
art. To be sure, there has been a strong modern tendency (some would
call it postmodern) to destroy the aura and see art as another
commodity of technological civilization. The insistence on the quotidian in all its actuality as an appropriate subject matter for art opened
art to the possibility of an aesthetic of boredom and banality. But the
complementary interest of the classic moderns, for example, Eliot and
Joyce, in a formal transformation of art means that the aura or sense
of aura is retained. The insistence on the autonomy of form presupposes a desire to discover in art a region of radiance and wholeness
missing from modern life. That the purely formal proves to be a
vulnerable fortress against the destruction of the aura is paradoxically
shown in the work of Greenberg and of *some* of the painters he has
championed. The purity Greenberg champions is too impoverished
for the sense of transcendence.

The common enterprise of modern artists and critics to decontami-
nate art of its extra-aesthetic religious and moral concerns and to assert the autonomous integrity of the aesthetic structure of a work of
literature has succeeeded only too well. For while it is necessary to
locate the peculiarly aesthetic function of a work apart from any religious, political, or moral ends to which it may be put, it may very
well be that the activity of art is the expression of a profound spiritual
or therapeutic impulse, the acknowledgment of which may enrich
rather than undermine our understanding of art. The very action of
symbol- or myth-making may be understood in terms of the self-co-
herent structure that results from the activity, or it may, without pre-
cluding such an understanding, be seen as an expression of a human
aspiration or need in history.

One finds such a view in Friedrich Schiller's Kantian letters on *The Aesthetic Education of Man,* a book, incidentally, that had significant influence on recent cultural revolutionaries like Marcuse and Brown. The consequence of this view is not the intransitive separation of disciplines one finds in the work of modern formalists, but rather the development of an aesthetic medium as a particular integration of human faculties, distinguished from political and moral integrations. Schiller regards the aesthetic as an autonomous realm of values, but this autonomy is not insulated from moral and political questions. Rather, the aesthetic is made to stand in a critical relation to the moral and the political. The aesthetic, in Schiller's view, is the medium for nonutilitarian play, a condition of being for which men strive as an end in itself. It is the integration of sensuousness and spirit, of spontaneity and responsibility, in which neither term suffers at the expense of the other—in short, the ideal of human freedom. The letters were written in 1795 and intended in part as a perspective on the despotism (masked as political freedom and justice) which the French Revolution had engendered.

I stress the translational possibility in the exercise of Kantian criticism because it is by no means inevitable that such criticism leads to the purifications and minimalizations that Greenberg seems to imply is the logic of art. For what Greenberg leaves out of account is the possibility of a critical activity conducted in behalf of an idea of an integral humanity, in which such translations are not violations but the natural movement of the discipline.

Greenberg's account of the "logic" of the modern history of art may provide a basis for making critical, evaluative discriminations among works of art, but it is uncritically accepting of its own logic. Greenberg refuses to consider the possibility that extraartistic pressures may produce changes in the history of art. Surrealism responds to discoveries in psychology, futurism to the ascendancy of the machine. Change may be a response to fatigue with the familiar: it may mean refreshment, new excitement, not necessarily discovery or invention. Greenberg's theory would exclude such evidence as irrelevant. Anything that does not fit the "medium logic" does not belong to the history of art. Since Greenberg's idea of history is exclusively confined to the medium itself (or his conception of the medium), he is unable to give a historical account of how such a logic was able to prevail. Why, for example, doesn't "radical self-criticism," to use Fried's phrase, take

the form of questioning the idea of the medium as constitutive of flatness, pigment, and picture support, or, more radically, as a source of
values or of standards of judgment? Such an account might entail a
sociological understanding of how the idea of autonomy in the modern world has been conflated with fragmentation and separateness,
how, in short, the very idea of an integral humanity has become severely problematic. To place the modern history of art in such a context might imply a critical perspective on the purist claims of much
modernist art—for example, on its adequacy, its integrity. It might
undermine the implicit idea that the course of modern art is essentially
one of human progress.

In "The Renaissance Conception of Artistic Progress and Its Consequences," E. H. Gombrich has shown that the idea of progress in the
arts, with its assumption of "originality," started in Renaissance Florence.[13] In contrast, the schools of Siena and Venice were governed by
an artisanal ideal. There artists learned their craft by imitating the old
masters; their goal was to achieve the perfection of traditional art in
its highest form, not to compete with or to overcome the past. Gombrich illustrates this difference by distinguishing between Lorenzo
Ghiberti's imitative attitude toward the making of the first door of the
baptistery and his attempt to "make progress" in his work on the second door. Gombrich is performing the role of historian in putting the
idea of progress in a historical perspective. But he is also providing a
historical rationale for the modern art historian. Gombrich seems less
certain of the objective historical reality of the progressive idea than
he does of its mythic power, its capacity to stimulate artists and his-
torians alike.

It would seem that Gombrich and Greenberg are one in their view
of art as a historical continuum and an autonomous realm of values.
But their conceptions of what the medium of art is and of what constitutes the historical development of art are radically different from
each other. The view that the history of art is a progress does not entail a belief in a particular sequence of artistic events. Critics who
share a belief in progress may have radically different views about the
nature of that progress. The difference may be based on differing
views of the nature of the medium. For Gombrich, painting is concerned with the problem of fidelity to nature. To be sure, Gombrich
does not believe that a painting simply must be faithful to nature, for
the perception and conception of the natural world are extremely

complicated matters. The eye can never be innocent. Gombrich, nevertheless, sees the business of painting as essentially involved with the representation of nature. The history of art for Gombrich is engendered by the discovery of the ambiguities inherent in the "act" of perception. The artist does not imitate a fixed object out there. He rather creates clues which perception organizes into the various possibilities of representing the protean aspect of the visible world. The future of art is open to the inexhaustible possibilities of "representation." Since the ideal is not the achievement of perfect representation, the history of art is not a progress toward perfection but a continuous unpredictable unfolding of the possibilities of art. Gombrich's aesthetic, with all its sophistication, is squarely within the mimetic tradition. In Greenberg's view, representation in the old masters is the great diversion from the true vocation of art. Gombrich's conception of the medium entails an interest in psychology—the medium of painting directly implicates the psychology of perception. Greenberg's conception of the medium entails nothing more than the materials of painting itself.

It is difficult to arbitrate between the two views because one is strong where the other is weak and vice versa. Greenberg's view has verisimilitude in relation to modern painting, indeed seems to provide the appropriate theory for a practical criticism of much modern painting, implying a sense of embarrassment in the presence of nonillusionist art. Gombrich, on the other hand, is not reduced, like Greenberg, to the disingenuousness of denying the real intentions of the old masters. Gombrich's concern with illusionism represents their real critical concern.

One way of mediating between Greenberg and Gombrich would be to take the view of Pierre Francastel, who describes a radical break from the Renaissance conception of the problematics of the medium with the advent of the impressionists. Francastel sees the source of that break not in the exhaustion of the possibilities of the medium, but in a change in man's or society's relation to the world. "The modern era, having refused to take things as primary data in nature, has perforce changed its notion of the relations between subject and object as well as between objects themselves."[14] Francastel does not deny the problem-solving aspect of the history of art, but by introducing the pressure of an external force, the change in man's relation to his environment, he has undermined the idea of an iron inner logic that one finds in Henri Focillon and Greenberg, among others. My own interest in the presence of an external force is not to introduce another version of historical determinism, but rather to fortify my own sense of art as a function of changing human interests. This enables a critic, inward with the demands and requirements of art, to stand at the same time outside the internal history of art and make judgments and discriminations.

The contrast between Gombrich and Greenberg is intended to show that the issue of what constitutes the proper business of criticism is not settled by an appeal to the medium. For the issue then becomes: What constitutes the medium? Indeed, one might say that the conception of the medium reflects the particular development of art one is interested in and not, as Greenberg puts it, that the development of art is determined by an increasing self-consciousness about the medium itself. Greenberg's "historicism" is not intended: it is the inadvertent consequence of his interest in a certain kind of painting. (Whatever its particular accomplishments, the current structuralist ambition to discover linguistic models which will establish the rules of literary discourse for creative and critical works strikes me as an exercise in futility precisely because the medium is conceived abstractly as a given, unaffected by real historical life.)

If the constitution of the medium is not self-evident, one might want to consider how one's conception of it is determined. How does it reflect a vision of human life and society? For example, the interest in life-likeness may represent an interest in an integral humanity. The idea of a medium purified of effects from other media may imply a view of society based on a careful and systematic division of labor. Marxist criticism may be helpful here. In any event, Kantian self-criticism, as Greenberg understands it, rests on uncriticized (and criticizable) presuppositions. Perhaps what is needed is an Enlightenment criticism from the outside, to use Greenberg's distinction, which at the same time is sensitive to the virtues and constraints of the medium, for the ultimate logic of medium purification which is immune to criticism from the outside is triviality.

The history of modern art, according to the formalist avant-garde, is rational and, in a surprising way, conservative. Gone is its revolutionary fervor, the belief in discontinuities and ruptures, which characterized the various avant-gardes of the nineteenth and early twentieth century. Missing too is the mixture of motive, the "impure" concern with politics and morals that characterizes the prototypical avant-garde. Art in its pure unfolding becomes a monastic utopia against which the fallen world can be judged. The fallen world may be variously characterized as the quotidian, the ordinary, the philistine. Or art can be viewed as an autonomous realm incommensurate with the real world and hence beyond the capacity and the desire for criticism and judgment.

The antiphilistinism of the formalist avant-garde should be distinguished from the original inspiration of the Enlightenment, in which the philosophes conceived themselves as the agents of light battling the forces of darkness in the general interests of mankind. This heroic world-transforming strain has persisted in the political realm in the Bolshevik idea of revolution, though even in the political realm the heroic strain has suffered a radical loss of authority. In the realms of art and intellect, the avant-garde has tended to take the route of an elitist formalism in great part because of a strong disillusionment (if there was an illusion) with the possibility of any transformation of the world.

The ambiguous development of the avant-garde is missed, for instance, by Richard Chase in his plausible account of the history of the avant-garde. Chase writes in 1957:

> Historically the avant-garde is the heir to the aristocratic coterie or court circle of artists and intellectuals. But whereas the aristocratic coterie of medieval and Renaissance times had no commitment, except to itself and posterity and consequently felt free to cultivate the disinterested pursuit of art and ideas apart from the rest of society, history has imposed upon the modern avant-garde the duty not only of disinterestedly cultivating art and ideas but of educating and leading an aimless body of philistine taste and opinion.
>
> The historical role of the avant-garde was thus necessitated by the breakdown of the aristocratic class and by the spread of literacy. After the eighteenth century, the democratization of culture and the new literacy confronted the advanced intelligence with a newly arisen welter of taste and opinion, which, left to itself, found no other standards than conformism, at once aggressive and complacent, of the bourgeoisie.[15]

The formalist view develops in part because the masses in a postrevolutionary democracy are seen as impervious to education, particularly in aesthetic and intellectual matters. Moreover, the perniciousness of the new philistine culture generates in the artist and the intellectual a self-protective ascetic commitment to their own ideas, for fear they will be contaminated. Unlike the avant-garde of the Enlightenment, which fosters the general interests of mankind, the antiphilistine cultural elitist enjoys a privileged access to the truth.

A judgment of the formalist avant-garde cannot be made exclusively in terms of its own valuation of philistine culture or its obsessive need to cultivate exclusively the artistic medium. What I have called its ascetic character has its own corrupt source: a deep and inextinguishable hatred of life itself. The classic exemplification of it is the artistic will of Gustave Flaubert.

7

Aristocrats and Jacobins: The Happy Few in *The Charterhouse of Parma*

BEFORE TURNING to Flaubert, in whom aestheticism has a strong ascetic motive, it would be illuminating to consider the work of his great predecessor Stendhal, in whom an ascetic motive is in conflict with an affinity for natural and social vitalities. In Stendhal's work art is exalted but not necessarily at the expense of life. In *The Charterhouse of Parma*, Stendhal's greatest work, the fate of the artist has not yet been resolved to the condition of alienation that becomes a cliché in modern culture. The artist is still in combat, engaged in *la chasse au bonheur*. He feels intensely the unsatisfactoriness of the new social condition, but he has not lost confidence in the possibility of inventing a congenial life for the happy few who constitute the community of artists. Such a reading of *The Charterhouse* is necessarily allegorical, for if the happy few are not artists by vocation, they have the spiritual gifts of the artist.

The Charterhouse of Parma was written in 1839, fifty years after the first French Revolution. However one wants to distinguish him from other writers of the nineteenth century, Stendhal shared with them a preoccupation with the greatest event in modern French history. Indeed, for the nineteenth century French writer, the revolution was a permanent fact of life: the events of 1830, 1848, and 1871 could be viewed as resurfacings of the revolutionary impulse that had exploded on the stage of European political life in 1789. In *The Charterhouse*, Stendhal gives us post-Napoleonic Europe in which the counterrevolution has for the moment triumphed, but the energies created by the revolution and Napoleon have not been extinguished. Or at least the postrevolutionary aristocratic imagination is obsessed with the fear that Jacobin energies are always potentially explosive. As Conte Mosca remarks: "Our policy for the next twenty years is going to consist in fear of the Jacobins—and such fear, too! Every year, we shall fancy ourselves on the eve of '93 . . . Everything that can in any way reduce this fear will be *supremely moral* in the eyes of nobles and bigots."[1] So intense is the fear that a condition for survival in the court of Parma is to be able to refrain from showing "enthusiasm" and "spirit," which in the eyes of the despotic prince are Jacobin emotions.

Of course, the identification of the revolution with Napoleon is achieved only in a foreign perspective, so to speak. If one judges Napoleon from the point of view of events within France, his connection to the revolution, let alone to its Jacobin manifestation, is highly problematic. By creating the empire and restoring the aristocracy, Napoleon betrayed the revolution. This view, to be sure, should be modified by his contribution to the institutionalization of certain accomplishments of the revolution—the codification of equality before the law, for example. As an imperialist, however, Napoleon is the unequivocal champion of revolutionary idealism. The French army marched into Europe under the rhetorical aegis of liberty, equality and fraternity. Whatever Napoleon intended, the impact of his conquests in Spain, Italy, and Germany was to stir, if not start, the fires of revolution.

Stendhal's creative strategy is to dramatize the incoherence that permeates political life in the post-Napoleonic world, a legacy of Napoleon's own rule. If we try to understand the politics of the novel according to the spectrum of the National Assembly—from left to right, from republican to monarchist, from liberal to conservative—we are confounded. Though their political roles are ultraconservative, Mosca and Gina (in whom Stendhal seems to have made a large personal investment) are suspected of Jacobinism by the prince because of their intellectual freedom and their susceptibility to unfamiliar ideas. Fabio Conti, a leader of the liberal faction,[2] is a jailer in the service of an ultraconservative regime. He must make the choice between lenity to satisfy the principles of his party and severity to satisfy the demands of the despotic prince, who gives and takes away power. It is clear that Fabio Conti will act, or try to act, in such a way as to assure the confidence of the prince. Moreover, the doctrine of the liberal party hardly exists. Like the ruling party, the liberal party is primarily interested in acquiring and holding power. Virtually everyone in the novel seems to be concerned with gaining or holding power. In the aftermath of the French Revolution, political positions have been increasingly emptied of moral content. One lives in a world of power or its absence. The questions are: Who has power, how does one keep it, how does one get it if one doesn't have it, how does one protect oneself from the tyranny of someone else's power? The poet Ferrante Palla is an anomaly in the novel because his political behavior is principled. But he is a madman. Stendhal makes it unequivocally clear that a state in which the Tribune of the People would be dictator is unthinkable. Even Ferrante Palla, like his ultra rival Count Mosca, is willing to give up his radical republicanism for the love of the ultra duchessa.

One result of this incoherence is a cynicism only partly redeemed by honesty and lucidity. In response to Gina's characterization of Mosca's extravagant proposal that she marry the Duca Sanseverina-Taxis as immoral (she gets everything and gives nothing), Mosca says with perfect cynicism:

> No more immoral than everything else that is done at our court and a score of others. Absolute Power has this advantage, that it sanctifies everything in the eyes of the public: what harm can there be in a thing that nobody notices? Our policy for the next twenty years is going to consist in fear of the Jacobins—and such fear, too! Every year, we shall fancy ourselves on the eve of '93. You will hear, I hope, the fine speeches I make on the subject at my receptions! They are beautiful! Everything that can in any way reduce this fear will be supremely moral in the eyes of the nobles and the bigots. And you see, at Parma, everyone who is not either a noble or a bigot is in prison, or is packing up to go there; you may be quite sure that this marriage will not be thought odd among us until the day on which I am disgraced. This arrangement involves no dishonesty towards anyone; that is the essential thing, it seems to me.[3]

The education of Fabrizio counseled by Mosca and Gina is completely Jesuitical in the metaphorical as well as literal sense of the term. Indeed, some of the most remarkable passages in the novel are the long speeches of advice given by both Mosca and Gina to the innocent Fabrizio on the necessity of masking one's true thoughts and desires.

The importance of seeing Mosca's cynicism as a species of self-honesty is that it effectively separates Mosca from his Machiavellian wisdom. Mosca is observing a truth of postrevolutionary political life,

not identifying himself with it. He is of necessity compelled to act as
the political agent of the nobility and the bigots, but he will do his best
to mitigate the noxious consequences of his role. Better Mosca than
Rassi! One must be grateful for the unmasking lucidity of his political
vision. Indeed, in the lucidity, in the absence of pretense, one senses
the man who is capable of throwing everything over for love.

But the cynicism is not the deepest note struck by the novel. The
passion of Gina, the high-mindedness of Fabrizio, the disdain of the
courtier spirit are, I think, the deepest notes in the novel. Indeed, there
is a range of aristocratic values which remains unscathed by the political cynicism of the novel: liberty, heroism, gaiety, brio, intelligence,
high feeling (the supreme expression of which is *amour passion*).
These values manifest themselves in the court of Parma, but they are
not to be identified with the life of the court. The court of Parma gives
opportunities for brio and the exercise of intelligence, for example, but
they are exercised in a hostile relation to it. Oddly enough, the despotism of Parma is an ideal opportunity for Fabrizio, Gina, Mosca, and
even Ferrante Palla. There is sufficient danger or menace in the environment to occasion heroic acts. And the despotism is vulnerable,
porous, farcical, so that characters have an extravagant freedom of
movement.

Though Stendhal affirms aristocratic ideals, he deplores the historical class which produced the ideals. The aristocracy of the eighteenth
and nineteenth centuries is seen as bigoted and stupid. In his dicta,
Mosca couples the nobles and the bigots. The Marchese del Dongo, a
typical representative of the historical aristocracy before and after the
revolution, is a mean-spirited character who has found in his eldest
son Ascanio a true heir. And the meanness is not fortuitous; it is inextricably bound up with class attitudes.

To understand Stendhal's politics, we need a perspective not provided by the progressive doctrine of the Enlightenment, but one which
tries to understand the doctrine. Such a perspective is given by Alexis
de Tocqueville in his study of political men of letters in the eighteenth
century.[4] Tocqueville's portrait of the literary man is in the context of
an interpretation of the relationship between the old regime and the
society produced by the revolution. This historical interpretation represented at the time a fundamental revision of the conventional view
that 1789 created a radical discontinuity in French political and social
history. He argues (and to an extent demonstrates) that the revolution
continued the process of centralization started by the monarchy.

Promising liberty, equality, and fraternity, the revolution betrayed the cause of liberty to centralized power and a majoritarian despotism, which egalitarianism tends to become. Tocqueville, it should be recalled, was among the first to signal the advent of the tyranny of the majority.

In Tocqueville's view, the spirit of liberty in the old regime was fostered by the aristocracy, which feared the monarchy more than it feared the insurgent revolutionary classes and their ideas. Indeed, attracted to the libertarian ideas of the philosophes, the most idealistic elements of the aristocracy became allies of the revolution only to find the aristocracy afterwards cast in the role of enemy together with the monarchy. Tocqueville, the aristocrat, appreciates the reasons that would turn the aristocracy into an enemy of the insurgent classes (he has few illusions about the exploitativeness and actual corruption of the French aristocracy in the late eighteenth century), but he is more interested in the irony of a class inviting and encouraging its own downfall under the illusion that its friends and not its enemies were making the revolution. Tocqueville's feelings of aversion for the philosophes, a nonpossessing, envious intellectual elite, excluded from the places of power and authority, and consequently given to abstraction and innovation, prevents him from appreciating the plausibility in the attraction the aristocracy felt for this intellectual elite. The boldness, originality, and intransigence of the ideas of the philosophes are the intellectual correlatives of the aristocratic spirit. By stressing the affinity between the aristocracy and the political men of letters, Tocqueville complicates the simple notion of a progressive vanguard contending with reaction in the name of liberty, fraternity, and equality. There existed an affinity not only between the philosophes and the aristocracy, who patronized them, but also between the philosophes and what I would call aristocratic ideals.

Tocqueville's supreme value is liberty, but no simple definition provides us with his conception of liberty. Richard Herr argues persuasively that the historical root of Tocqueville's conception is the aristocratically dominated commune, which attempted without much success to resist the incursions of authority centralized in the monarchy.[5] The members of the commune felt free to express their grievances, assert their rights, though they were dependent on the noblesse oblige of the aristocrat. The aristocratic root of Tocqueville's conception of liberty suggests that one of its negative ideals would be freedom from restraint by the despotism of centralized authority. Of course, this ideal does not necessarily entail a corresponding sensitivity to freedom of the lower classes from the despotism of the aristocracy. Aristocratic freedom does not include equality among classes. The positive ideal of aristocratic liberty may be glimpsed at moments in the life of old aristocracies—a life at once spacious, grand, filled with heroic risk, the life of the knight-errant. In the modern period such a life tends to take a literary form. The principal measure of a society for Tocqueville is its cultural achievements: its accomplishments in the arts and sciences. If Tocqueville often prefers democracy to aristocratic society, it is because of democracy's superior capacity to diffuse the benefits of the cultural life, which incarnates aristocratic values. Aristocratic liberty enables the individual to express his worth, his energy, his talents. Its motto is "Distinction."

However accurate Tocqueville is as a historian, he is presenting a version of prerevolutionary history that reflects his own nineteenth century view of politics and society. Tocqueville, the aristocratic libertarian of the nineteenth century, refuses to accept the role of conservative which progressive doctrine would impose upon him. By suggesting the uneasy, indeed sometimes antagonistic, relation between liberty and equality, he tries to undermine progressive doctrine and in effect propose another idea of "progress" (for want of a better word), which is to keep alive the spirit of liberty that the bourgeoisie, the heirs of the revolution, are trying to destroy.

The hatred of ideas, of new ideas, that marks the aristocracy after the French Revolution, expressed by the Marchese del Dongo in *The Charterhouse*, is a belated wisdom that the aristocracy could not have been expected to have before the revolution. "The Marchese del Dongo professed a vigorous hatred of enlightenment: 'It is ideas,' he used to say, 'that have ruined Italy.' "[6]

The year is 1796, the French Revolution has already occurred, and the finger of blame is understandably pointed to the ascendancy of new ideas. The Marchese is merely expressing a sentiment widely shared by members of his class.

> For the last half-century, as the *Encyclopedia* and Voltaire gained ground in France, the monks had been dinning into the ears of the good people of Milan that to learn to read, or for that matter, to learn anything at all was a great waste of labour, and that by paying one's exact tithe to one's parish priest and faithfully reporting to him all one's little misdeeds, one was practically certain of having a good place in paradise.[7]

If the Marchese represents the norm of his class, Mosca, Gina, and Fabrizio exemplify the natural affinity of the aristocracy at its best for bold ideas boldly expressed. Even when Mosca and Gina advise Fabrizio to mask his thoughts, they encourage him to preserve his intellectual conscience, to keep alive his courage to think unfamiliar thoughts. Stendhal's idealized aristocracy is reactionary in its antiegalitarianism, but liberal in its love of liberty.[8] "The happy few" is a perfect exemplification of the tension between liberty and equality that Tocqueville noted in postrevolutionary society. To be sure, the despotism against which Stendhal's "aristocratic libertarians" contend is not the tyrannical majority in Tocqueville's account, but a tyranny parodying the monarchy of *le roi soleil*. Nevertheless, there is a feeling throughout the book, occasionally made explicit, that the critical spirit of the happy few is simultaneously directed against monarchical despotism and the tyranny of the majority.

> [Fabrizio] loved Napoleon, and, in his capacity as a young noble, believed that he had been created to be happier than his neighbor, and thought the middle classes absurd.
>
> The fashion and cult of the greatest good of the greatest number, after which the 19th century has run mad, [was] nothing in his eyes but a heresy which, like other heresies, would pass away, though not until it had destroyed many souls.
>
> "Believe me," [the Duchessa warns Fabrizio], "for you just as much as for myself it would be a wretched existence there in America." She explained to him the cult of the god Dollar, and the respect that had to be shown to the artisans in the street who by their votes decided everything.
>
> "In despotic courts, the first skillful intriguer controls the *Truth*, as the fashion controls it in Paris."[9]

It is as if Stendhal were confirming the view of Tocqueville that the tyranny of the monarchy, with its mistrust of energy and distinction, was analogous to the tyranny of the majority.

Tocqueville's contempt for the "new ideas" of the philosophes might suggest that his sympathies would be with the Marchese del Dongo. But the Marchese's hatred of the Enlightenment is sheer vulgarity, as the Duchessa's advice to Fabrizio makes clear.

> "Do not fall into the vulgar habit of refuting Voltaire, Diderot, Raynal and all those harebrained Frenchmen, who paved the way for the Dual Chamber. Their names should not be allowed to pass your lips, but if you must mention them, speak of these gentle-

men with a calm irony. They are people who have long since been refuted and whose attacks are no longer of any consequence."[10]

Tocqueville's quarrel with the philosophes is not directed at the intellect but at the passion for innovation which proceeds from an abstract relation to reality. Tocqueville, like Burke, took the view that society is an organism too complex and too subtle in the interconnections of its elements to allow for constructive change based on abstract general ideas different from the received and therefore time-tested ones. Tocqueville's own performance in *Democracy in America* as well as *The Old Regime and the Revolution* shows an intellectual originality, a predilection for the unfamiliar idea and a freedom from cant, that would have made him suspect of Jacobinism in the court of Parma. Both Tocqueville and Stendhal wrote at a time when the idea of progress had already become a piety. The opinions of the conventional postrevolutionary liberal in the nineteenth century are no more bold or original or true than those of their conservative adversaries. Tocqueville and Stendhal belong to a new small breed of philosophes of the nineteenth century. Their discovery of the tyranny of the majority or of public opinion reflects the political enlightenment of the nineteenth century.

Stendhal's relation to the Enlightenment is more complex than the foregoing remarks indicate. Certainly, the spirit of Stendhal's language and style suggests a strong affinity between him and the philosophes. He virtually raises lucidity and wit, hallmarks of Stendhal's style, to an ideological principle against the involuted romanticizing of Chateaubriand and De Maistre. The lucidity is expressive of Stendhal's passion to demystify reality. Here he is at one with the spirit of the philosophes. If Stendhal's heroes mask their desires and ambitions to achieve power, his prose unmasks those ambitions, so that we are never under any illusions about their characters and motives. Nonetheless, Stendhal retains what I would call a mystical feeling for personality. He is unlike the rationalistic Biblical critics of the eighteenth century whose materialism and literalism led them to destroy—or to want to destroy—the authority of the Bible; he is like the higher critic of the nineteenth century whose atheism does not prevent him from perceiving and appreciating irreducible mystery. Stendhal is a secularizer, not a materialist.

Since the rule of the majority is not constituted by a passion for justice, Stendhal's attack upon this rule should not be construed as an attack on the idea of social justice. Indeed, Stendhal is keenly aware of how hardened the historical aristocracy is to any suffering other than its own. The need to dissociate high feeling and style from the exploitativeness that defines the actual performance of the aristocracy and was a major provocation of the revolution is exquisitely expressed through Stendhal's fine irony in Fabrizio's thoughts on aristocratic privilege:

> "After all," he said to himself at length, with the lustreless eyes of a man who is dissatisfied with himself, "since my birth gives me the right to profit by these abuses, it would be a signal piece of folly on my part not to take my share, but I must never let myself denounce them in public." This reasoning was by no means unsound; but Fabrizio had fallen a long way from that elevation of sublime happiness to which he had found himself transported an hour earlier. The thought of privilege had withered that plant, always so delicate, which we name happiness.[11]

The snobbery of a Rassi or a Gonzo ("everyone not of noble birth was absolutely nothing in the eyes of this courtier")[12] is mocked as evidence of the contemptible spirit of the courtier. And there is no doubt as to where our sympathy should be in Stendhal's characterization of the Marchese del Dongo's hatred of Conte Pietranera, Gina's first husband.

> [The Marchese] execrated Conte Pietranera, his brother-in-law, who, not having an income of 50 louis had the audacity to be quite content, made a point of showing himself loyal to what he had loved all his life, and had the insolence to preach the spirit of justice without regard for persons, which the Marchese called an infamous piece of Jacobinism.[13]

The tyrannical majority, like the tyranny of the prince, operates through mistrust of energy and distinction, not, as I have already remarked, through the love of justice. Napoleon, who rose from humble origins, was made possible by the revolution, and he is valued principally for his great-souled heroism, which the mean-spirited philistinism of the counterrevolution connects with Jacobin enthusiasm. The counterrevolution has instituted "a state of boredom," to which Stendhal's happy few stand opposed. Notwithstanding doctrinal differences among themselves, they feel an instinctive affinity for the energies and enthusiasm of the revolution and of the Napoleonic period. "His most appalling act of tyranny," Stendhal remarks of Napoleon in a letter, "was less harmful to the people than the present inertia."[14]

If the French Revolution continued the process of centralization begun by the monarchy, as Tocqueville argues, we might see the critical
reaction of intellectuals and artists of the nineteenth century (like
Stendhal or Tocqueville himself) to the consequences of the revolution
as a continuation of the libertarian tradition of the aristocracy. Under
the old regime this tradition is not obviously libertarian, because it
had been in possession of those who have power. Indeed, the liberty
of the historical aristocracy is the oppression of its vassals and servants, and the invidious justice implied by aristocratic liberty creates
resentment in those who are not above the law. But with the triumph
of the Criminal Code and the Civil Code, there is a sudden contraction
of the space in which the aristocratic individual is free to act. The
Criminal Code and the Civil Code apply to the bourgeoisie, but the
absence of law protecting the economically exploited from their ex-
ploiters means, as Marx has taught us, that a liberty exists for the
bourgeoisie in post-revolutionary society comparable to the liberty
possessed by the aristocracy under the old regime, a power to do its
will greater than the law's capacity to constrain it. The oppressor then
is the unrestrained entrepreneur and the aristocrat becomes the victim
of oppression.

What I am suggesting is that the libertarian element in the aristocratic tradition becomes clear and desirable when the aristocracy loses
its power. Only then can we see more clearly what values have been
lost—brio, grace, intelligence, imagination—because they are not ob-
scured by oppressiveness. Indeed, because these values must find a
new embodiment, the old practical consequences of such qualities as
energy and brio become less important, less distracting. True liberty
for Stendhal, as F. C. Green points out, exists "in the absence of oblig-
atory relationships."[15] That this might entail a certain cruelty toward
others is less important than the enervations of spirit that are the consequence of a society oppressed by the spirit of obligation. The cruelty
of Conte Mosca and the Duchessa de Sanseverina is dismissed as an
aberration, in fact is deliberately fudged by Stendhal himself when he
has Mosca declare that he never killed anybody and speak of a conscience troubled by the memory of two alleged spies whom he had
shot in Spain, "perhaps a little lightly."[16]

One of the most difficult things to determine is the degree of tension
that exists in the imagination of the novel between rival moral claims.
The difficulty consists in part in defining the terms of the claims. If

liberty is on one side, what is on the other side? Is it the despotism of the monarchy or of public opinion, or is it rather equality and justice? How are we to render the moral anxiety of Fabrizio, when he meditates on Mosca's "immoralist" dictum that the "risks a man runs are always the measure of his rights over his neighbors"?[17] This could provide Fabrizio with a justification for killing a servant and taking his horse, for Fabrizio after all is a hero. But that would be "a horrible thing to do." At least in this case, the opposite side of liberty is justice or simply humaneness. The sensitive Stendhalian hero usually recoils from the cruelty that might result from his freedom to act. The touch of cruelty in Gina is the spot of corruption that results in her deterioration in the novel. The crucial episode, of course, is her scheme of revenge upon Parma. But she already betrays her cruelty when she says that the death of a Giletti cannot be held against a del Dongo. It is an unnecessary remark, for Fabrizio is justified in having acted from the motive of self-defense. Had Fabrizio simply acted from the code of risk proposed by Mosca, the death of Giletti, from the point of view of justice, could be held against him. If Stendhal affirms the heroic or libertarian ideal, he is at the same time concerned to show a sensitivity to its dangers. Nevertheless, the focus is not on the dangers.

The aristocrat has lost his privileges, and the intellectual and imaginative effort to compensate for the loss becomes an affirmation for the cause of liberty and distinction. This accounts for what seems an anomaly: that Stendhal and Tocqueville, whose hearts are with the aristocracy (an idealized aristocracy, to be sure), are at the same time liberals. If Stendhal's hero is Napoleon, his antagonist is Metternich,[18] which means that Stendhal is alienated from the available political positions. He is in fact in a dilemma, which, as Balzac notes in his "Study of M. Beyle," he presents as the moral of his tale.

> From the whole business one can derive this moral, that the man who mingles with a court compromises his happiness, if he is happy, and in any event, makes his future depend on the intrigues of a chambermaid.
>
> On the other hand in America, in the Republic, one has to spend the whole weary day paying serious court to the shopkeepers in the street, and must become as stupid as they are; and there one has no opera.[19]

Happiness cannot be obtained through aristocracy or democracy. What then are the conditions of happiness, a word powerfully charged with utilitarian connotations in the nineteenth century, to which Stendhal was nonetheless attached?

As an artist, Stendhal has recourse to the imagination. That is to say, he can invent a world which projects an invisible community of kindred spirits who, while living in the "real" world, are able to enjoy a happiness that exists essentially apart from the world. "The happy few," a phrase Stendhal borrowed from Shakespeare's *Henry V*, is a classless elite, distinguished not by their political or economic "functions," by domination or exploitativeness, but by the aesthetic and spiritual ambience in which they live. The elite is constituted by Mosca, Gina, Fabrizio, and Ferrante Palla. Ferrante Palla's "membership" in the happy few is crucial because it focuses the classless and apolitical character of Stendhal's elitism. Ferrante Palla's willingness to give up his republicanism for the Duchessa is identical in spirit with Mosca's willingness to quit as prime minister and live on the fourth floor with her, should she so desire. The two gestures express the community of spirit between the ultra prime minister and the revolutionary poet.

In a sense, the happy few do not constitute a true community. Though they have affinities for one another, each is engaged in a lonely quest for personal fulfillment, one might say for a transcendence, which he wishes to inhabit with his beloved. In Fabrizio, for example, there is an odd admixture of asceticism in his love for Clelia, which betokens a desire to remove himself from the world. Fabrizio's priestly habit turns out to have a certain appropriateness: his sermons are indistinguishable from his love for Clelia. Stendhal recalls the love of the troubadour poets of the twelfth and thirteenth centuries, the poets who spiritualized secular love between man and woman.[20] Fabrizio, a latter-day Petrarch, writes sonnets:

> To die near what one loves! expressed in a hundred different fashions, was followed by a sonnet in which one saw that this soul, parted, after atrocious torments, from the frail body in which it had dwelt for three-and-twenty years, urged by that instinct for happiness natural to everything that has once existed, would not mount to heaven to mingle with the choirs of angels as soon as it should be free, and should the dread Judgment grant it pardon for its sins; but that, more fortunate after death than it had been in life, it would go a little way from the prison, where so long it had groaned, to unite itself with all that it had loved in this world. And "So," said the last line of the sonnet, "I should find my earthly paradise."[21]

The dream of earthly paradise is in opposition to life at court. These aristocrats, born and bred at the court, have immortal longings to which the artifice of courtly life is finally inimical. The love between Fabrizio and Clelia can almost be expressed in Christian terms, free of the frailty of flesh. However, the suggestion is pervasive and clear throughout the novel that the ascetic impulse would not have asserted itself if the world had provided occasions for spiritual fulfillment. Stendhal sees the situation of his hero and heroine as a matter of the historical moment. His private diaries, for example, correlate the vagaries of erotic passion with the politics of the moment.

> It's quite obvious that the Frenchman of today, not being occupied in the forum, is driven to adultery by the very nature of his government.
> Since it isn't within the power of love such as I conceived it to bring me happiness, I began some time ago to be in love with glory.[22]

The psychological metaphysics of both statements are inconsistent. In the first statement, politics (or the absence of it) is the cause for adultery, in the second the incapacity of love to satisfy makes for political or military ambition. What is consistent is Stendhal's concern for the relations between political and spiritual or psychological events.

The aristocrat, freed of his historical circumstances, becomes a metaphor for the spiritual life. That the aristocracy once existed in association with a powerful and authoritative church is evidence that the metaphor is not an arbitrary expression. In the novel Fabrizio develops from the role of aristocratic hero to the high priest of Parmesan society. The development, to be sure, is complicated by masking and role-playing. Fabrizio uses the church for his own ends, though it is essential to note for his own *spiritual* ends. The role of archbishop (one of the highest the church can confer), however, is finally inadequate to Fabrizio's spiritual aspiration.

There is no surety, no resting place for the soul in Stendhal or his heroes. The Stendhal character is an irrepressibly restless spirit whose forms are endlessly changing. The religious "fulfillment" at the end of the novel would be as provisional as every other role, if it were not for the intervention of death. Stendhal implicitly acknowledges the inadequacy of this aestheticized religion by showing it to be precariously dependent on the individual soul whose qualities must remain invisible to the world and hence cannot find any external and communal form to express itself. The overt religious symbolism is a mask, a concealment, a lie that precariously protects the hero and heroine from a spiritually coarse and threatening world. Religion is another role for the displaced aristocrat.

If Stendhal can be said to affirm a historical aristocracy (which, after all, is a multitude), it is the Italian aristocracy of the sixteenth century.[23] The energy of the sixteenth century aristocrat becomes enfeebled and overrefined in the eighteenth and nineteenth centuries. But Stendhal's concern is not that of the conventional historical novelist, which is to create nostalgia for a particular time and place, for a particular world that actually existed. His Parma is not a real place, or rather its relation to an actual Parma is oblique. The city is composed of historical reminiscences (Renaissance Italy, seventeenth century France), but in a fashion that places it outside of historical time.[24] By liberating the depiction of Parma from any obligation to verisimilitude, Stendhal enables his characters to act out their powers to the full.

Stendhal depicts neither an actual past nor an actual present. He rather affirms values imperfectly realized in the past, which the present is dedicated to destroying. The terms "conservative" or "reactionary" are irrelevant. Stendhal frees certain values from their historical context—a privilege of the imagination—as an act of resistance to losses incurred through historical "progress."[25] The act of freeing these values is in a sense an act of transmutation. There are differences between the sixteenth century aristocrat and the idealized aristocrats in whom Stendhal tries to pack the energy of the sixteenth century. It has been noted, for example, that the characters of *The Charterhouse* would all be condemned by the Criminal Code and the Civil Code. Viewed in the perspective of the sixteenth century, the nineteenth century codes can be seen as an advance in civilization, for they represent an increase in justice and an attempt to minimize barbarism and cruelty. But in the perspective of the nineteenth and twentieth centuries the codes can be regarded as bourgeois creations, designed to protect the emerging interests of the new ruling class. The immoralism implicit in Stendhal's work is therefore a kind of weapon against the insipidity of bourgeois law and order. Stendhal suppresses the sixteenth century perspective—as the artist is free to do—by neutralizing the noxious effects of immoralism through fantasy and farce. The imagination does all it can to focus on the virtues of energy liberated from constraints.

Aestheticism is one version of the transmutation of aristocratic ideas or attitudes in a postrevolutionary society.[26] The modern artist, whatever his political persuasion, lacks the plebeian element so strong in the bourgeois spirit. The poet Ferrante Palla's revolutionary republicanism does not prevent him from despising the prospect of an America in which he would have to dine with a grocer. This is no mere snobbery on Ferrante Palla's part. It reflects the strong aesthetic feeling against commonness and ordinariness which characterizes the artist. Indeed, the aesthetic transformation of aristocratic feeling can be grasped, if we think of the object of aesthetic condescension as being a quality rather than a person embodying the quality: commonness rather than the common people, ordinariness rather than the ordinary people. (In fact, the ordinary people are capable of distinction in, for instance, a revolutionary situation. Stendhal says of those who were on the barricades on July 28, 1830, "The lowest rabble was heroic, and after the battle was full of the noblest generosity.")[27] To be sure, Ferrante Palla speaks with contempt for the grocer. But the person is here only as a metaphor. The quality, not the person, is fixed as an object of contempt. The aesthetic transformation of aristocratic feeling has passed into our common discourse and feeling. Only in our militantly populist moods do we suspect that we therefore carry within us the poison of reaction.

In this respect, Stendhal's feeling for revolution is not unlike that of Rimbaud, whose support for the Paris Commune of 1871 was emotional rather than ideological. Like Rimbaud, Stendhal responds not so much to the doctrines or even idealism of the revolution as he does to the opportunity for energetic and courageous action which the revolution creates. Stendhal's response to those on the barricades in 1830 is reenacted by Tocqueville in the strange and anomalous pleasure he takes in the revolt of 1848, when he descends into the barricade-lined streets of Paris with a brace of pistols ready to do battle, exhilarated by the pulsing energy of the streets, which he contrasts invidiously with the dullness of parliamentary life. Tocqueville's preference here, of course, is emotional and not political or ideological. He responds to the barricades against his better political judgment.

That Stendhal has reinvented the aristocrat for the modern period is clear from the social position in which he and his characters are placed. Stendhal's heroes, as well as Stendhal himself, have all the marks of the *parvenu*. The supreme instance of the type is, of course, Napoleon himself. The Stendhal hero—Julien Sorel, for example—is a man of the lower classes possessed of an aristocratic dream. Paradoxically, the revolution represents the possibility of aristocratic liberty for him. Given the meanness of objective bourgeois life, its insufficiencies and overpowering resistance to greatness and distinction which constitute the aim of aristocratic liberty, the freedom of the Stendhalian character can be achieved only in imagination—in the reveries of the Stendhalian character and the literary achievement of Stendhal himself.

Fabrizio apparently does not fit this description. But on closer inspection, Fabrizio's condition is like that of Julien Sorel and Stendhal. Though Fabrizio is, to be sure, an aristocrat by birth, he is the second disinherited son of the Marchese del Dongo. It is possible to view his status in a symbolic way. The aristocratic class has been disinherited by the revolution and the aristocrat must find his place in a new world by revealing himself as a true aristocrat. Fabrizio in effect is freed from the taint of association with the meanness and corruption of the actual historical aristocracy. His nobility, distinction, brio, are for the most part inward, and Stendhal in utopian fashion contrives the world to create opportunities for the expression of these qualities. Fabrizio's aristocratic character is Julien's character, given a dreamlike license.

There is in Stendhal an aristocratic confidence in the spiritual life that survives disillusionments and frustrations. It becomes aesthetically the principle of improvisation and the tone of gaiety. Discontinuities in the unfolding of the narrative correspond to the disillusionments. The sudden energy with which a new episode occurs reflects the recurrence of confidence and vitality. To see this clearly, one has only to compare the brio of the Stendhal novel with the repressive structuring of the Flaubert novel.

Stendhal is willful with his narrative line, as if the narrative represented the repressive reality of fate. Fate does impose itself on character—more so in *The Red and the Black* than in *The Charterhouse of Parma*—but common to both novels is the refusal of the hero to accept his fate. In the spiritual sense, character triumphs, though the triumph is qualified by the volatility of character. Fate, represented by plot, is the boring bourgeois world that Stendhal detested. Despite his modernity, of which his conception of the volatility of character is a powerful example, he rebels against a modern fate in behalf of values embodied in a disappearing past.

If Stendhal is read under the aegis of Tocqueville rather than Marx or Marxism, we are free to respond to the claims of Stendhal's imagination on its own terms. The impoverishment of Stendhal's meaning that occurs as a consequence of viewing him from a progressivist standpoint can be seen in the work of the Marxist Georg Lukacs, in particular his treatment of Stendhal in *Studies in European Realism*. Lukacs devotes a chapter to Balzac's review of *The Charterhouse* and Stendhal's reply to it. For Lukacs, Stendhal is a romanticist, despite a capacity for realistic representation which he shared with Balzac. And Balzac is a realist, despite the romantic tendency of his style. "Thus the Stendhalian conception comes into being, a gallery of heroes who idealistically and romantically exaggerate mere tendencies and dawnings into realities and hence can never attain the social typicality which so superbly permeates the Human Comedy." "Idealistically" and "romantically" are, of course, pejorative terms in Lukacs' materialistic vocabulary, and they effectively prevent him from responding to the positive value-bestowing capacity of the imagination. Lukacs faults Stendhal for his refusal to accept "the fact that the heroic period of the *bourgeoisie* was ended."[28] Stendhal's monumental figures in *The Charterhouse*, far from being heroic representations of the bourgeois, are attempts to revive an older aristocratic possibility for the new unheroic bourgeois world.[29]

Marx himself might have shown a certain sympathy for this view. He was too much rooted in the Hegelian tradition, with its sentiment about spiritual accretion that occurs through the dialectical process, simply to repudiate the past. It constitutes his humanism. In fact, both Hegel and Marx stand as a corrective within the Enlightenment tradition to that aspect of progressivism which has as its aim the liquidation of the past. But Marx and the tradition that flows from him do not entirely escape what I would call the antihumanist aspect of progressivism. In *The Eighteenth Brumaire of Louis Napoleon* the ideological stress unquestionably falls on the dead hand of the past. And this stress is a symptom of an inability or unwillingness to see the future as enriched by values of the past, values that were embodied in historically discredited societies and institutions. This is so for two related reasons. First, there is a tendency in Marxism to overdefine the past as a time of exploitation. ("The history of all hitherto existing society is the history of class struggles.") Second, if the cultural life is an epiphenomenon, "superstructure" in the Marxian idiom, it becomes difficult, though perhaps not impossible, to separate the ideals from the historical class that produced them. Such a separation would imply an autonomy to the cultural life that would threaten the Marxian view of experience.

It is perhaps unfair to assimilate Marx to the vulgar materialism that comes to be associated with Marxism after his death. The culprit may well be Engels, who destroyed the tension between the idealist metaphysics of Hegel and the heritage of French materialism which distinguished Marx's thinking and spurred the development of the ideological materialism that characterizes certain versions of Marxism to this day. Engels' materialism insists upon the absolute relativism of values. "The demand for final solutions and eternal truths ceases once for all." As George Lichtheim incisively points out: "How in the absence of normative standards ('eternal truths') [is it] possible to qualify the long-term development [of history] as 'progressive'?"[30] If normative standards are indeed required to sustain a progressive view of history, an open acknowledgment of this fact might lead to a wholly unexpected valuation of the past. For it is probable that the past is the repository of values or ideals which have never achieved historical realization. One of the virtues of the literary imagination, as I have tried to suggest in my discussion of *The Charterhouse*, is its capacity for abstracting or disengaging values from the past and, by implication if not explicitly, its capacity for proposing those values in the new context of the present.[31]

Stendhal has had his share of admirers among the great—Nietzsche and Gide, to name two. But as a novelist, he is sui generis. No tradition emanates from him as it does from Flaubert, for example, from whom we can draw a line through Mann and Joyce and the *nouveau roman*. Stendhal, great as he is, has not been seminal because the quality of soul or spirit that he cherishes resists the modern realistic tendency toward the flattening or the materializing of character. For all his aestheticism, Flaubert encourages the tendency. Stendhal combines his vision of spirituality with a thoroughly modern sense of the instability of character as it manifests itself through role-playing, the effect of which is to create original characters who suggest a future rather than represent past or present. The "futurist" Nietzsche must have perceived this. It is a future still beyond our modernity.

8

Flaubert and the
Powerlessness of Art

THE EXACERBATED self-consciousness of modernist art and literature
tends to become ideological. Through an ascetic impulse toward
order, art divides itself from life and engages in what appears to be active combat with its disintegrative tendency. The work of Flaubert is
particularly illuminating because the fiction itself, virtually without
discursive statement, generates the ideology of modernist art. Flaubert
stands behind Joyce, Beckett, and the new novelists.

The opposition between art and life proves to be illusory. Before
either the appearance of opposition or its illusory character can be
understood, it is necessary to consider Flaubert's—that is, the artist's
—hostile view of the bourgeois, the victor in the revolutionary struggles of the nineteenth century. It is not fortuitous that *Madame Bovary* concludes with Homais, the philistine incarnate, receiving the
Legion of Honor.

The hatred of the bourgeois is a peculiarly French phenomenon, a
product of the continuous stresses of the revolution in the nineteenth
century. Having triumphed in the revolution but having failed to realize the promise of liberty, equality, and fraternity, the bourgeois became a universal object of resentment and hatred. They were, of
course, hated by the members of the class they had overthrown and
deprived of their privileges and wealth. Some members of the aristocratic class attempted to accommodate themselves to the new reality
by making financial alliances with the new entrepreneurs (Balzac's
novels are filled with the dramas of such alliances), though even success in such enterprises rarely extinguished the contempt and fear the
aristocrats felt for the bourgeois. As for the working class, by 1848 the

illusion of solidarity between the bourgeoisie and the emerging working class is destroyed irrevocably. Marx's *Eighteenth Brumaire of Louis Napoleon* is a brilliant exposition of the shattering of illusions, in the first half of the nineteenth century, that the bourgeoisie spoke and acted in the interests of the workers, who marched in the ranks of the bourgeois revolution. The working class had discovered that the slogans of the revolution served the interests of the bourgeoisie by masking their exploitation of the working class. The keenest hatred of the bourgeoisie, however, is that of sensitive, imaginative members of the bourgeois class itself.

The polarization of consciousness that marks French political and cultural life is alien to English consciousness. In the imaginative writers and social critics of the nineteenth century in England, the most severe scorn heaped upon the middle class is qualified by the sentiment that whatever its moral and spiritual failures, the middle class (or individual members of the middle class) constitutes the hope for the future. Carlyle, in *Past and Present*, begins by contrasting the virtues of the medieval community of St. Edmund to the disintegrative, inorganic society of the modern period, only to celebrate the captains of industry as the aristocrats of the future. Ruskin's prophetic condemnation of the moral and aesthetic corruption of English life assumes the possibility of persuasion. And Matthew Arnold's satiric view of the middle class in *Culture and Anarchy* is continuously checked by a profound feeling for middle class virtues. The great English social critics were as intransigent and as uncompromising as any French critic of the bourgeois esprit, but their intransigence contained a belief in the moral power of their criticism. They believed that they could change or help bring about a change in the character and quality of social life.

If there is a term of evil in Flaubert's vocabulary, it is "bourgeois." "To hate the bourgeois is the beginning of all virtue."[1] Flaubert's hatred of the species that included "those in overalls as well as in a frocked coat" is the master passion of his life and work.[2] Flaubert is, of course, not the only writer of bourgeois origins to despise the species. One has only to invoke the names of Stendhal, Gide, and Sartre, among others, to perceive that in France, at least, there is a notable literary tradition of bourgeois self-hatred. Bourgeois self-hatred may be a unique phenomenon in the history of classes, since bourgeois ideology is particularly hostile to moral idealism. Though liberty, fraternity, and equality belong to the heroic past of the bourgeoisie, its ideal is moneymaking, the cash nexus. The poverty of idealization in bourgeois life makes the sensitive bourgeois vulnerable to self-hatred.

The phrase self-hatred suggests that there is no order of positive experience or values outside the orbit of bourgeois life to which the self has access. This is certainly not the case with Stendhal, whose feeling for distinction, energy, and talent derives in part from an empathy with aristocratic values. Nor is it the case with Sartre, whose continuous combat with the bourgeois in himself as well as in others is rooted in a strenuously willed commitment to a synthesis of existentialist and proletarian values, which in his view embody the ideas of personal integrity and social justice. Flaubert, on the other hand, never seems to stand securely outside the world he condemns. In *Madame Bovary*, for instance, the aristocracy is present but not as a valuable contrast to the bourgeoisie. Flaubert's depiction of the ball at Vaubyessard is not only a devastating portrait of the aristocracy, it is a major stimulus to Emma's romanticism and hence a destructive force. The charms of Vaubyessard will poison Emma's consciousness. In depicting those charms Flaubert elicits the brutality and sensuality that underly them.

> Those who were beginning to grow old had an air of youth, while there was something mature in the faces of the young. Their indifferent eyes had the appeased expression of daily-satiated passions, and through all their gentleness of manner pierced that peculiar brutality that stems from a steady command over half-tame things, for the exercise of one's strength and the amusement of one's vanity—the handling of thoroughbred horses and the society of loose women.[3]

Emma's romanticism, it becomes clear, is filled with an ignorant desire for aristocratic luxury and excitement. Indeed, romanticism in Flaubert can be viewed as the bourgeois pretension to aristocratic gratifications, and one detects in this view an almost puritan fascination with and revulsion from those gratifications. I mean by the term "puritan," with its connotations of austerity and repression, to suggest Flaubert's bourgeois character.[4] As for the proletariat, the significance of including overalls in the definition of bourgeois is that in Flaubert's view a proletarian future offers no prospect of change. The proletariat differs from the bourgeoisie in circumstance and not in spirit. Its real ambition is to be enriched like the bourgeoisie.

The order of values outside of bourgeois life to which Flaubert is committed is embodied in the word "art." Indeed the cult of art that comes to be denominated aestheticism receives its major inspiration from the work of Flaubert. Does art liberate Flaubert from the mere negativism of bourgeois self-hatred? Despite the exalted place it occupies, art is curiously vulnerable to its bourgeois adversary. Conversely, despite the despicable character of the bourgeois, he is the most formidable of adversaries. The bourgeois is small-minded, dull, cliché-bound in his speech, and impervious to enlightenment. "Charles Bovary's conversation," Flaubert tells us, "was commonplace as a street pavement, and every one's ideas trooped through it in their everyday garb, without exciting emotion, laughter or thought."[5] What makes him formidable is his identification in Flaubert's imagination with life itself.[6] He may be a historical species, but for all practical purposes he exists as the exemplar of normal humanity in a present to which there is no end in sight. Art then must reckon not only with the bourgeois but also with life itself.

The identification of bourgeois reality and life itself increases the sense of potency of bourgeois reality and drains art of its vitality, for if bourgeois reality has preempted life itself, the very ideal of vitality has been contaminated. Art must insulate itself from the impure energies of life. In Stendhal, by contrast, bourgeois reality is not all of life, and so his valuing of art is at the expense of the bourgeois but not at the expense of life qualities: liberty, brio, and gaiety. There is in *The Charterhouse of Parma*, for instance, a certain carelessness about art, expressing itself as spontaneity and love of improvisation. The action of the novel is a continuous improvisation that reveals at the same time the daring and ingenuity of the characters and of the novelist himself. The action of the novel shows Stendhal's love of life despite his sense of estrangement from the historical moment in which he lives. He invents a world against the world into which he has been born because the historical world has not preempted his imagination.

The writing of *Madame Bovary* makes clear the antivitalist imperative under which Flaubert worked. It has been noted how Flaubert deliberately divested his first version of the novel of a wealth of sensuous detail and psychological observation (comparable to what one might find in a Proustian novel), an act that led Proust to doubt Flaubert's capacity as a novelist in the final version. In a fine essay, Albert Beguin documents this process of divestment. Beguin accurately characterizes the original version of *Madame Bovary* as "uneven and frequently faulty" in its style, "though amazingly free in invention. The human content, however, is infinitely richer than in the printed version." Beguin offers as instances the following passages which Flaubert excised in the final version in the interest of an austerity of style.

> Then they faced each other; they looked at each other, touching with their hands, their faces, their breasts, as if they didn't have senses enough with which to savor the joys of love, burning with desire, stamping their feet while staring at each other with lascivious laughs, until they could no longer wait for the moment of possession.
>
> The pleasures of the senses did not invalidate this ideal image; to the contrary, they made it stronger. Emma reconquered happiness in this blonde-colored passion and knowing how uncertain it was, tried to increase it by means of all the artifices of her tenderness, savoring it with the craving of the poor, the thirst of the sick, the avarice of the elderly.[7]

But Beguin fails to give an adequate account of the motive for the excisions.

> If it were not a vain game, one would like to dream of a Flaubert born fifty or seventy years later, who could have accepted without further ado the gift of a style beyond rules and a way of writing capable of recapturing exactly the inner movement it was expressing. Writing at the time of Proust, he would perhaps have known a happiness that was refused to him as long as he worshipped the idol of Art, to which he sacrificed his soul and his blood. But, in that case, we would not now have that irreplaceable great book *Madame Bovary*, the book of the impossible escape, the heavy-hearted poem of eternal *ennui*.[8]

The reference to Proust's happiness in his art suggests Stendhal, who pursued and found on occasion happiness in his writing. ("Beauty," Stendhal remarked, "is the promise of happiness.") Flaubert's decision to prune his earlier work, however, cannot be simply explained by a desire to conform to rules, as Beguin remarks. The Proustian freedom of imagination (Beguin's implicit ideal), which allows for the involuntary floodings of memory, presupposes a belief in inspiration, the sublime mood of the poet. And inspiration in turn presupposes a love of life, literally, a breathing in of a greater life than one's daily, ordinary life. Flaubert was without this faith and thus exhibited a profound mistrust of inspiration. Rather, Flaubert sought to rid himself in his diction, in the cadences of his prose, of the suggestion of any contamination with the energies of life. That is why it is the heavy-hearted poem of eternal ennui.

Flaubert's expression of his hatred of life is explicit and frequent in the correspondence.

> Do you know what boredom is? Not that common, banal boredom that comes from idleness, but that modern boredom that eats the very entrails of a man and turns an intelligent being into a walking shade, a thinking ghost.[9]

> I have a hatred of life. Yes, of Life and of everything that reminds me that life must be borne. It bores me to eat, to dress, to stand on my feet, etc.[10]

One might guess that this hatred of life is dialectically related to an inordinate expectation of life, even expressed as a love of life. The hatred is the result of a sense of betrayal: the stupidity and banality it offers instead of the fulfillment of one's wildest romantic dreams.

We can see the process of expectation and disappointment graphically in Flaubert's adolescent fantasy *November*, an adumbration of *Madame Bovary*. Happiness in Flaubertian terms presupposes a godlike condition—that is, omnipotence, the ubiquitous experience of a variety of pleasure.

> I loved Life, a life expansive, radiant, irradiate. I loved it in the furious gallop coursers, in the glitter of the stars, in the rushing of the waves toward the shore. I loved it in the surge of lovely naked bosoms, in the flutter of amorous glances, in the vibrations of the chords of the violin, in the swaying of oak trees, in the setting sun when it turns the windows to gold and calls up thoughts of the balconies of Babylon on which the queens rested their arms as they looked toward Asia.[11]

> I wished that I were an emperor for his absolute power, for his numerous slaves, for the wild enthusiasm of his devoted armies. I wished that I were a woman for her beauty. I wished that like her I might strip myself naked, let my hair fall to my heels, mirror and admire myself in the stream. I lost myself when I would in limitless reveries. I imagained myself sitting at the noble feasts of antiquity. I imagined myself King of the Indies.[12]

And in the midst of these effusions there is suddenly the most extreme expression of nihilistic despair.

> I was born with the longing for death. Nothing seemed more stupid than life, nothing more shameful than to cling to it.

> Brought up, like all my contemporaries, without religion, I had
> neither the dry satisfaction of the atheist nor the nonchalant irony
> of the skeptic.[13]

Flaubert's longing for happiness is bound to be disappointed because
its intensity and ambition make it insatiable. And the disappointment
is as bitter as the longing was intense. Small wonder that Flaubert
identifies himself with Madame Bovary, meaning that he wishes to
exorcise the demon of romanticism from his soul.

Flaubert's unsatisfied Faustian love of life leads through a dialectical
reversal to a hatred of it. The same dialectic converts a passion for art
to a hatred of it—or at least a feeling of its ultimate inadequacy. Flaubert knows from bitter intimate experience an enthusiasm for life; he
also has the capacity to express it. His letters and the first draft of
Madame Bovary have a richness of utterance which suggests a complicity with the longing for happiness, a complicity which he never
fully overcame in *Madame Bovary*. Art for Flaubert becomes an exercise in enervation, a way of weakening and undermining the pernicious desire for happiness. The effect of what might be called the
aesthetic of enervation is to allow tedium to enter the very substance
of art. Flaubert is perhaps the first modern writer to reproduce the
boredom of life into the work itself through a deliberate act. Flaubert
at once creates the cult of art and demystifies it, or invites the critical
reader to demystify it.

THE OSTENSIBLE subject of *Madame Bovary* is the futility of romanticism. But to see the subject of the novel as romanticism is at once
limiting and misleading. The subject of *Madame Bovary* is life itself—
that is, life under the *apparently* antithetic guises of romance and reality, for the antithesis is a demonstrable illusion.

The illusion is that romance represents transcendence or the possibility of transcendence.[14] Flaubert's imaginative effort is to reveal the
futility of such transcendence. It would put the case too crudely to say
that reality is an insurmountable obstacle to romantic ambition. Flaubert shows that romantic fantasy, like reality, is subject to conditions.
Emma is as much a prisoner of her fantasy life as Charles is of pedes-
trian notions that determine his view of life. What they see and understand is determined by temperament, desire, and need. What they fail
to see is the result of the exclusions, the crowding out of the needs and
desires of others, which the very fact of personal temperament im-

plies. This is not an accident of the particular personalities of Charles
and Emma. It is the condition of all the characters in the novel. Reality
in *Madame Bovary* is hardly ever seen apart from the distorting lens
of each character's subjectivity—whether it is the pedestrianism of
Charles, the enflamed temperament of Emma, the greed of Lheureux,
or the pompous vanity of Homais.

Moreover, the effect of this extreme subjectivity (one is tempted to
call it solipsism) is to coerce—or attempt to coerce—the character who
is the object of fantasy. A particularly interesting instance of this is
Emma's plan for her elopement with Rodolphe, her first lover:

> It was the next month that they were to run away. She was to
> leave Yonville as if she was going on some business to Rouen.
> Rodolphe would have booked the seats, obtained the passports,
> and even written to Paris in order to have the whole mailcoach
> reserved for them as far as Marseilles, where they would buy a
> carriage, and go on from there straight by the Genoa road. She
> would have sent her luggage to Lheureux, from where it would be
> taken directly to the "Hirondelle," so that no one would have any
> suspicion. And in all this there never was any allusion to the
> child. Rodolphe avoided the subject; it may be that he had for-
> gotten about it.[15]

It is Rodolphe, of course, who has been the seducer, the obvious co-
ercer, but Flaubert shows that the seduction was accomplished by
stimulating a fantasy in Emma to change her life, which must necessarily occur through the instrumentality of Rodolphe, regardless of his
intentions. Emma's fantasy about Rodolphe is coercive, as coercive as
Rodolphe's fantasy about Emma. Indeed, under the aspect of fantasy,
there is no difference in their coerciveness. One might add that her af-
fair with her other lover, Leon, openly betrays Emma's coerciveness,
for in effect she turns Leon into a mistress.[16]

The solipsism has its expression in the incommunicability between
people. And one version of this incommunicability is the cliché. All
the characters in the novel speak clichés of one kind or another. In the
famous episode of the Agricultural Fair, Flaubert deliberately counter-
points the romantic cliché of private life and the "realistic" cliché of
public life in order to dramatize the spiritual vacuity of both. The politician, speaking the rhetoric of national pride:

> Everywhere commerce and the arts are flourishing; everywhere
> new means of communication, like so many new arteries in the

body politic, establish within it new relations. Our great industrial centers have recovered all their activity; religion, more con-
solidated, smiles in all hearts; our ports are full, confidence is
born again, and France breathes once more!

The seducer, speaking the language of romance:

Don't you know that there are souls constantly tormented? They
need by turns to dream and to act, the purest passions and the
most turbulent joys, and thus they fling themselves into all sorts
of fantasies, of follies.

And the politician again:

You, farmers, agricultural laborers! You pacific pioneers of a
work that belongs wholly to civilization! You, men of progress
and morality, you have understood, I say, that political storms
are even more redoubtable than atmospheric disturbances![17]

And so on.

To dismiss the cliché simply as an exercise in stupidity is to under-
estimate its power in Flaubert's imagination. The cliché is the expression of the conditioned character of our speech. It is speech hardened
into incorrigible habit, the mind expressing itself without tension or
anxiety. The absence of anxiety may be a form of repression, for what
the cliché does is avoid the interesting, possibly threatening aspects of
reality. As Leo Bersani remarks, the cliché "articulates the real by impoverishing it."[18] It is a pathological condition, a contagious disease of
the mind of epidemic proportions. Like original sin, it is incurable.
Flaubert's work is in a sense the archetype for a good deal of modern
fiction, which is nourished by the cliché of everyday life just as psychoanalysis is nourished by psychopathology. Cliché is impenetrable
substance, the verbal counterpart of the solipsistic minds of the characters. It is impossible for a thought or idea to enter a cliché-domi-
nated mind and move it to another kind of attention. The nondra-
matic character of *Madame Bovary* is the outcome of the impenetra-
bility of one clichéd consciousness by another. The soul of a Flaubert
character is hardened into habit, damned because it is incapable of
fundamental change. By the dramatic I mean an encounter between
characters in which something happens which transforms reality for
the characters involved. What we get in *Madame Bovary* are disturb-
ing juxtapositions of the subjectivities of the characters rather than
dramatic interactions.

The presentation of the power of the cliché is one of Flaubert's notable achievements. But he makes excessive claims for its power. Most people, perhaps all people, speak in clichés, but they do not speak only in clichés. Moreover, not all people are dominated by them. The effect of Flaubert's artistic obsession with cliché is to repress the unfamiliar idea, the unexpected thought. There is even a moment in *Madame Bovary* in which Flaubert indirectly and perhaps unwittingly raises a question about what seems his stridency in presenting human speech in the form of cliché. It is the passage in which Flaubert condemns Rodolphe's coarseness, which consists of his failure to hear the accent of true feeling underneath the stock romantic phrases of the still innocent Emma.

> He had so often heard these things said that they did not strike him as original. Emma was like all his mistresses; and the charm of novelty, gradually falling away like a garment, laid bare the eternal monotony of passion, that has always the same shape and the same language. He was unable to see, this man so full of experience, the variety of feelings hidden within the same expressions. Since libertine or venal lips had murmured similar phrases, he only faintly believed in the candor of Emma's; he thought one should beware of exaggerated declarations which only serve to cloak a tepid love; as though the abundance of one's soul did not sometimes overflow with empty metaphors, since no one ever has been able to give the exact measure of his needs, his concepts, or his sorrows. The human tongue is like a cracked cauldron on which we beat out tunes to set a bear dancing when we would make the stars weep with our melodies.[19]

One wonders whether the "similar phrases" and the "empty metaphors" are a function of personal failure (the failure of Emma) or the necessary limitations of human speech or some curious, perhaps willful, self-limitation in Flaubert. It is significant that a writer whose passion for *le mot juste* is almost his defining characteristic never creates either a character or, for that matter, a narrative voice that would finely distinguish in language those differences in feeling that Flaubert apparently believes exist. Flaubert in his fashion shares the guilt of Rodolphe. His search for the right word is not the search for words which perfectly express true feeling; it is a search for the words we use as counters for feeling. If Flaubert's own language implies an ironic distance from the "empty metaphors" that express or conceal the "monotony of passion," there is no promise of an alternative language that would suggest a life free of the weariness and banality which the novel depicts. Indeed, the failure has suggested to some critics that the reality concealed by the cliché is an emptiness or absence, despite Flaubert's claim to the contrary.

The critical faculty asserts itself with energy, but it is not rooted in any firm conviction of a more valuable life. All the alternatives meet in a common banality and Flaubert can only allow it to speak through him. His famous impersonality may be no more than inability to find a moral or spiritual perspective from which to view his world. He does have the gift of art, which means the shaping gift for form and phrase to distinguish him from the presented world, but it is an art divested of the power of transcendence. It is significant, I think, that Flaubert is incapable of imagining a character of genuine creativity within his realistic fiction. Emma Bovary and Frederic Moreau are artist types, but there is no complicity between novelist and character (as there is in Joyce's *A Portrait of the Artist*) that their fantasies of fulfillment or creation will come to anything. Flaubert's ironic manner anticipates defeat in the incipience of any wish or promise.

I here take issue with Erich Auerbach's discussion of the passage describing Emma and Charles at the dinner table in which Emma experiences disgust with Charles while he obliviously eats his meal.

> But it was above all at mealtimes that she could bear it no longer, in that little room on the ground floor, with the smoking stove. The creaking door, the oozing walls, the damp floortiles; all the bitterness of life seemed to be served to her on her plate, and with the steam from the boiled beef, there rose from the depths of her soul other exhalations as it were of disgust. Charles was a slow eater; she would nibble a few hazel-nuts, or else, leaning on her elbow, would amuse herself making marks on the oilcloth with the point of her table-knife.

Auerbach presents this paragraph as an instance of Flaubert's objectifying Emma's subjectivity. It is not simply a matter of Flaubert's representing the content of Emma's consciousness, "of *what* she feels as she *feels* it." As Auerbach convincingly argues, Emma herself is situated within the picture and consequently judged, or at least understood, as she does not understand herself. The evidence for this is that Flaubert expresses her consciousness in language she would not have been capable of: "the creaking door," "the oozing walls," "the steam from the boiled beef," "all the bitterness of life seemed to be served to her on her plate." To be sure, Flaubert is the artist with the gift for expression and Emma is not. But the difference hardly justifies Auerbach's conclusion that if Emma had Flaubert's power of expression "she would have outgrown herself and saved herself." For if there is nothing of Flaubert's life in these words, but only Emma's, as Auerbach concedes, Flaubert's power of mature expression simply articulates Emma's subjectivity without changing it. The capacity for expression does not necessarily have the power to change what it expresses. At least the case has to be made that it does, and Auerbach fails to make it.[20]

Auerbach's view depends, I think, upon an untenable assumption about the creative process. He ignores the incommensurability between novelist and character. Flaubert is not a character within the fiction to be compared with Emma. Indeed, Flaubert for all practical purposes vanishes within Emma's consciousness. He is simply the agent of articulation.

On the evidence of *Madame Bovary* and Flaubert's other great realistic masterpiece *The Sentimental Education*, one could hardly make the argument that art redeems the reality that it works so hard to render. Art proves to be an ineffectual resource against the weariness with life to which both novels so powerfully testify. Art in Flaubert becomes not a countervalue to bourgeois reality, to life itself, but its perfect expression. *Le mot juste* implies that perfection in art is the perfect rendering of reality. If Flaubert does not intend celebration, he nonetheless shows implicit deference to that reality. Flaubert's deadly ear for the commonplaces of bourgeois life has a parodic effect, which we find in his realistic fiction and quintessentially in *The Dictionary of Accepted Ideas*. It would be misleading to say that Flaubert loves what he hears and sees, but when there is no alternative to the object of parody (except for Flaubert's skill at parody), then its effect becomes a kind of pleasure, perhaps akin to celebration. Indeed, doesn't Flaubert confess as much in speaking of his attraction to stupidity?

> Such a wide gap separates me now from the rest of the world that I am often surprised at hearing the simplest and most natural-sounding statements. The most ordinary word fills me at times with boundless admiration. Certain gestures, certain inflections of voice fill me with wonder, and certain types of ineptness almost make me dizzy.[21]

Roland Barthes has provided a lucid and succinct description of Flaubert's "transcendence" of the ironic attitude.

The writer's only control over stereotypic vertigo (this vertigo is also that of "stupidity," "vulgarity") is to participate in it without quotation marks, producing a text, not a parody. This is what Flaubert did in *Bouvard et Pecuchet:* the two copyists are copiers of codes (they are, one may say, *stupid*), but since they too confront the class stupidity which surrounds them, the text presenting them sets up a circularity in which no one (not even the author) has an advantage over anyone else; and this is in fact the function of writing: to make ridiculous, to annul the power (the intimidation) of one language over another, to dissolve any meta-language as it is constituted.[22]

This new tolerance of the plenitude of reality or of the codes that represent reality is not as self-justifying as Barthes seems to imply. If the author loses his advantage as a consequence of the stupidity of the copyists and the surrounding class stupidity, what is the authority and pleasure in the presentation? The negative capacity of "writing . . . to annul the power . . . of one language over another" becomes perversely a celebration of contemptible reality. Perhaps, more pointedly, in Barthes's own terms, the new tolerance offers itself as another arbitrary authority. If irony is a privileged language or vantage point, it is because it is the incarnation of intelligence. To deny authority to intelligence, as Barthes's version of Flaubert does, is not to unmask a false power or corruption but to assert a claim that need not be credited. Indeed, if it were credited the status of Barthes's own account of Flaubert (or of anything) would lose whatever authority it might have, for its intelligence would have no advantage, no privilege over someone else's stupidity.

Jonathan Culler provides an extraordinary answer to this challenge by arguing for "the exhilaration of Flaubertian stupidity."

The stupidity which refuses to comprehend objects in accordance with received modes of understanding but prefers to seek freedom and enrichment in reverie, the irony which explores alternative views both as polemical activity and as a way of enlarging horizons, are both attempts to enact, in the novels, the allegory of mind striving to avoid the limitations of particular social modes of understanding and to win through to something of the purity and inviolacy of the sacred, which one may define as arbitrary meanings guaranteed not by man but by God.[23]

Following Sartre and Barthes, Culler seeks to transvalue stupidity into the highest form of intelligence, though he confuses the matter by connecting stupidity with irony. What does this transvaluation amount to? Essentially, an undermining of conventional assumptions about mimesis. "Flaubert's realism provides firm links with an empirical world and draws the reader into a process which appears very familiar, only to expose him to the drama of the sentence and to the demystification of his role in making sense of the text."[24] The winning "through to something of the purity and inviolacy of the sacred" becomes nothing more than a sensitivity to the problematics of fictional representation. That such a claim can be made without irony or self-irony by an intelligent critic is symptomatic of the present state of criticism.

Flaubert's attraction to banality is a sort of displacement of the artist's generic relation to the literary language of the past. As Hugh Kenner reminds us in *The Pound Era*, "writing is largely quotation, quotation newly energized, as a cyclotron augments the energies of common particles circulating."[25] Kenner is, of course, characterizing a modern condition of writing. The richer the tradition, the greater the opportunity and the burden of quotation.[26] Moreover, the modern novel has as its field not simply the literary tradition but reality as a whole. Hugh Kenner invokes Joyce, who said of *Finnegans Wake:* "Really, it is not I who am writing this book, it is you, and you, and that man over there, and that girl at the next table."[27] The result of this process is inevitably the cliché, or rather the disclosure of the "magical" properties of the cliché.

By an odd reversal, art and bourgeois reality exist in a kind of complicity with each other in Flaubert as it is subsequently to exist in Joyce. However hard Flaubert may have tried to insulate the artistic idea from the banality of everyday life, the banal infects the ideal. The cult of banality that I described in the first chapter is already implicit in Flaubert.

Flaubert's work contains the paradox of the symbiosis of avant-garde formalism and the conviction of the banality of everyday life. Formalist innovation presupposes the banality of reality, which can only be overcome by innovation—by what Claude Levi-Strauss might call *bricolage*. Those who regard reality as changeful or intrinsically interesting do not put much stock in formalist innovation. Modern creativity has become linked to a view of experience as banal and has invested much of its energy in parody, pastiche, "quotation"—paradoxically, in repetition. The avant-garde learns from cliché its gift for parodic repetition. The search for the new entails a devaluation of what exists, of what is old. Averse to the habit of meditation upon the given (a meditation that might enrich the given), the avant-garde, having no place to go, turns to parody-pastiche-repetition, which has the paradoxical effect of enriching the given. Contemporary versions of the aesthetic complicity with the banal are without Flaubert's rancor, as if they have acknowledged what Flaubert was reluctant to acknowledge—a new principle of enrichment.

In a review of *Death in Venice*, D. H. Lawrence brilliantly characterized the pleasure experienced by the artist and the reader in the aesthetic acquiescence in the banal.

> Thomas Mann seems to me the last sick sufferer from the complaint of Flaubert. The latter stood away from life as from a leprosy. And Thomas Mann, like Flaubert, feels vaguely that he has in him something finer than ever physical life revealed. Physical life is a disordered corruption, against which he can fight with only one weapon, his fine aesthetic sense, his feeling for beauty, for perfection, for a certain fitness which soothes him, and gives him an inner pleasure, however corrupt the stuff of life may be . . . And so, with real suicidal intention, like Flaubert's, he sits, a last too-sick disciple, reducing himself grain by grain to the statement of his own disgust, patient, self-destructively, so that his statement at least may be perfect in a world of corruption.[28]

This pleasure, of course, is a world apart from emotions that are provoked by an art that is sacred, redemptive, life-enhancing. I am not asserting that art ought to provoke these emotions. I am saying that the Flaubertian cult of art creates an expectation of holiness and redemption through art, which it fails utterly to satisfy.

Sartre notes the paradox that though Flaubert despised realism and loved only "the absolute purity of art . . . the public decided at the outset that Flaubert was a realist."[29] Flaubert the aesthete and Flaubert the realist: the paradox is only verbal, for "the absolute purity of art" in the great realistic novels turns out to be very little to the extent that it does not depend for its substance on the despicable reality which it renders. Flaubert's influence on modern aestheticism has been duly noted, indeed has been felt by writers like Baudelaire and Joyce, for whom Flaubert represented "the absolute purity of art." But Flaubert's protégés, it should be remembered, were Maupassant and Zola, whose legacy from Flaubert is naturalism, which asserts the triumph of reality.[30]

Is it merely fortuitous that aestheticism would have as a major out-

come a crushing triumphant realism? In his essay "The Dehumaniza-
tion of Art" Ortega y Gasset suggests that the enthusiasm for pure art
is a mask which conceals surfeit with art and hatred for it. Ortega sees
this hatred as a concomitant of a hatred of science, hatred of the state,
hatred, in sum, of civilization as a whole. We might go further and see
the fanatical enthusiasm for and consequent hatred of art as a symptom of a hatred of life itself.

Ortega is not the first to have perceived the self-undermining character of fanatical aestheticism. We have it on the authority of Baudelaire himself—who felt its temptation as powerfully as did Flaubert. In
his essay "The Pagan School," Baudelaire remarks on the immoderate
love of form.

> Immoderate love of form leads to monstrous and unknown dis-
> orders. Absorbed by the fierce passion for the beautiful, the
> amusing, the pretty, the picturesque—for there are different de-
> grees—notions of the just and the true will disappear. The fren-
> zied passion for art is a canker which devours all else; and since
> complete lack of the just and the true in art is equivalent to a lack
> of art, the whole man shrinks; the excessive specialization of one
> faculty ends in nothingness [even if that faculty claims to be de-
> voted to the depiction of the whole man].[31]

Baudelaire is describing fanaticism, a quality which aestheticism in its
Flaubertian form shares with political ideology. Flaubert introduces
the party spirit into the vocation of art. He is to art what Robespierre
is to politics—fanatical, incorruptible, autocratic. His, like Robespierre's, is a vision without alternatives. Like that of Robespierre
again, it is a self-betraying vision. Robespierre's purism, his principled
beheading of his adversaries, for example, sowed the seeds of his own
destruction. Flaubert's purism, his exclusive passion for art, has
within it the seeds of a disgust with art, an undermining of any edify-
ing, redemptive, life-enhancing claim for art.

The analogy between aestheticism and the party spirit may not be
fortuitous. The French Revolution brought into existence the political
and the ideological spirit—which then permeates social and cultural
life. Since politics suffuses the daily atmosphere in which people live
in a historically unprecedented way (the enormous vogue of journalism
is to a great extent responsible for this), the cultural life itself takes on
the forms of the political life. Just as a party cannot exist without an
ideology, a cultural or artistic "school" needs, or feels it needs, an

ideology, even if the ideology is anti-ideological. The modern aesthetic hostility to the cliché may be seen as an act of resistance to the ideological reduction of ordinary life, which the cliché represents.[32]

The specialism of art entails the exclusion of morality, religion, politics as offering the basis for a point of view in fiction, the effect of which is to deplete as much as to purify the resources of art. No longer seen as entertainment or moral instruction or the *via media* toward salvation or an imaginative spur toward social or communal change, art becomes a pitiful life resource even for the most gifted and accomplished. One has only to invoke the lives of Flaubert and Kafka. The impulse toward aesthetic purity impoverishes the works of art themselves.

Kafka's equivocal relationship to aestheticism is illuminating. He is the aesthete par excellence who understands the poverty of art. Or at least that is how I read the story "The Hunger Artist." The ascetic commitment to art is an ineluctable compulsive condition for Kafka. The panther, bursting with life, that appears at the end of the story is an unmistakable emblem of the limits of art. Yet Kafka, like the hunger artist, can as soon force himself to participate in the feast of life as the panther can choose to refrain from eating. It may be that Flaubert himself was as sensitive to the impoverishment of art as Kafka but simply could not help himself.

Max Brod, Kafka's friend and literary executor, writes:

> I shall never forget the deep emotion with which Kafka read to me the last paragraph of *Souvenirs intimes* by Flaubert's niece, Caroline Commanville. The passage describes how Flaubert sacrificed to his idol "La Littérature," everything—love, tenderness —everything, and the author asks if he never toward the end of his life regretted this departure from the "route Commune." She is inclined to believe he did. A few excited words that Flaubert once said to her on one of their last walks together led her to think so. They had been to see a woman friend of theirs, and found her in the midst of her charming children. As they were walking back home along the Seine, Flaubert said, "Ils sont dans le vrai . . . [Commanville explains] en faisant allusion a cet intérieur de famille honnête et bon. 'Oui,' se repetait—il a lui—même gravement, 'ils sont dans le vrai' . . ."[33]

The difference between Flaubert and Kafka is in the continuous sentiment of Kafka's work expressed in Flaubert's statement: "Ils sont dans le vrai." Flaubert did not live, sleep, and eat the regret Kafka suffered that he could not live the ordinary life of a bourgeois.

The anti-aesthetical view should not be confused with a disrespect for a serious concern with the formal properties of art. Nor should it serve as an excuse for bad art. Tolstoy and Dostoevsky, who did not have the aesthetical view (Tolstoy was in fact militantly anti-aesthetical), were as serious as Flaubert in their devotion to the careful construction of their novels, and Tolstoy struggled with language as passionately as did Flaubert. The issue between them is not respect for art, but the matter of art as fetish. Aestheticism is the fetishizing of art and not the logical consequence of a belief in the value of art. This distinction lies at the root of the perceptions of Baudelaire and Ortega.

Just as it would be wrong to identify Flaubertian aestheticism with the proper valuation of art, it would be wrong to see Flaubert as representing a willful and perverse deviation from the proper route of art. Flaubert does not so much separate art from morality, religion, politics: his art is a response to the fading authority of morality, religion, and politics. The Dantean integration of the various modes of human knowledge and art is no longer possible. Flaubert's art is *faute de mieux*, given—and this is an important qualification—a temperament which lacks moral, political, and spiritual adventurousness. It is a defense against the movement and change common to both romanticism and revolution. Art, the vocation of the valetudinarian, turns realities into fixities (the fixities of despair) because the artist as a human being cannot bear the disappointments of reality. To mitigate despair he anticipates disappointments. It is not fortuitous that art achieved its apotheosis in a country where for a century political revolution became the dominant fact of life. Flaubert, with all his poetic genius, did not have the capacity to see in the profound instability of nineteenth century life anything other than failure. He lacked the ambition and gift of a Stendhal or a Nietzsche to search for new values, new institutions, or to imagine ways of reviving old values. Flaubert's modernism is at once filled with a sense of present failure, future hopelessness, and hatred of the past. His is a vertiginous imagination, precariously poised on itself.[34]

One of the ways in which Flaubert destroys the sense of possibility is by making us feel that what he is presenting is an eternal condition. The romantic expectations and disillusionments of his heroine and hero in *Madame Bovary* and *The Sentimental Education*, respectively, belong to the eternal rhythm of the soul—or of a certain kind of soul.

In his view, they may be intensified by the historical moment but not determined by it. Thus Flaubert shows as much contempt for the continual efforts to revive revolution in the nineteenth century as he shows for the conservative heirs of the first revolution, for, as in the case of Senecal in *The Sentimental Education,* he hears in the clichés of revolutionary discourse the tyranny of utopian logic and detects in the desires of the insurgent proletariat the vulgarity and greed of the class it is trying to overthrow.

> He was familiar with Mably, Morelly, Fourier, Saint-Simon, Comte, Cabet, Louis Blanc, the whole cartload of Socialist writers—those who wanted to reduce mankind to the level of the barrackroom, send it to the brothel for its amusement, and tie it to the counter or the bench; and out of this mixture he had evolved an ideal of a virtuous democracy, half farm and half factory, a sort of American Sparta in which the individual would exist only to serve the State, which would be more omnipotent, more absolute, more infallible and more divine than any Grand Lama or Nebuchadnezzar. He had no doubt that this idea would soon be realized, and anything which he considered hostile to it he attacked with the logic of a mathematician and the faith of an inquisitor.[35]

Flaubert dehistoricizes the events of 1848 (makes them seem like moments in a process of eternal recurrence) by presenting them as a part of a fatal Cartesian logic from which nothing new could possibly emerge.

So systematic is the spirit of nihilistic reduction in Flaubert that nihilism itself becomes the object of irony. After presenting Deslauriers as a corrosive critic of the pretensions of the political parties, which represent "those who have, those who used to have and those who are trying to have . . . all united in the imbecile worship of Authority," Flaubert says of Deslauriers and his friends what could be said of Flaubert himself.

> They must attack all accepted ideas, the Academy, the Ecole Normale, the Conservatoire, the Comédic Française, anything which bore any resemblance to an institution. In this way they could provide their review with an overall doctrine. Then, once it was solidly established, it would suddenly turn into a daily paper; and after that they could start attacking individuals.[36]

The line from Flaubert to the New Novel through Joyce and Beckett has often been remarked. Perhaps no one has put better the almost programmatic and, one should add, paradoxical powerlessness of

Flaubert's art than Samuel Beckett in describing his own ambition. "I speak of an art turning from it[self] in disgust, weary of its puny exploits, weary of pretending to be able, of doing a little better the same old thing, of going a little further along a dreary route." And the interviewer asks: "And preferring what?" "The expression that there is nothing to express, nothing from which to express, together with the obligation to express."[37]

What is the source of this weariness but the effort to redeem (or, as Beckett puts it, the pretence of redeeming) commonplace reality. It was Henry James who was troubled by the commonplaceness of Flaubert's subject in *The Sentimental Education*. He did not feel, as many later critics feel, that the mere fact that the artistic will is strenuously at work, creating and shaping structure, formulating and refining language, redeems the commonplace material. It is an interesting fact that the two novelists who have found fault with Flaubert in this respect are James and Proust, who shared with Flaubert a certain estrangement from life. The critical difference from Flaubert is that for them life was a supreme value, which they sought to capture in their art either by imagining its presence or by dramatizing the horror of its absence. In James's *The Beast in the Jungle*, for example, there is a passionate refusal to allow the fact that nothing happens to the central character in the work to penetrate the aesthetic of the story. The aesthetic interest of the work staves off the tedious and the banal. Flaubert surrenders even in his aesthetic to the tedium of life, fascinated as it were by the abyss. It is true of both James and Proust, as it is not of Flaubert, that their imaginations have their sources in a life other than the immediate historical moment they face. Flaubert remains the perfect exemplar of the self-hating bourgeois imagination condemned to the reality which it loathes. The very purism of Flaubert's aestheticism, which deprives art of the energy of transcendence, is itself a symptom of Flaubert's bourgeois character.

Art in its formalist manifestation is austere and repressive, it stimulates the senses only to deny them. Art in its exalted formalist version is as hostile to pornography, for example, as the most hostile puritan censor and like the puritan censor it is in a kind of covert dalliance with pornography. Form is a shield against the abyss, not a spiritual journey through the abyss. Artists preoccupied with form do not emerge from an ordeal transformed, cured, renewed. They disintegrate unless they learn to halt before the abyss. Formalism is the avoidance of the tragic; it is art's declaration that the gods have abandoned it. Its power of survival depends upon sheer human will, a will without moral or spiritual inspiration.

The *locus classicus* for the career of formalism is *Death in Venice* by Thomas Mann, "the last sick sufferer of the complaint of Flaubert." The artist Aschenbach embodies in full, vulnerable strength the principle of form per se, which proves to be ineffectual against the unleashed chaotic Dionysian forces of life. The tale, fully conscious of its meaning, reveals form's equivocal relation to the moral life. Divided between an immoralist fascination with the abyss and a need for order, form in Aschenbach is disembodied and hence demystified. Not being in the service of anything greater than itself, whether it be religious mystery or life, its fragility is exposed.

Unlike Aschenbach, Flaubert managed to preserve the integrity of his commitment to form, but there is no transfiguration of his personal misery, which becomes cosmic despair. The things of the world are homogenized into reality, and art becomes an impotent magic. It is lucid only as a revelation of the triumph of reality. The historical moment (1848 in *The Sentimental Education*) is simply the medium for Flaubert's metaphysical meditation. It is nevertheless significant that the abyss opened in a time of revolution and fundamental social transformation. Flaubert's vision, no matter how hard he tries to mute the historical element, inhabits a historical period in which a new class has come to power, devoted to the acquisition of wealth and unconcerned with distinction and beauty, a period in which another class is achieving a sense of its own identity and threatening to overturn the world in the name of justice and brotherhood so that it too can enjoy the material fruits of the world and thus emulate the despicable class it has overthrown.

Flaubert's view of the bourgeois soul as incorrigible, trapped in solipsism and cliché, and his retreat into the consolations of art would make him an ally of Ernest Renan, the great nineteenth century ideologue of cultural elitism, who was willing to sacrifice the development of the masses for "the creation of geniuses and of an audience capable of understanding them."[38] The diffusion of the cultural life among the people (the ambition of democracy) is an impossibility because the people are insusceptible to the truths of that life. In Flaubert's case, there is the poignant irony that the truths of art are incapable of saving either the geniuses or the audience capable of understanding them. Flaubert appears in the strange role of an ideologue of an untranscending art.

9

The Blasphemy
of Joycean Art

JOYCE'S AFFINITY for Flaubert was explicit and strong. Filled with
sensitive types who never achieve the condition of art, *Dubliners*,
Joyce's most Flaubertian work, reveals in the fastidiousness of its language, in the control exercised by the symbolic imagination, the su-
premacy of the artistic imagination and its incapacity to redeem the
world. The destiny of the Dubliner, like that of Emma Bovary, is an-
nunciated and determined by an unrelenting symbolism. The "blindness" of North Richmond Street guarantees the failure of the boy in
"Araby" to escape Dublin squalor through imagination just as the
pricking of Emma's finger by the wire of the wedding bouquet binds
the fate that will make her an adulteress. The significance of Flaubert's
presence in Joyce's imagination is in the high value which Flaubert placed on art, and in the countertendency, which made Flaubert
deeply suspicious of its powers. "Bourgeois reality" is conceived as too
formidable to be overcome by its adversary, art. In *A Portrait of the
Artist* Joyce presents an alternative language to the weariness and banality of everyday life, but it is a language already in the process of
becoming banal itself. Joyce echoes the vaporous prose of Pater,
whose spiritual authority can hardly compete with the language of the
church either in its heavenly or in its infernal versions. Indeed, the
power of art finally is in its complicity with reality. In the Nausicaa
and Oxen of The Sun episodes of *Ulysses*, Joyce evinces a gift for the
parodic enactment of human speech and attitude surpassing that of
Flaubert. And like the parody of Flaubert, Joyce's parody is a form of
celebration.

The profanity of Joyce's art is the outcome of a curiously unresolved struggle with his Catholic heritage. There is even a sense in which Joyce remained a Catholic artist through his defiances and indifferences. If there is a "classical" touchstone for Stephen Dedalus, the artist-hero, it is Dante, the poet-pilgrim of *The Divine Comedy*.

Dante, of course, is explicitly present in his imagination. Hélène Cixous notes that "between 1903 and 1906 Joyce was going through his Dante phase. He had learned Italian from Father Ghezzi at the university and quoted Dante at every opportunity, to the extent that Gogarty nicknamed him Dante."[1] Richard Ellmann remarks early in his biography that "Dante was perhaps Joyce's favorite author," though he strangely qualifies this remark by noting that Joyce "put aside Dante's heaven and hell, sin and punishment, preferring like Balzac to keep his comedy human, and he relished secular, disorderly lives which Dante would have punished or ignored."[2] Ellmann's statement is either a frivolous paradox or a profound and obscure truth about Joyce's imagination. Did Joyce prefer Balzac to Dante or did he enjoy a profoundly antithetical and yet nourishing relationship to Dante, which both Balzac and Joyce shared? I think the latter is true. Both Joyce and Balzac stand in a modern relationship to their great medieval precursor. Joyce himself acknowledges this when he says: "I love Dante almost as much as the Bible. He is my spiritual food, the rest is ballast."[3]

Joyce turned to Aquinas for ambivalent inspiration: both as a source of ideas and as an occasion for energetic rebellion. Stephen draws upon Aquinas (as Dante did before him) for an aesthetic that offers itself as an alternative dispensation to that of which *The Summa Theologica* is a supreme expression. Dante is the implicit rival of Stephen, and through Stephen of Joyce. It is not fortuitous that *A Portrait of the Artist* virtually begins with Stephen's terrible maiden aunt, Dante. She is the meanest expression of the Irish Catholic spirit in the novel, who provides Stephen with one of his earliest threatening memories.

> Pull out his eyes
> Apologise
> Apologise
> Pull out his eyes.
>
> Apologise
> Pull out his eyes
> Pull out his eyes
> Apologise.

This is the burden of original sin (the birthright of every man and woman) of which Stephen will have to divest himself to become an artist. Guilt, punishment, the mutilation or mortification of one's vision of the world: Stephen must free himself of the whole burden of religious commitment, of which the poet Dante is the supreme artistic embodiment.

In *A Portrait of the Artist* Stephen's childhood humiliations, his perception of hatred around the Christmas table, his sense of the spiritual vacuity of the priests at Clongowes provoke the countervision of art. But art is not yet a way of life; it is rather a promise in the rhapsodic cadences of Paterian prose.

Joyce is in competition with Dante on the same spiritual terms, for he conceives of his aesthetic as a rival to Catholic theology, an alternative theology offering a new integration of the spiritual and material aspects of life. He is trying to find in the vocation of art itself the workings of spirit unsanctioned by a superior agency. Thus in *A Portrait of the Artist* Stephen journeys through hell and purgatory to achieve a glimpse of paradise, guided by a parodic Virgil in the figure of his father Simon and by the sublimated female objects of his desire, who are stripped in Platonic fashion of all particular attributes and become a sort of collective Beatrice whose promise is the heavenly bliss of art.

> Her image had passed into his soul forever and no word had broken the holy silence of his ecstasy. Her eyes had called him and his soul had leaped at the call. To live, to err, to fall, to triumph, to recreate life out of life! A wild angel had appeared to him, the angel of mortal youth and beauty, an envoy from the fair courts of life, to throw open before him in an instant of ecstasy the gates of all the ways of error and glory.[4]

By sublimation I mean to suggest that the erotic quality of the female figure is residual in the idealized "object," just as Francesca da Rimini is remembered in Beatrice Portinari. What is at stake is nothing less than the emergence of the artist-hero in the work of Joyce, a figure already present in the *Vita Nuova* and *The Divine Comedy*, though there shackled from the romantic point of view to a servitude from which there can be no escape. In Dante freedom and beatitude consist in the graced acceptance of the condition of servitude to God. Joyce is bent on changing the terms of artistic freedom.[5]

Dante's journey is a poet's journey aided by another poet, Virgil, both in turn guided by a divine being from above. Virgil's departure from the poem before Dante enters Paradise can be interpreted as a symbolic statement of the inadequacy of the ungraced poetic imagination, a condition underlined by the confinement of the great pagan poets in Limbo. Virgil is a likely guide for Dante not because he is the greatest poet of classical antiquity (Homer, even in Dante's time, was considered the greater poet)[6] but because in his work (the *Fourth Eclogue* and the *Aeneid*), dogmatic Christianity found anticipations of the coming Christ. Virgil is the pagan poet who comes closest to a vision of Christianity. In the typology of Christianity, *The Divine Comedy* can be regarded as the fulfillment of the promise of the *Aeneid*. Nevertheless, though he deserves the admiration and affection Dante bestows upon him, he lacks the saving grace of Christianity. He is not privileged to enter the circles of Paradise. The presence of Virgil and the pagan poets in Limbo is necessary to establish the limits of the powers of the poetic imagination. It is not poetry alone that can lead the pilgrim out of the Dark Wood. The pilgrim Dante must depend upon Beatrice, who in *The Divine Comedy* has transcended the role of poetic muse which she performs in the *Vita Nuova*. In *The Divine Comedy* she has become the via media to God.

By simply identifying Virgil with "the powers of the poetic imagination," I am perhaps distorting Dante's conception of his great predecessor in the light of the postromantic preoccupation with poetic heroism. For Dante, Virgil embodied the quintessence of human reason untransformed by Christian grace. It is Statius, inspired by the prophetic Fourth Eclogue, a lesser poet who embodies a graced human reason and who leads Dante into Paradise. But the very fact that Virgil remains the great poetic presence in Dante's imagination means that the conceptual translation of his significance into human reason may not be sufficient to account for his power in Dante's imagination. It suggests that Virgil embodies the energies of poetry for Dante at their fullest, energies which are not coextensive, despite affinities, with human reason. The energies of poetry are insufficient to enable the pilgrim to achieve paradise.

In *A Portrait of the Artist*, paradise is the poet's imagination which means that the Other is merely a function of consciousness. Stephen exudes contempt or self-pity, almost never compassion. This is even more marked in *Ulysses*, in which his claim on us is severely reduced to the benefit of the suffering and compassionate Leopold Bloom. In his walk on the Strand, Stephen tries to establish the reality of the world beyond the senses, beyond subjective consciousness. But Stephen's assertion of faith is unconvincing, for it is his opened eyes that tell him that the world has been "there all the time without you: and ever shall be, world without end." There is no use in simply sneaking a look, for what one sees depends entirely upon the act of seeing and hearing, which are ineluctable in two senses: they are the only paths to the world and to thought and they are paths one cannot avoid. "At least that if no more, thought through my eyes."[7] Stephen's world remains a solipsist's world. It is a world based entirely on the senses mediated through language, but unredeemed by a Berkleyan faith that individual sensory experiences occur in the greater mind of God. It conjoins radical empiricism and radical egoism. Though the novel itself is inevitably determined by this radical subjectivity, the very presence of Bloom is an effort to overcome the limitation.

The Divine Comedy, of course, is a consummate expression of the objective imagination in which the egoism of the hero (even when it takes the form of a displaced, though moving, compassion for the sufferers in hell) is checked by the justice of the Divine Other. In *A Portrait of the Artist* the artistic imagination undergoes a spiritual ordeal. Like the pilgrim Dante, Stephen must learn to resist the self-diminishing lures of the sensuous life. The egoism implied in Stephen's exalting of the imagination is unbridled. It is not the poet who submits himself to a world greater than himself, as in Dante, but it is the world that must submit itself to the poet. By absenting himself in creating Stephen Dedalus, Joyce makes for a moral indeterminacy in Stephen's behavior. From a moral point of view, we do not know what to think of Stephen, since there is no Other against which to measure or judge him.

If the imagination is regarded exclusively as a faculty immanent in man, its powers and weaknesses dependent wholly on human capacity, it is susceptible to abysmal visions of existence. The despair of the poet becomes the meaninglessness of the world. But if transcendence or the myth of transcendence prevails, then at least a portion of the imagination is sufficiently stabilized so that we can conceive of a meaningful world external to the personal imagination, however deep one's despair might be. The pilgrim Dante may be lost in the Dark Wood, but the straight path remains to be found, and it leads, though the pilgrim himself may fail, to the radiant order of Paradise. The world is meaningful to Joyce only if and when the personal imagination of the artist-hero is confident and vital. In contrast to Dantean piety, Joyce makes Lucifer's presumption that the unaided imagination can "forge within the . . . soul the uncreated conscience of his race." Stephen's *non serviam* echoes Lucifer's refusal to accept the authority of anyone or anything other than himself, in this case his poetic imagination.

The consummate expression of the self-exaltation of the artist is the romantic version of Shakespeare, who unlike Dante lacked the humility that comes from a confident place in the cosmic order. An artist, lacking a sense of limitation, may through a fear of vertigo substitute himself for the cosmos. At least this is the way Shakespeare looks to the romantic and postromantic poet. This may be part of the explanation of why Shakespeare haunts Joyce's imagination (as in the Scylla and Charybdis episode in *Ulysses*).

From the Catholic point of view, Stephen's triumphant progress in *A Portrait of the Artist* is a journey through hell: a wholly legitimate view, if one is clear first that this is not Joyce's view and if the critic has made the effort to grasp from within the claim of the adversary imagination—that the beauty and energy of Stephen's effort at transvaluation is his attempt to replace divine grace with art. The hell-fire sermon at once moves Stephen to his sincere but abortive surrender to the church and then to his aesthetic consummation, suggesting not so much an opposition as a spiritual affinity between art and the church. Joyce here again is in a sort of competition with Dante, evoking in a microcosmic way a genuine vision of eternal perdition. Joyce does not reject the church because it possesses this imagination. On the contrary, the sermon is a goad toward communion with the church. The rejection is based rather on the church's failure to sustain an adequate countervision to damnation. Stephen's backsliding results from ineradicable perceptions of hollow, moribund expressions on the faces of the priests, unseemly twitchings, breath soured by the drinking of the wine of communion: a vision of the church as part of the common squalor of Dublin life. Against these experiences, art seems to offer the possibility of transcendence.

The sermon, to be sure, has none of the spiritual imagination of Dante's conception of hell; it disengages the literalism of the *Inferno* from the continuous illuminations of Dante's poem, and therefore can be seen as parody.[8] This is a judgment that goes deeper than the con-

sciousness of Stephen himself, a consciousness virtually coincident
with the narrator's mind. Stephen does not reject the church out of the
perceived moral squalor of the sermon. Indeed, the intensity of the
Christian imagination of pain is an impressive fact for him. It may be
associated with the punitive aggressiveness of the Dublin environment, the pandybatting at the hands of the priests, for example, but it
becomes in Stephen's mind a convincing provocation for fearing God.
Moreover, Stephen's communion with the church occurs after the
hell-fire sermon. If the sermon were simply grotesque parody as some
readers believe, Stephen would not have been so susceptible to it.
That the fear is insufficient to sustain communion with God is indisputable, but it is not the cause of the failure of the communion. If irony is intended, it is a structural irony, which the reader discovers
when he rereads the chapter in the light of his knowledge of the whole
work. The church has at least this in common with aestheticism: they
are both the rearguard of the presumption of order in the bewildering
chaos of the modern world. From the Catholic point of view, Joyce's
aestheticism in *A Portrait of the Artist* has the seriousness of heresy
like Protestantism: it is not an alien Other.

Yet there is an absence of self-confidence in the heresy which provokes the suspicion that Stephen (Joyce) will never free himself of the
Catholic influence. The conversation between Stephen and Cranly is
crucial.[9] On their walk together, Stephen speaks of an "unpleasant
quarrel" with his mother about religion. Cranly immediately assumes
the role of provocateur, responding to Stephen's assertion that he will
not do his Easter duty (the occasion for the quarrel with his mother)
with a question about whether he believes in the eucharist or not. Stephen's response is agnostic: "I neither believe in it nor disbelieve in it."
To Cranly's question whether he does not fear the everlasting fire, Stephen expresses disdain for the alternative of "an eternity of bliss in the
company of the dean of studies." Stephen's response here is characteristic: his "agnosticism" never impels him beyond the idiom of
Christianity. (Even in his rejection of the church, he parrots Lucifer's
non serviam.) Cranly anticipates Buck Mulligan's characterization of
Stephen as an inverted Jesuit with the remark: "Your mind is super-
saturated with the religion in which you say you disbelieve."

But it is not simply the idiom of Christianity which retains its hold
on Stephen's mind. In defending his apparent callousness to his
mother, Stephen argues from authority, citing first Pascal who

"would not suffer his mother to kiss him as he feared the contact of her sex," and then Jesus himself "who seems to have treated his mother with scant courtesy." There is, to be sure, a vein of irony in Stephen's use of authority, but it is weak against the shock he feels when Cranly, playing the devil's advocate, dismisses Jesus as a conscious hypocrite and blackguard. Stephen reprimands him with priestly severity: "I am curious to know are you trying to make a convert of me or a pervert of yourself?"

The shock releases in Stephen the confession that he is not indifferent to the matter of belief. He is by no means certain that Jesus is not the son of God and he fears the possible truth that the host is "the body and blood of the son of God and not a wafer of bread." The fear expresses Stephen's continuing sense of not simply the power of the Church but its venerable authority. More than damnation, Stephen fears "the chemical action which would be set up in my soul by a false homage to a symbol behind which are massed twenty centuries of authority and veneration." Stephen is afraid of profaning the church by pretending to a faith that he has lost. When Cranly concludes that Stephen "does not intend to become a protestant," Stephen again reveals a grudging admiration for the church: "I said that I had lost the faith . . . but not that I had lost selfrespect. What kind of liberation would that be to foresake an absurdity which is logical and coherent and to embrace one which is illogical and incoherent?"

THE POET-PILGRIM of *The Divine Comedy* shows a capacity for spiritual progress because he has harnessed his poetic gift to a power greater than himself. The power of Dantean art is in its modesty, in its knowledge of its own limits. The paradox in the respective claims of Dante and Joyce is this: an art that conceives itself with humility is more powerful than an art that has assumed the complete burden of the spiritual life. To presume to possess a power greater than one is capable of is to embrace emptiness. There are already indications in *A Portrait of the Artist* that Stephen's aesthetic heresy will fail. At the conclusion, when the note of release and liberation is continuously struck, irony and self-irony are subtly counterpointed to the dominant music of affirmation. In a diary entry of April 15, Stephen meets E. C. "point blank in Grafton Street" and in answer to her question of why he writes poems, he opens "the spiritual-heroic refrigerating apparatus, invented and patented in all countries by Dante Alighieri." Stephen goes on in disarmingly self-ironic fashion to view his revolutionary gestures as the action of "a fellow throwing a handful of peas into the air."[10] Such self-irony is disarming because it anticipates the reader's view of the pretentiousness of such gestures: in knowing himself in the act of making such gestures, he is free to make them. The phrase "refrigerating apparatus" is nonetheless particularly telling, for it suggests the absence of warm life (the kinetic element) in the making of art.

In *Ulysses* Stephen discovers what artists have always discovered about their daily lives: disappointed friendships, family betrayals, only fitful inspiration, wayward, thwarted imaginings, alcoholic distraction from the pain of the dull quotidian. It is worse for the artist than for the ordinary man because his expectations are greater than those of *l'homme moyen sensuel*. His dissatisfactions with the given are more intense, partly because his human capacities are in a sense less developed, for his imagination chills his involvement with life.

Kafka's hunger artist, Mann's Aschenbach or Faustus, Proust's Marcel, Gide's counterfeiters declare the failure of the artist while they implicitly celebrate the triumph of art. One cannot live by art alone, so that it is not the ineffectual artist type alone who fails but the successful artist as well. Does one have to do more than appeal to the actual lives of artists to establish this truth? The career of modern artistic heroism dramatizes art's incapacity to save, however great its promise.

It is surprising that speculation about Joyce's view of Stephen in both *A Portrait of the Artist* and *Ulysses* usually fails to account for the inherent logic of this development. Joyce's intentions to generalize his portrait beyond the particular artist-type named Stephen should be clear from the title of the novel: *A Portrait of the Artist As a Young Man*. Hélène Cixous says typically, and I think misleadingly, that Joyce "defines the conditions of creation for one particular writer named Stephen Dedalus."[11] To be sure, Joyce gives us one of many possible portraits, but the portrait represents his understanding of the "logic" of artistic heroism. It is not simply an exercise in naturalism. (Lawrence provides an alternative view. He presents the artist-type who rarely makes art—indeed, whose art is a gift for life, a forming, breaking, and remaking of relations. The very sense of incompleteness, imperfection, inconclusiveness in Lawrence's work is deliberately opposed to the finished and hence life-denying work of art.)

Ulysses begins as if it were picking up from the conversation between Stephen and Cranly in *A Portrait of the Artist*. Stephen, Buck Mulligan tells us in a memorable phrase, has "the cursed Jesuit strain," only "injected the wrong way."[12] In *Ulysses*, Joyce's art will be a profane analogue, a parodic inversion of the order and coherence of Catholicism. In his wayward and incisive ruminations on "Dante . . . Bruno. Vico..Joyce.," Beckett makes some neat contrasts between Dante and the Joyce of *Ulysses* and *Finnegans Wake*.

> Dante's purgatory is conical and implies culmination. Mr. Joyce's is spherical and excludes culminations.
>
> Dante's purgatory is progressive, Joyce's "nondirectional or multidirectional" . . . A step forward is a step backward.
>
> Dante's terrestrial Paradise is the carriage entrance to a Paradise that is not terrestrial. Mr. Joyce's terrestrial paradise is the tradesmen's entrance onto the sea shore.[13]

The contrasts are within Joyce's art and generate a dialectic between the Christian and the profane.

The Nestor episode in *Ulysses* provides an illuminating instance. While teaching a class on the battle of Tarentum, the archetype of the pyrrhic victory, Stephen reflects on events in history.

> Time has branded them and fettered they are lodged in the room of the infinite possibilities they have ousted. But can those have been possible seeing that they never were? Or was that only possible which came to pass?[14]

In a subsequent conversation with the schoolmaster Deasy, Stephen states his personal anguish in world-historical terms:

> —History . . . is a nightmare from which I am trying to awake.
>   From the playfield the boys raised a shout. A whirring whistle: goal. What if the nightmare gave you a back kick?
> —The ways of the Creator are not our ways, Mr. Deasy said. All history moves towards one great goal, the manifestation of God.
>   Stephen jerked his thumb towards the window, saying:
> —That is God.
>   Hooray! Ay! Whrrwhee!
> —What? Mr. Deasy asked.
> —A shout in the street, Stephen answered, shrugging his shoulders.[15]

In denying Mr. Deasy's orthodoxy, Stephen is asserting, if not affirming, a profane view of history.

Is the shout in the street an occasion for despair (a shrug of the shoulders, the back kick of a nightmare) or is it an occasion for an affirmation against an imprisoning teleology? If *Ulysses* itself constitutes Joyce's liberation as an artist and if Stephen *at this moment* can be viewed as a surrogate for Joyce himself, then we might see in that gesture toward the indeterminate noise of actuality the modern artist's desire to liberate himself from the nightmare of teleological history. *Ulysses* allows the possible that has not come to pass in history to come to pass in the imagination. Whether Stephen can bear the rich inconsequential detail (of freedom from the constraints of providential patterning) becomes increasingly doubtful as the novel develops.

If one reads Joyce's work under the aegis of Stephen, the artist, it is hard to avoid negativism and despair. The opening chapters of *Ulysses* unravel the "heroic" artist promised at the end of *A Portrait of the Artist*. The ghost of his mother returns to haunt Stephen's conscience, and he speaks the language of guilt without resentment in the manner of the self-knowing sinner. "Who has not sinned against the light?" Stephen replies to Mr. Deasy's antisemitism in the Nestor episode. It is clear that Stephen himself has not flown the nets of church, home, and country. In the Proteus episode he is afraid of his own shadow, uncertain of the objective reality of the world, his mind wrapped in the protective garment of language and literary allusion. Stephen's insufficiency as man and artist is unmistakable from beginning to end. But *Ulysses* is the "record" of Joyce's discovery of a way out. Stephen's insufficiency is the raison d'être for the creation of Bloom, whose sensibility paradoxically has the heroic capacity promised in *A Portrait of the Artist*. Problematic man that he is, Bloom courageously encounters reality again and again, forging the conscience of his race, though not in the terms in which Stephen speaks at the conclusion of *A Portrait of the Artist*. Unlike Stephen, he is an exile by necessity, not by choice, and this means that he yearns to be part of the life of Dublin. The yearning expresses itself as an abundant curiosity, which Bloom's off-center existence turns into fresh observations about the people of Dublin, its geography and history. In Bloom's voyeurism, androgyny, indeed, his ineffectuality as a man, we discover the sources of Joyce's strength as an artist. The sensibility of Bloom is the key to Joyce's ability to come to terms imaginatively with the world that he rejected in his life.

Yet it would be false to convert Bloom's triumphant presence in

Ulysses into a statement about the world or self-transforming power of art. Joyce's acceptance, even celebration, of reality is made possible by an exercise of the imagination, which acknowledges the intractability of personal and social reality. Joyce, the artist, neither escapes nor transcends; he "triumphs" through immersion—the only victory possible to a renegade Catholic and modernist.

In order to accept the world, Joyce must abandon the Thomistic aesthetic of *A Portrait of the Artist* with its stress on *claritas, quidditas,* and *stasis.* He must abandon the ordering, epiphanizing impulse that characterizes Dante's art. According to Erich Auerbach, Dante presents historical man in the supernatural world in order to give us his essential character.

> The meaning that Dante gives us is for the most part very simple, often stated in a short sentence; but even when it is so simple as to seem almost threadbare, a well-nigh superhuman penetration was required to find it, and it gains its richness from the abundance of events which surround it and from which it is distilled; only a small part of the man's experience is expressed, but that small part is the essential, what is omitted is present in it by implication. When the elder Montefeltro says: *"Io fui uom d'arme, e poi fui cordigliero"* ("I was a man of arms and then became a Cordelier"), Dante has put his finger on the essential character of that hard, crafty man with his secret but insufficient yearning for purity; and when of all the episodes of his life only a single one is related, the story of how he could not resist the temptation to exercise his often tested guile one last time, that one event not only determines his ultimate fate but also characterizes the man, and all the rest of his life remains unexpressed—the struggles, the hardships, the intrigues, and the days of vain repentance—is implicit in the characterization.[16]

The theory of the Joycean epiphany (the point of light at which the events of a person's life and character converge) is implicit in the series of encounters between Dante and the "dead," whose lives are given quintessential form by their places in the other world. The epiphany in Joyce's early work is the "divine" illumination of one's secular experience.

The effect of the supernatural framework in *The Divine Comedy* is to liberate historical experience from randomness and inconsequence. I am expressing the effect in a modern idiom—it is certainly not Dante's—in order to suggest where the modern failure lies. In his early

work Joyce tried to substitute an aesthetic sublimation of the supernatural framework but found it ineffectual against the reality it is supposed to encompass. So he "surrenders" to the experience of randomness and inconsequence. The continuous stream of association is the
correlative of the infinite possibilities suppressed by providential history. Dante the poet does not suffer pangs of conscience at the sup-
pression of those possibilities because his teleology has a divine sanction. Dante the pilgrim may occasionally yearn for the possibilities,
but he is subject to the corrections of the poet's confident spiritual
imagination. In *Ulysses* Joyce fills the world with an abundance that
cannot be epiphanized.

The "supersaturation" of human detail and language in *Ulysses* has
the look and feel of naturalism, but a naturalism to the ultimate degree—as if Joyce were once and for all exhausting the possibilities of
representation in terms of form and content. The motive for the supersaturation, I am trying to suggest, is at the very heart of Joyce's imaginative enterprise. Between *A Portrait of the Artist* and *Ulysses* Joyce
seems to have discovered the artistic principle that could "redeem" or
liberate reality: the promise of the concluding pages of *A Portrait of
the Artist*. The principle runs counter to Stephen's aesthetic in *A Portrait of the Artist* and to that of the novel itself. Irrelevant to it is the
classical feeling for wholeness and harmony, the fitting of parts to the
whole, of content to form, and irrelevant too is the romantic feeling
for luminousness and radiance crystallized in the concept of the epiphany. Indeed, much of *Ulysses* reads like a demystification of early
Joycean art and thought. The Ithaca episode in *Ulysses*, significantly
the ugly duckling of the novel and Joyce's favorite episode, gives us
one "epiphany" after another but without the luminousness. The career of Joyce contains the irony of a formalism that is available to the
inchoate debris of the world and consequently undermines itself.

The effect of the presentation in *Ulysses* is of an extraordinary en-
veloping density. Judgment (condemnation or approval) may be a
relevant response, but it is not adequate. Joyce is giving us life or the
illusion of life itself, an illusion that is supposed to overcome any literary distancing that would enable us to make judgments. The clichés in
the Nausicaa episode, for example, are presented with such abundance
and ingenuity that any irony we are tempted to direct toward them is
neutralized. We are even moved by Gerty MacDowell's hackneyed
fantasies. It is as if Joyce succeeded through the very density of detail

to elicit the authentic voice of feeling which Rodolphe in *Madame Bovary* had failed to hear. Gerty's consciousness expresses itself in the only language it knows: the cliché of romantic pulp magazines. Her fantasy moves easily from an imagination of her *beau idéal* to griddle cakes done to a golden brown hue. She combines in a comic and poignant way romantic sentiment and a lip-smacking complacency at the prospect of domestic bliss. But the effect of the juxtapositions is not so much ironic contrast as a naturalistic effort to represent the texture of actual consciousness. The attempt is to redeem the content, to convert the poverty into richness.

One can mark the distance Joyce has come from *A Portrait of the Artist* simply by recalling a scene in which Stephen dramatically presents art as a contrast, if not an alternative, to the squalor of Dublin life, its politics, its church life, its domesticity. In his room, trying to shut out the noise from the street (the shout that is God in *Ulysses*), Stephen makes a gesture at once ascetic and aesthetic, the gesture of the artist-priest. "Shrinking from the life [Stephen] turned towards the wall, making a cowl of the blanket and staring at the great overblown scarlet flowers of the tattered wallpaper."[17] The gesture is futile, because the tattered wallpaper is unavoidable. The progress of *Ulysses* is in allowing the wallpaper to become an acceptable element in the texture of life.[18]

The four levels of interpretation of every event that Dante elaborates in his famous letter to Can Grande (the literal, the allegorical, the moral, and the anagogical) give Dante an opportunity for a remarkable richness of effect concentrated within the most restricted space. The richness is hierarchical and coherent. It assumes what Joyce cannot assume, a stable system of values. Joyce inherits the detritus of the breakdown of the medieval synthesis, which may be the occasion for despair or for an exhilarating freedom of opportunity. The ambition to present or to incarnate the totality of civilization remains, but the presentation is a parody of the integration and coherence that one discovers in Dante. In the poem "Correspondances" Baudelaire defined the very enterprise of the poetic imagination as a seeking out of correspondences between the visible and the invisible world. The Joycean mediation becomes a riot of correspondence, an indeterminate matrix of symbol, an exercise in the limitlessness of the symbolic power.

If events in *Ulysses* do not terminate in a higher significance, a moment of revelation, an epiphany, they risk meaninglessness. What is substituted for meaninglessness is the symbolic activity itself or the linguistic pleasure of symbolic activity. It is as if the vernacular becomes invested with the energies of the sacred. In this respect Joyce recalls the achievement of Dante in establishing the literary legitimacy of the vernacular against the traditional authority of Latin. By the time he wrote *The Divine Comedy*, Dante clearly preferred the living quality of Italian to the artificiality of Latin. Understood as a spiritual fact, the commitment to the vernacular is an assertion of worldliness. Dante's imagination of the afterworlds of Hell, Purgatory, and Paradise is not at the expense of his attachment to the people and politics of Florence. The Apocalypse exists in a distant indefinite future for Dante. He deals with Florence as if it were a permanent realm coexistent with other worlds of his imagination. *The Divine Comedy* assumes that the corrupt world of the vernacular is for all practical purposes an abiding fact.

Joyce's legacy, of course, is the vernacular, but in *Ulysses* and even more radically in *Finnegans Wake* he reacts toward the received tradition as if a new literary vernacular had to be invented—that is, a language for literature that corresponds to the language actually used by men and women in the world. Joyce attempts to produce the illusion not simply of uttered speech but of the speech of the mind in the condition of silence. Language has in a sense always been the hero of Joyce's work. In *A Portrait of the Artist*, the play on words (belt, suck) or the use of rhyme ("apologize," "pull out his eyes") is part of the impersonalizing therapy of art which enables Stephen to harden himself against the assaults of adult authority and childish malice and still the destructive kinesis of desire. In a sense then Joyce never abandoned the persona of the word-obsessed Stephen. In *Finnegans Wake* he goes beyond or beneath natural language itself to a kind of (invented) *ur-sprache*: poetic, mythic, musical, expressive of the sacred origins of our being. If the sacred manifests itself in the activity of language, the mimetic or referential character of language is no longer interesting. Language becomes self-referential or a-referential, what Derrida calls an unbounded play of signification. Or language may be said to generate surplus signification, a kind of higher meaninglessness. *Finnegans Wake* is the ur-text of postmodern criticism. Language becomes for Joyce, as the supernatural is for Dante, "the point of view" from which the world of Dublin is seen and justified.

The theme of exile illuminates the communities and differences between Joyce and Dante. Ellmann notes that Joyce's "feeling of ostracism lacked, as he was well aware, the moral decisiveness of his hero Dante's exile from Florence, in that he kept the keys to the gate. He was neither bidden to leave nor bidden to return."[19] Florence and Dublin are more than geopolitical entities for Dante and Joyce. They are Cities of Man and therefore emanations of the City of God. Corrupt as they may be, they are the objects of an indestructible allegiance. As Alessandro Passerin d'Entreves remarks, "Dante was and remained to the end . . . a proud Florentine, a son of the greatest and proudest of medieval Italian cities."[20] Florence provides the historical and political arena, the necessary vale of tears, in which the spirit must travail and be tested. In contrast, Dublin is the microcosm of the world from which all spirit has been evacuated—to be miraculously concentrated in the soul and imagination of the artist. The artist must leave his city in order to "forge the uncreated conscience of his race." This somewhat pretentious phrase, as I have tried to show, does not clearly point to the fulfillment that *Ulysses* and *Finnegans Wake* represent. The Dublin of *Ulysses* is certainly not invested with the spirit promised by Stephen at the conclusion of *A Portrait of the Artist*. The scraps of life, the debris of natural language are transmuted into a linguistic medium which provides a curious justification of Dublin life. Joyce remains her spiritual son—or should I say father?

The defiant heretic of *A Portrait of the Artist* turns into the self-indulgent blasphemer of *Ulysses* and *Finnegans Wake*.[21] Blasphemy enables Joyce (as well as Stephen) to maintain the ambivalence toward Dublin and all that it represents. He leaves Dublin not to found a new order (the promise of *A Portrait of the Artist*) but to free himself sufficiently of its oppressions so that he can embrace it linguistically in love and hatred. Dante had the supernatural world as "the place" from which to exercise his expatriate sympathies and aversions for the only earthly existence that mattered to him. Joyce had only his linguistic virtuosity.

When Joyce revolts against Catholicism, he cannot find within Catholicism itself an adequate principle of revolt. Revolt weakens into blasphemy. In contrast, when Lawrence revolts against puritanism in behalf of an idolatry of the flesh, he finds the impulse for revolt in puritanism itself. The principle of reform animates every version of Protestantism, which in turn becomes the object of reform when it materializes and corrupts itself.[22]

The moral failure of art in Joyce's work may have something to do with the modern condition of Catholicism—particularly in backward countries where it tends to perform a reactionary role. Lacking the Protestant freedom to invent and reinvent the symbolisms of the spiritual life, the only path for the unconverted Catholic is a blaspheming atheism which leaves him forever bound to the Catholic dispensation. The gain is an aesthetic richness, serving as a surrogate for fulfillment; the loss has been the subject of this book.

Notes

Introduction

1. F. R. Leavis, *For Continuity* (Cambridge, Mass.: Gordon Fraser, The Minority Press, 1933), p. 49.

2. Ibid., p. 77.

3. "The Scholar-Gypsy," line 202.

4. Van Wyck Brooks, "On Creating a Usable Past," *The Dial* (April 11, 1918), p. 340.

5. R. H. Super, ed., *The Complete Prose Works of Matthew Arnold*, 10 vols. (Ann Arbor: University of Michigan Press, 1960-1974), III, 271-274.

6. Wayne Booth has shown how unstable irony has become in the modern period, so that the positive basis implied in a stable ironic judgment has, in the work of Beckett, for example, either disappeared or appeared against the artist's will in the imaginative playfulness and energy of the art. The effect of this loss of control is to undermine Beckett's ostensible animus against the very process of living. See Wayne Booth, *A Rhetoric of Irony* (Chicago: University of Chicago Press, 1974), chaps. 8 and 9.

7. Roland Barthes, *S/Z*, trans. Richard Miller (New York: Hill and Wang, 1974), p. 206.

8. Jonathan Culler, *Structuralist Poetics: Structuralism, Linguistics, and the Study of Literature* (Ithaca: Cornell University Press, 1975), p. 248.

9. Phillipe Sollers, *Logiques*, trans. Jonathan Culler (Paris: Seuil, 1968), p. 248.

10. Stanley Fish, "Interpreting the Variorum," *Critical Inquiry* (Spring 1976), p. 474.

11. See T. S. Eliot, *After Strange Gods: A Primer of Modern Heresy* (London: Faber and Faber, 1934), p. 38.

1. Modernism and the Critical Spirit

1. I. A. Richards, *The Principles of Literary Criticism* (New York: Harcourt Brace, 1925), p. 60.

2. There is an irony, of course, in the collector's acquisition of works that have had their moment of fame and in the increasing value of these works with time. The older conception of the eternity of art prevails in the habit of consumption or connoisseurship.

3. See Wylie Sypher, *Loss of the Self in Modern Literature and Art* (New York: Random House, 1962) and my *The Cult of the Ego* (Chicago: University of Chicago Press, 1968), pp. 196-200. Walter Benjamin's famous discussion of the destruction of the aura of a work of art in an age of mechanical reproduction provides another perspective on the phenomenon. The very conditions of the modern production of books and painting contribute to the sense of the flatness of art. See Walter Benjamin, *Illuminations*, ed. Hannah Arendt (London: Jonathan Cape, 1970), pp. 219-269.

4. There are, to be sure, canting versions of these virtues which produce their own forms of mystification.

5. *On Poetry and Poets* (New York: Farrar, Straus and Giroux, Noonday Paperback, 1957), p. 127. There is a tension in this sentence between what is sensed to be inevitable and what is felt to be undesirable. The sentence does not postulate cause and effect, but there is the implication that uncertainty dissolves the taboos, whereas the case may be the reverse. The absence of taboos may generate uncertainty. Eliot was committed to the modernist venture because of and despite his religious commitment.

6. See John Henry Newman, *The Grammar of Assent* (New York: Doubleday, 1955); Michael Polanyi, *Personal Knowledge: Towards a Post Critical Philosophy* (Chicago: University of Chicago Press, 1958); Michael Oakeshott, *Rationalism in Politics* (New York: Basic Books, 1962).

7. The irrationalist element in modernism is too strong to allow the identification of modernism with rationalism to pass without comment. Modern irrationalism has at least this in common with rationalism—its impiety in the presence of mystery or silence. Nothing, for instance, is sacred to dada or surrealism. The surrealist André Breton turns to Freud because he wishes to demystify reality, to disabuse mankind of illusions.

8. Quoted in Stanley Edgar Hyman, *The Tangled Bank: Darwin, Marx, Frazer and Freud as Imaginative Writers* (New York: Grosset and Dunlap, 1966), p. 98.

9. Quoted in David McLellan, *Karl Marx: His Life and Thought* (London: Macmillan, 1973), p. 90.

10. Marx, *Economic and Philosophical Manuscripts of 1844*, ed. Dirk J. Struik, trans. Martin Milligan (London: Lawrence I. Wishart Ltd., 1973), p. 141.

11. It is a paradox of the work of the Frankfurt school (particularly that of Theodor Adorno, Max Horkheimer, and Herbert Marcuse) that in its assault on Enlightenment rationalism in the interests of freedom, it continues the relentless work of demystification inaugurated by the Enlightenment. Marcuse writes: "Self-consciousness and reason, which have conquered and shaped the historical world, have done so in the image of repression, internal and external. They have worked as the agents of domination." *Eros and Civil-*

ization (Boston: Beacon Press, 1955), p. 57. The antidote to this domination is to be found in the deepest motive of Frankfurt critical theory: the unremitting search for and assertion of the negative. One may view the work of the Frankfurt school as a kind of modernist outgrowth of and reaction against Marxism, a version of Enlightenment rationalism working often, though not exclusively, within the assumptions of Marxism. The Frankfurt school dissolves them into uncertainties without necessarily abandoning them. The Frankfurt philosophers are the blasphemers, if not the heretics, of Marxism.

12. And, of course, the place of its greatest triumph is America. America is modernism.

13. In great modernist writers like Eliot and Yeats the antimodernist impulse is still strong. One can avoid the obvious semantic difficulty by following Frank Kermode's distinction between "two phases of modernism, our own and that of fifty years ago," a tradition-oriented strain, which has ended, and our antitraditional one. *The Sense of an Ending* (New York: Oxford University Press, 1967), p. 103. My only objection to Kermode's formulation is that the temporal division is too neat. The antitraditional strain was present fifty years ago, in the futurists, for example.

14. Wyndham Lewis, *Time and Western Man* (Boston: Beacon Press, 1957), p. 422.

15. Nonmoralistically, nondidactically, objectively, disinterestedly: one is free to choose the word or words which cover both art and science.

16. Northrop Frye, *The Critical Path* (Bloomington: Indiana University Press, 1971), p. 115.

17. Ibid., p. 109.

18. Ibid., pp. 74-75.

19. Ibid., p. 99.

20. Northrop Frye, *Anatomy of Criticism* (Princeton: Princeton University Press, 1957), p. 346.

21. Ibid., p. 347.

22. Geoffrey H. Hartman, *Beyond Formalism: Literary Essays, 1958-1970* (New Haven: Yale University Press, 1970), p. 30.

23. Frye does on occasion write with an apparently Marxian bias.

24. Terry Eagleton, "Criticism and Politics: The Work of Raymond Williams," *New Left Review* (Jan.-Feb. 1976), p. 23.

25. F. R. Leavis, *The Common Pursuit* (New York: New York University Press, 1952), p. 193.

26. Jonathan Culler, *Structuralist Poetics* (Ithaca: Cornell University Press, 1975), p. viii.

27. Lionel Trilling, *Beyond Culture* (New York: Viking Press, 1965), pp. 3-31. R. P. Blackmur once remarked of Trilling that he cultivates a mind not his own and therefore is vulnerable to a reality that might be resisted if he simply acted from his own conviction. But Trilling's conviction includes the effort to understand a reality larger or other than his own personal moral commitment and this effort can create strength as well as weakness. The question becomes: What makes for a critical understanding that results in control

and what makes for an understanding which results in being seduced or in capitulating? Trilling, it seems to me, manages to remain in control, very much his own man and exemplary in not presenting this control as a triumphant achievement. See R. P. Blackmur, *The Lion and the Honeycomb* (New York: Harcourt Brace, 1955), pp. 32-42.

28. Needless to say, Frye, Bate, and Bloom take up different positions vis-a-vis the burden of the past. Bate speculates in a "conservative" spirit: "Why, when a standard had been established (and it had), should one not try to work in, through, or at least near it rather than to cultivate difference for its own sake?" *The Burden of the Past and the English Poet* (Cambridge, Mass.: Harvard University Press, 1970), p. 38. Bloom, on the other hand, sees the strong poet as necessarily denying his precursor and the standard he incarnates. Frye shares Eliot's view of the characteristic benignity of the tradition, though he acknowledges the element of anxiety.

29. The view of the avant-garde as a destroyer of the preceding avant-garde is contradicted by Clement Greenberg, the art critic, and his followers (see Chapter 6).

30. This is not a satiric distortion of the case, for what Solzhenitsyn considers to be justice and decency are dismissed contemptuously by Soviet authorities as bourgeois values. Actually, Solzhenitsyn is in a sense a feudalist —from the positive point of view.

31. See Trotsky's *Literature and Revolution* (Ann Arbor: University of Michigan Press, 1960).

32. See Clive Bell, *Art* (New York: Capricorn Books, 1958).

33. Much radicalism is the expression of guilt of morally sensitive members of the oppressor class. This may disfigure the sense of justice as much as the resentment born of deprivation.

34. F. R. Leavis is quite right to point out C. P. Snow's ignorance of the moral history of the literature of the past two hundred years when Snow refers to literary intellectuals as natural Luddites.

2. English Social Criticism and the Spirit of Reformation

1. Lionel Trilling, "The Uncertain Future of the Humanistic Educational Ideal," *The American Scholar* (Winter 1974-1975), pp. 52-67.

2. Philip Rosenberg, *The Seventh Hero: Thomas Carlyle and the Theory of Radical Activism* (Cambridge, Mass.: Harvard University Press, 1974).

3. Thomas Carlyle, *On Heroes and Hero-Worship*, in Thomas Carlyle, *Sartor Resartus and On Heroes and Hero Worship* (New York: Everyman's Library, 1964), pp. 354, 355.

4. The same judgment applies to Ruskin. As John Rosenberg remarks, Ruskin "remained too radically an individualist, too protestantly insistent upon his own interpretation of God's word, ever to have become a Catholic," despite his gothicizing and medievalizing. *The Darkening Glass: A Portrait of Ruskin's Genius* (New York: Columbia University Press, 1961), p. 55.

5. Ernst Troeltsch, *Protestantism and Progress* (Boston: Beacon Press, 1966), pp. 85, 86.

6. Herbert Lüthy, *Calvin to Rousseau* (New York: Basic Books, 1970), p. 59.

7. John Ruskin, "Traffic," in *The Crown of Wild Olive* (Lecture II).

8. "On the Nature of the Gothic," in *The Stones of Venice* (vol. II).

9. American literature proposes a comparable phenomenon. Puritanism becomes for certain American social and literary critics a major reason for America's stunted cultural development, and yet one could say, with Lewis Mumford, that "the critical examination of men, creeds, and institutions . . . is the vital core of Protestantism." *The Golden Day* (New York: Boni and Liveright, 1926), p. 92.

10. R. H. Super, ed., *The Complete Prose Works of Matthew Arnold*, 10 vols. (Ann Arbor: University of Michigan Press, 1960-1974), VI, 351.

11. Ibid., VI, 352.

12. Super, *Prose Works of Matthew Arnold*, VI, 353.

13. For all his severity toward Luther, Arnold regards him as one of his spiritual ancestors. For example, he notes in *Literature and Dogma* that Luther's idea of the good is *the best that man knows or can know*, virtually Arnold's own definition of culture. Ibid., p. 171.

14. Ibid., VII, 389.

15. Ibid., VI, 58.

16. Ibid., IX, 161.

17. According to Weber in *The Protestant Ethic and the Spirit of Capitalism*, the ascetic discipline of the monastic orders penetrated social and economic life in a manner which supported the development of industrial capitalism. (I leave aside the much vexed question of cause and effect.) "Faith in machinery," which Carlyle, Ruskin, and Arnold see as the besetting danger of the spiritual life, has, on this view, its origins in the spiritual life. English social criticism can be understood as an attempt to separate the original inspiration of Christianity (and Protestantism) from this particular worldly application of it. It is in a sense misleading to speak of the original inspiration of Protestantism (and Christianity) since, as Weber for one has shown, there is a variety of intention in Luther, Calvin, pietists, Baptists, Methodists. Moreover, each figure and group underwent a history of changing intentions. But what all the worldly asceticisms had in common, and what could therefore be generalized into an "original inspiration," was a sense of the discipline as an end in itself, not as an instrument of material gain and earthly satisfaction. It is interesting to note that the main evidence for Weber's thesis comes from English puritanism, which is Calvinist (Wesleyan) in inspiration. Luther, in this context, represents an emotional, unsystematic type of Christianity. "Wesley felt the emotional element in the Herrhut religion inspired by Luther to be mysticism and branded Luther's interpretation of the law as blasphemous. This shows the barrier which existed between Lutheranism and every kind of rational religious conduct." *The Protestant Ethic and the Spirit of Capitalism*, trans. Talcott Parsons (New York: Charles Scribner's Sons, 1958),

p. 257. Arnold uses Luther in his inwardness (not quite the same thing as emotionality) against the materialistic logic of English puritanism. He sees Luther as inconsistent in his emotional Christianity.

18. Indeed, Arnold's critique of Hebraism from the point of view of Hellenism is misleading to the extent that it diverts us from Hebraism's own critique of the barbarism of a materialistic civilization. Intellectual and aesthetic consciousness alone cannot generate the moral horror that Arnold feels when he reads the newspaper squib about Wragg in custody. The inspiration of the passage about Wragg is not Arnold's cultivation (which gives it its intellectual and verbal distinction) but its ethical passion (which gives it its character).

19. Super, *Prose Works of Matthew Arnold*, III, 265-266.

20. Arnold's valuing of Hellenistic consciousness, which is primarily an expression of the intellectual and aesthetic sides of our nature, does not represent an antithetic strain to Protestantism. "Spontaneity of consciousness" as well as "strictness of conscience" were both present in the Reformation, "though all which Protestantism was to itself clearly conscious of, all which it succeeded in clearly setting forth in words, had the character of Hebraism rather than Hellenism." Ibid., V, 172. Hellenism, in Arnold's view, must be cultivated in the interests of Protestantism itself.

21. Ibid., VI, 87.

22. Ibid., V, 135.

23. Ibid., III, 267.

24. One of the most impressive visualizations of the organic society is in Coleridge's *A Lay Sermon*. See R. J. White, ed., *The Collected Works of Samuel Taylor Coleridge* (London: Routledge and Kegan Paul, 1972), VI, 127: "The administration of the laws; the almost continual preaching of moral prudence; the number and respectability of our sects; the pressure of our ranks on each other, with the consequent reserve and watchfulness of demeanor in the superior ranks and the emulation in the subordinate; the vast depth, expansion, and systematic movements of our trade; and the consequent interdependence, the arterial or nerve-like *network* of property, which make every deviation from outward integrity calculable loss to the offending individual himself from its mere effects, as obstruction and regularity; and lastly the naturalness of doing as others do:—these and the like influences, peculiar, some in the kind and all in the degree, to this privileged island, are the butresses on which our foundationless well-doing is upheld, even as a house of cards. The architecture of our infancy, in which each is supported by all."

25. John Gross, *The Rise and Fall of the Man of Letters* (New York: Collier Books, 1970), p. 32.

26. Raymond Williams, *The Country and the City* (New York: Oxford University Press, 1973), pp. 78-79.

27. Ibid., p. 36.

28. I have already dealt with the risks of the historical enactments of abstract ideas in "Utopia and the Irony of History," in *Culture and the Radical Conscience* (Cambridge, Mass.: Harvard University Press, 1973).

29. Kenneth Burke, *A Rhetoric of Motives* (New York: Prentice Hall, 1950), p. 110.

30. Super, *Prose Works of Matthew Arnold*, V, 158.

31. Arnold nowhere elaborates a vision of a classless society, though he gives us glimpses of the possibility. "But if we say, on the one hand, that the Bible utterly condemns all violence, revolt, fierceness and self-assertion, then we may safely say, on the other hand, that there is certainly communism in the Bible. The truth is, the Bible enjoins endless self-sacrifice all round; and to any one who has grasped this idea, the superstitious worship of property, the reverent devotedness to the propertied and satisfied classes is impossible." Ibid., VII, 72. Arnold's Christian sentiment against "the superstitious worship of property" is qualified by a politically conservative sentiment about the value of property as a stabilizing force in society. See ibid., p. 285.

32. Lionel Trilling, *Matthew Arnold* (New York: Columbia University Press, 1949), p. 253.

33. Eliot perceives the equivocation in *Notes Towards the Definition of Culture*. See *Notes*, in *Christianity and Culture* (New York: Harcourt Brace, 1940), p. 94.

34. "Roots of Honour," in *Unto This Last* (1860).

35. Super, *Prose Works of Matthew Arnold*, II, 324.

36. "Bishop Butler and the Zeit-Geist," ibid., VIII, 25.

37. Ibid., p. 153.

38. Elie Halévy, *A History of the English People in the Nineteenth Century. England in 1815* (New York: Barnes and Noble, 1961), p. 425.

39. Ibid., p. 476.

40. My account of English literary and social criticism of the nineteenth century contradicts Tocqueville's low view of the moral energy of literature in England. "In a nation where wealth is the sole, or even the principal foundation of aristocracy, money, which in all societies is the means of pleasure, confers power also. Endowed with these two advantages, it succeeds in attracting towards itself the whole imagination of man . . . In such a country literature is little cultivated, and literary merit therefore scarcely attracts the attention of the public." Quoted in Seymour Drescher, *Tocqueville and England* (Cambridge, Mass.: Harvard University Press, 1964), p. 121.

41. Super, *Prose Works of Matthew Arnold*, VI, 152.

42. Ibid., p. 168.

43. Ibid., VIII, 148.

44. T. S. Eliot, *Selected Essays* (New York: Harcourt Brace, 1950), pp. 385, 387.

45. Carlyle, *Sartor Resartus*, p. 330.

46. Walter Pater, "Wordsworth," in *Appreciations*.

47. Catholicism, with its powerful feeling for symbolism, would seem to allow for the possibility of secularization. The effect of the Protestant appeal to the scriptures is to liberate the spirit from subjection to dogma, which is what Catholic symbolism becomes. The fact that Protestant fundamentalism became dogmatic does not alter the original liberating significance of Lutheran

subjectivity. Another way of seeing the difference between Protestantism and Catholicism with respect to the possibility of social change is to compare the conservatisms of Burke and De Maistre, the former progressive, the latter reactionary.

48. Troeltsch again is illuminating here (*Protestantism and Progress*, pp. 168-169). However, his instancing of Ruskin's aestheticizing of modern England as representing the end of puritanism overlooks the tension in his work between the puritan and the aesthetic.

49. It is not necessary to have been born in a Catholic country to make an imaginative Catholic response to life. Thus in his "On Goethe as Sage" (1954), Eliot characterizes himself as having "a Catholic cast of mind, a Calvinist heritage and a Puritanical temperament."

3. The Reality of Disillusion in T. S. Eliot

1. *The Enemy* (January 1927), pp. 16-17.

2. *The Idea of a Christian Society*, in *Christianity and Culture* (New York: Harcourt Brace, 1940), p. 25.

3. William Chace, *The Political Identities of Ezra Pound and T. S. Eliot* (Stanford: Stanford University Press, 1973), pp. 155-156. In a careful study of *T. S. Eliot's Social Criticism* (New York: Farrar, Straus and Giroux, 1972), Roger Kojecky tries to show that Eliot's imagination of a Christian society is not a rootless abstraction. Eliot belonged to clubs and was involved in journals that spoke to real or potential elites in the political life of England. One club, the Moot, included men of political stature and influence such as Anthony Eden and Richard Crossman, as well as intellectuals like Karl Mannhein and Michael Polanyi. It is difficult for Americans, with their experience of mass democracy, the diffusion of power, and the relatively weak influence of intellectuals on political life, to imagine that a club devoted to the discussion of social issues in a philosophical manner would have a real influence on the political life of a country. But England, with its strong Oxbridge legacy, now extended to places like the University of London and the London School of Economics, is remarkable for its susceptibility to such influences. Moreover, as Kojecky shows, the belief in the possibility of restoring a genuinely Christian society after World War II (on the Anglican model) was shared by no less a figure than Winston Churchill: "By our combined exertions we have it in our power to restore the health and greatness of our ancient continent— Christendom as it used to be called. No longer a breeding ground for misery and hate, Europe shall arise out of her ruins and troubles, and, by uniting herself, carry the world a step further to the ultimate unity of all mankind" (as quoted on pp. 212-213). Yet Kojecky's argument is finally unpersuasive. Churchill's declaration is a piece of rhetoric—and Eliot's sustained speculative commitment to Christianity remains an enclosed intellectual exercise in its effect rather than a serious response to a challenge.

4. Moreover, his doctrinal allegiance is to Anglo-Catholicism and not to Roman Catholicism, a fact that makes the unqualified characterization of

Eliot as Catholic even more difficult to maintain.

5. Charles Baudelaire, *Intimate Journals*, trans. Christopher Isherwood, introduction by T. S. Eliot (New York: Random House, 1930), p. 20.

6. *The Idea of a Christian Society*, in *Christianity and Culture*, p. 53.

7. Ibid., p. 75.

8. Ibid., p. 77.

9. Ibid., p. 39.

10. R. H. Super, ed., *The Complete Prose Works of Matthew Arnold*, 10 vols. (Ann Arbor: University of Michigan Press, 1960-1974), V, 106.

11. Eliot's view may appeal to the popular cultists of recent years who have attacked high culture's evangelical presumptions. "Error creeps in again and again through our tendency to think of culture as group culture exclusively, the culture of the 'cultured' classes and elites. We then proceed to think of the humbler part of society as having culture only in so far as it participates in this superior and more conscious culture. To treat the 'uneducated' mass of the population as we might treat some innocent tribe of savages to whom we are impelled to deliver the true faith, is to encourage them to neglect or despise that culture which they should possess and from which the more conscious part of culture draws vitality; and to aim to make everyone share in the appreciation of the more conscious part of culture is to adulterate the cheapen what you give." *Notes Towards the Definition of Culture*, in *Christianity and Culture*, pp. 183-184. Note that high culture does not function in a reciprocal relation to popular culture. Popular culture nourishes high culture, but high culture cheapens and adulterates popular culture when it tries to return the favor.

12. Elsewhere in the poem, the past stutters ineffectually in the present.

13. I. A. Richards, *The Principles of Literary Criticism* (New York: Harcourt Brace, 1925), p. 295.

14. James Joyce, *Ulysses* (New York: Random House, 1946), p. 162.

15. *The Family Reunion*, in *The Complete Poems and Plays* (New York: Harcourt Brace, 1934-1952), p. 234.

16. Allen Tate, "On Ash Wednesday," in Hugh Kenner, ed., *T. S. Eliot: A Collection of Critical Essays* (New York: Prentice Hall, 1962), pp. 132-133.

17. *The Family Reunion*, in *The Complete Poems and Plays*, p. 242.

18. Tolstoy, it seems to me, is a more complicated case than Trilling allows. To be sure, the life of the common middle class routine is deficient for Tolstoy, but not the ordinary life of the peasant—for instance, that of Gerasim in *The Death of Ivan Ilych* or that of the peasants whom Levin admires and tries to emulate in *Anna Karenina*.

19. Denis Donoghue, "The Cocktail Party," in Kenner, ed., *T. S. Eliot*, p. 181.

20. Chace, *Pound and Eliot*, pp. 148-150.

21. Eliot, I think, mistakenly identifies the inner voice with individualism. Even the Church Catholic depends upon the inner voice for spirituality. Yet Eliot's classicism has a particular value for the modern period. In an age which is losing its past, it is valuable to insist on the virtues of the classical—

for, though one can recover the past through other modes (romantic, baroque), such a past is bound to be partial, distorted by the anxieties of personality.

22. *Ulysses*, p. 21.

4. The Organic Society of F. R. Leavis

1. F. R. Leavis, *Revaluation* (New York: George W. Stewart, 1947), pp. 30-31.

2. If one follows Ferdinand Tonnies, who made the classic distinction between *Gemeinschaft* and *Gesellschaft*—community and society—organic society is an anomalous phrase. It is community, not society, that is by definition organic.

3. F. R. Leavis and Denys Thompson, *Culture and Environment* (London: Chatto and Windus, 1933), pp. 70-71.

4. Ibid., pp. 78-79.

5. "For the healthy know not of their health, but only the sick . . . We may say, it holds no less in moral, intellectual, political, poetical, than in merely corporeal therapeutics . . . In the Body Politic, as in the animal body, the sign of right performance is Unconsciousness." Carlyle, "Characteristics" (1831).

6. Leavis and Thompson, *Culture and Environment*, p. 80.

7. Leavis shares this view with I. A. Richards, who remarks, "as other vehicles of tradition, the family and the community, for example, are dissolved, we are forced more and more to rely on language." *Practical Criticism* (New York: Harcourt Brace, 1929), p. 321.

8. F. R. Leavis, *For Continuity* (Cambridge, Mass.: Gordon Fraser, The Minority Press, 1933), p. 216.

9. Leavis and Thompson, *Culture and Environment*, p. 81.

10. F. R. Leavis, *The Common Pursuit* (New York: New York University Press, 1952), p. 51.

11. Leavis's immediate source is Marjorie Grene's *The Knower and the Known* (Los Angeles: University of California Press, 1974). Behind Grene's work is Michael Polanyi, whose principal work is *Personal Knowledge: Towards a Post-Critical Philosophy* (Chicago: University of Chicago Press, 1958). See Leavis's *The Living Principle: English as a Discipline of Thought* (New York: Oxford University Press, 1975).

12. E. H. Gombrich, *Norm and Form* (London: Phaidon, 1966), pp. 1-11.

13. Edmund Burke, *Reflections on the Revolution in France* (New York: Holt, Rhinehart & Winston, 1962), pp. 38-39.

14. J. H. Plumb, *The Death of the Past* (Boston: Houghton Mifflin, 1970), p. 48.

15. Ibid., p. 49.

16. F. R. Leavis, *Lectures in America* (New York: Pantheon Books, 1969), p. 19.

17. *After Strange Gods* (London: Faber and Faber, 1934), pp. 18-19. See Leavis, *The Common Pursuit*, p. 256.

18. See F. R. Leavis, *English Literature in Our Time and the University* (London: Chatto and Windus, 1969), pp. 7-8.

19. Leavis, *The Living Principle*, p. 191.

20. Ibid., pp. 230-231.

21. Ibid., p. 21. Leavis says of the dogmatic version of humanism: "The belief that 'architectural' qualities like Milton's represent a higher kind of unity goes with the kind of intellectual bent that produced Humanism—that takes satisfaction in inertly orthodox generalities, and is impressed by invocations of order from minds that have no glimmer of intelligence about contemporary literature and could not safely risk even elementary particular appreciation." *Revaluation*, p. 61.

22. Leavis, *The Living Principle*, p. 10.

23. An exercise of which Lionel Trilling was capable.

24. "For to insist that literary criticism is, or should be, a specific "discipline of intelligence is not to suggest that a serious interest in literature can confine itself to the kind of intensive local analysis associated with 'practical criticism'—to the scrutiny of the 'words on the page' in their minute relations, their effects of imagery, and so on: a real literary interest in man, society and civilization, and its boundaries cannot be drawn; the adjective is not a circumscribing one." Leavis, *The Common Pursuit*, p. 200.

25. Donald Barthelme, *Snow White* (New York: Bantam Books, 1967), p. 138.

26. The sociologist Cesar Graña very effectively dissolves the sentimental distinction between "conscious and unconscious forms of social participation," between the rural mind and the city mind. "Rural life, a life where personal consciousness was a shared segment of the sustaining milieu, where social experience was the steady reenactment of daily understanding and where the momentary and the incidental had no significance or, in fact, reality [appeared to Simmel, the celebrated German sociologist], as more authentic and even more 'human.' And he also suggested that the city mind, being mobile, unanchored, and able to scatter its attention and interests, was, therefore, insubstantial and unnaturally rarified. He was, in other words, unwilling to accept that urban consciousness was simply a different order of consciousness. Not an inner ritual reaffirmation of social membership, not a thinning of 'genuine' social relationships, but a faculty capable of extracting a new human plot out of the city's 'gathering of fugitives' and for which passing events *were* passing, but also the not quite loose ends of many unstated meanings." Cesar Graña, *Fact and Symbol* (New York: Oxford University Press, 1971), p. 83.

27. "The Irony of Swift," in *Determinations*, with an introduction by F. R. Leavis (Folcroft, Pa.: Folcroft Press, 1934, 1969), pp. 104-105.

28. See "The Excremental Vision," in Norman O. Brown, *Life Against Death* (Middletown, Conn.: Wesleyan University Press, 1959).

29. Leavis, *The Common Pursuit*, p. 65.

30. See F. R. Leavis, *The Great Tradition* (New York: New York Uni-

versity Press, 1948).

31. Q. D. Leavis, *Fiction and the Reading Public* (London: Chatto and Windus, 1932), pp. 162-163.

32. Ibid., p. 114.

33. Ibid., p. 187.

34. Q. D. Leavis, who writes as her husband's alter ego, occasionally betrays their fundamentalist view of language when, for example, she makes a comparison between Dickens and Tolstoy "below the *superficial* level of the social, linguistic, economic, religious and historical differences in the two novelists' habitats" (italics mine). F. R. Leavis and Q. D. Leavis, *Dickens: The Novelist* (London: Chatto and Windus, 1970), p. 37.

5. A Postscript to the Higher Criticism: The Case of Philip Rieff

1. Philip Rieff, *Fellow Teachers* (New York: Harper and Row, 1973).

2. Philip Rieff, *The Triumph of the Therapeutic* (New York: Harper and Row, 1966).

3. Philip Rieff, *Freud: The Mind of the Moralist* (New York: Viking, 1959).

4. This term has affinities with Robert Lifton's Protean Man, but Rieff's elaboration of Psychological Man is intellectually more substantial and suggestive.

5. Rieff, *The Triumph of the Therapeutic*, p. 195.

6. Ibid., p. 98.

7. Ibid., p. 34.

8. R. H. Super, ed., *The Complete Prose Works of Matthew Arnold*, 10 vols. (Ann Arbor: University of Michigan Press, 1960-1974), IX, 161.

9. *The Triumph of the Therapeutic*, p. 261.

10. *Phoenix: Posthumous Papers of D. H. Lawrence* (London: William Heinemann Ltd., 1936), p. 728.

11. Northrop Frye, *Anatomy of Criticism* (Princeton: Princeton University Press, 1957), p. 27.

12. Rieff, *The Triumph of the Therapeutic*, p. 226.

13. Ibid., pp. 257-258.

14. There is an inherent ambiguity in viewing art as therapy. Do we mean therapy for the artist or therapy for the spectator or reader? The difference may be significant. For instance, the imaginative works of Kafka may be infernal—and thus hardly therapeutic for the reader—but Kafka's making of it may be an act of therapy for him. To the extent that the reader empathizes with the creative imagination of a writer, he may share the therapeutic satisfaction with the writer. When Rieff speaks of the therapeutic, he must have in mind its larger social implication, that is, the relation between art-work and audience. Of course, the fundamental problem in offering a therapeutic conception of art is that it is not always clear that the therapeutic can keep entirely clear of philistine connotations that always threaten to adhere to it. In the world of modern art, well-being that is the result of the therapeutic is not a

value for the artist if it is purchased at the cost of complexity or beauty or a certain wild and dark energy. The modern artist may court suffering, even deficiency (see Kafka's "Hunger Artist") as the purchase price of his art, though it could be argued from a psychoanalytic point of view that the artist never really chooses to do so, that he is rather compensating for the absence of well-being. Nevertheless, there is a suspicion of philistinism in the quest for well-being (legitimately shared by artists and nonartists alike), the sense that quality or meaningfulness or value is being surrendered. Well-being may turn out to be a mask for emptiness. Everything depends upon the substantive richness of the category of well-being.

15. Rieff, *The Triumph of the Therapeutic*, p. 207.

16. Frederick William Roe, ed., *Victorian Prose* (New York: The Ronald Press, 1947), p. 201.

17. Ibid., p. 194.

18. Rieff can speak of the priesthood of the intellect, mix terms which Newman would scrupulously keep separate, because Rieff's Jewishness has affinities with Protestantism.

19. Weber, "Science as a Vocation," in H. H. Gerth and C. Wright Mills, *From Weber* (New York: Oxford University Press, 1958), p. 146.

20. Doris Lessing, *The Golden Notebook* (New York: Bantam Books, 1973), pp. 227-228.

21. Ibid., p. 50.

22. Quentin Anderson, *The Imperial Self* (New York: Knopf, 1970), p. 240.

23. He means that Americans, lacking a temporal as well as spatial conception of community, do not think of their forebears as ancestors.

24. Actually, there has been in recent years strong evidence of a hankering after associated life in America, though it could be argued that the communities projected are utopian precisely in the sense that they involve no surrender of the imperial self—a case of having one's cake and eating it too. To have community is to be willing to give up a portion of the self's claim. Having fully enjoyed and suffered the experience of anomic individualism, Americans—or some Americans—now long for the experience of associated communal life. However, the American's habit of being egoistic persists in his or her imagination of community; in thinking of community he begins with the boundless self.

25. Kenneth Burke has argued that a term such as god "is required as a title of titles . . . spinning out the resources of language in a to-the-end-of-the-line way . . . It sums up the realm of duties and admonitions." *Language as Symbolic Action* (Los Angeles: University of California Press, 1960), p. 456.

6. The Formalist Avant-Garde and the Autonomy of Aesthetic Values

1. Rieff's claim for its spiritual authority notwithstanding.

2. Clement Greenberg, "Modernist Painting," in Gregory Battcock, ed.,

The New Art (New York: Dutton, 1973), p. 67.

3. Ibid., p. 68

4. Ibid., p. 75.

5. Irving Babbitt, *New Laokoon* (Boston: Houghton Mifflin, 1960), p. 204.

6. Greenberg, "Modernist Painting," p. 74.

7. See Hilton Kramer, "A Critic on the Side of History: Notes on Clement Greenberg," *Arts*, 37 (October 1962), 62.

8. Kramer himself provides evidence that his view of Greenberg is somewhat misleading, when he reports in a short piece on avant-gardism Greenberg's distinction between authentic "avant-gardeness" and inauthentic "advanced-advanced art." According to Greenberg, the strident will to originality, for which Marcel Duchamp is the archetype in Greenberg's account, is a false path of modern art. The result is ingenuity rather than inspiration, contrivance rather than creation, fancy rather than imagination. I am less interested in the justice of Greenberg's view of Duchamp and his epigones than I am in the fact that a commitment to historicism would hardly permit Greenberg to make such evaluative distinctions. The fact that they are history would itself be validating. Hilton Kramer, *The Age of the Avant-Garde* (New York: Farrar, Straus and Giroux, 1973), p. 530.

9. There is an analogous case in Hugh Kenner's tracing of the vector of literary development which produces the homemade world of American modernism. He is compelled to exclude major modern American writers because he is describing the evolution of a "medium" which differs from the medium in which the excluded writers work. Unlike Greenberg, however, Kenner does not read the exceptions out of history. See *A Homemade World* (New York: Knopf, 1975).

10. Thus Hilton Kramer can speak of the difficulty an audience trained to formalism may have appreciating the work of a painter like Max Beckmann, for "the visual arts today are so devoid of moral intelligence, so totally sealed off from any problem, idea or emotion that reaches beyond the dialogue that art conducts with itself, that a mind like Beckmann's seems more and more like a visitor from another civilization." *The Shape of the Avant-Garde* (New York: Farrar, Straus and Giroux, 1973), pp. 132-133.

11. Though I am suggesting the inadequacy of an aesthetic based on an empathic intimacy with the work of art, I want to stay clear of the philistine implications of a radical distinction between a "creator-oriented" and "user-oriented" art. The distinction is at the basis of at least one sociological discussion of what differentiates high from popular culture. See Herbert Gans, *Popular Culture and High Culture* (New York: Basic Books, 1975). User-oriented art implies the spontaneous gratification of the consumer's desires and the unproblematic confirmation of his values, whereas creator-oriented art solicits the imaginative will of the "consumer" to make the most strenuous effort to identify his imagination with that of the artist. My own view implies an alternative possibility, in which the consumer (spectator, reader, or listener) is challenged but not exclusively by the conditions of the creative act.

The work of art is seen to have spiritual or moral implications which may be in some degree rooted in the creative process but not exhausted by it. As Cesar Graña remarks, "What is a resolution of conflict to the artist, in the sense that he finds the form to state the problem, may be only the beginning of conflict for the viewer who finds himself challenged by the power of the artist's statement." *Fact and Symbol* (New York: Oxford University Press, 1971), p. 144. I would want to separate myself, however, from Graña when he writes: "In my view, whatever is happening culturally now is part of the cultural present, and therefore there is every reason to believe that if more people go to see Giorgione rather than Mark Rothko, the first is, in fact, more of a contemporary artist than the second; anything that is experienced and significantly recognized now is a 'now' thing." Ibid., p. 109. Graña's attempt (admirable in its intention) to defend the vitality of the tradition against the "cult of the new" leads him to a perversely philistine view of the history of art. The public decides what is contemporary and alive. The history of art becomes sociology.

    12. Greenberg, "Modernist Painting," p. 68.

    13. E. H. Gombrich, *Norm and Form* (London: Phaidon, 1966), pp. 1-11.

    14. Pierre Francastel, "The Destruction of a Plastic Space," in Wylie Sypher, ed., *Art History: An Anthology of Modern Criticism* (New York: Random House, Vintage, 1963), p. 397.

    15. Richard Chase, "The Fate of the Avant Garde," *Partisan Review* (Summer 1957), p. 363.

7. Aristocrats and Jacobins:
The Happy Few in *The Charterhouse of Parma*

    1. Stendhal, *The Charterhouse of Parma*, trans. C. K. Scott Moncrieff, 2 vols. (New York: Boni and Liverwright, 1925), I, 129-130.

    2. Since the political life occurs at court, the groups contending for power are factions, but they are clearly analogues to the parties produced by the French Revolution.

    3. Stendhal, *The Charterhouse of Parma*, I, 129-130.

    4. Alexis de Tocqueville, *The Old Regime and the Revolution*, 1856.

    5. Richard Herr, *Tocqueville and the Old Regime* (Princeton: Princeton University Press, 1962).

    6. *The Charterhouse of Parma*, I, 20.

    7. Ibid., p. 4.

    8. In his *Vie de Napoleon*, Stendhal notes with approval Napoleon's observation: "The French are indifferent to liberty. They do not understand it or love it. Vanity is their only passion; and political equality, which allows every one of them the hope of attaining every position, is the only political right which concerns them." Quoted in Joanna Richardson, *Stendhal* (New York: Coward, McCann and Geoghegan, 1974), p. 139.

    9. Stendhal, *The Charterhouse of Parma*, I, 110, 164, 146, 253.

    10. Ibid., p. 148.

11. Ibid., pp. 188-189.

12. Ibid., II, 315.

13. Ibid., I, 25.

14. To the Editor of *The Edinburgh Review*, April 10, 1818.

15. F. C. Green, *Stendhal* (Cambridge: Cambridge University Press, 1939), p. 266.

16. Stendhal, *The Charterhouse of Parma*, II, 245.

17. Ibid., I, 207.

18. When Stendhal was to be appointed to a consular post in Trieste in 1930, "the Austrian and political police commenced to prick up their ears and consult their files. As a result, Metternich refused Stendhal's *exaequatur* protesting against the appointment of this anti-clerical liberal." Green, *Stendhal*, p. 239. Like Stendhal, Tocqueville was opposed to Metternich and admired England. He expressed his disgust with the Austrian alliance against England. See Seymour Drescher, *Tocqueville and England* (Cambridge, Mass.: Harvard University Press, 1964), p. 166. If Metternich is Stendhal's antagonist, how does one account for the Metternichian side of Mosca, which Stendhal renders with a certain affection? There is no certain answer to the question, but I would venture a guess. Stendhal values the capacity to create and sustain political intrigue as a mark of intelligence, but also as a way of protecting certain values which otherwise would be exposed to the world and perhaps betrayed. Without Mosca's Metternichian capacity to control the politics of Parma, Gina, Fabrizio, and even Ferrante Palla would have no chance for survival, let alone being themselves. Stendhal proposes a Metternich who allows the *esprit Napoleonique* to survive, if only in aesthetic and intellectual form.

19. Stendhal, *The Charterhouse of Parma*, II, 243.

20. The various love relationships of the novel (Mosca-Gina, Ferrante Palla-Gina, Fabrizio-Clelia) have the chivalric theme in common, a legacy of aristocratic culture.

21. Stendhal, *The Charterhouse of Parma*, II, 194.

22. July 31, 1803, in *The Private Diaries of Stendhal*, trans. and ed. Robert Sage (New York: W. W. Norton, 1954), p. 36.

23. Aristocracy is an ambiguous term. It means at once the ruling class and the society it rules. It is a useful ambiguity, because the value of brio, for example, is not exclusively in the possession of the ruling class. It is shared by the whole society, though the values have been largely created and most fully expressed by the ruling class.

24. Stendhal's depiction of the battle of Waterloo is his magnificent concession to the fantastic world that he imagines in the pages that follow the "real" battle of Waterloo.

25. In an essay on *Bleak House*, Q. D. Leavis shows how Dickens distinguishes the value of the aristocrat Sir Leicester Dedlock from his noxiousness. "Sir Leicester and his set are retrograde politically . . . and want to run the country in the interest of their own class by personal influence . . . they bribe the electorate." Yet "Chesney Wold, Sir Leicester's estate, is beautifully or-

dered with contented servants and retainers and seems comparatively idyllic when measured against all the other places in the novel." More important is Sir Leicester's grace and generosity in his suffering. "When the disclosure of his wife's 'guilty' past is made to him, he declares unequivocally that he has nothing to forgive and thinks no less of his wife than before . . . He sees his privacy and family pride exposed to vulgar scandal, but he feels only for his wife as the sufferer, since he is capable of real, personal, unselfish feeling." Even more pertinent to the case of Stendhal is the view Mrs. Leavis takes of "Dickens, the artist, the poet, who mourns the loss of 'passion and pride,' which only can be nourished by such a cultural context, and who sees that 'dull repose' is the death of the spirit which the light of the drawing room had formerly kept alive." And she reminds us of Yeats, "who saw the great house as the creation and home of proud, passionate, violent men who thereby nourished the arts and inspired artists to creativity." F. R. Leavis and Q. D. Leavis, *Dickens: The Novelist* (London: Chatto and Windus, 1970), pp. 143, 144, 147, 148, 296.

26. The life-hating aestheticism of Flaubert is not comprehended by this statement. Nine-tenths of the world cannot live by Flaubert's art and the artists themselves can neither live without nor live with art, so difficult is the burden. Stendhal is one of the first instances of an aestheticism which does not pit art against life, but sees art and life as necessary to each other.

27. Letter to Sutton Sharpe, August 15, 1830, *Private Diaries*.

28. Georg Lukacs, *Studies in European Realism* (New York: Grosset and Dunlap, 1964), p. 81. Stendhal embraced Romanticism—though not in the sense attributed to him by Lukacs. Lukacs attributes to Stendhal an Enlightenment sensibility because of his austere, colorless style. Balzac is the romantic stylist. But Stendhal's alleged tendency to distort reality makes him an *inadvertent* romantic, according to Lukacs, despite, oddly enough, Stendhal's avowed Romanticism. Lukacs's unwillingness to make clear the difference between his categories and those of his subject is disconcerting because the same words are used to designate different things.

29. I do not think of Tocqueville as offering the possibility of a "systematic" interpretation of literature—as Marx and Freud seem to do. Tocqueville does not appear to have a general theory of human nature or of historical development, so he is not a competitor with Marx and Freud. And yet it strikes me that Tocqueville's speculations about aristocracy and democracy provide an insight into the political dimension of modern literature that one does not find in Marx or his followers.

30. George Lichtheim, *Marxism: An Historical and Critical Study*, 2d ed. rev. (New York: Praeger, 1964), p. 148.

31. I anticipate the charge that I have not begun to do justice to Marxist thought by not taking into consideration the work of Adorno, Horkheimer, and Marcuse, who would defy my assertions. The basis for such a charge is the unacceptable assumption that the Frankfurt philosophers are ideological Marxists. As I remarked earlier, though often working within the assumptions of Marxism, they cannot be characterized as Marxists. Martin Jay, the his-

torian of the Frankfurt school, remarks that "the great irony [of the development of the dialectic of its work] was that the Institute had abandoned many of its more radical ideas." *The Dialectical Imagination: A History of the Frankfurt School and the Institute of Social Research, 1923-1950* (Boston: Little, Brown, 1973), p. 248. But given the openness and undogmatic character of Critical Theory, the irony is not an unexpected development. For the Frankfurt school and its successors, Marx and Marxism are part of a heritage as Plato and Platonism are part of the heritage of Kantians. To assimilate the Frankfurt school to ideological Marxism would be to render both terms meaningless.

8. Flaubert and the Powerlessness of Art

1. Quoted in Francis Steegmuller, *Flaubert and Madame Bovary* (London: Collins, 1947), p. 25.

2. See letter to George Sand, Paris, May 10, 1867, in Francis Steegmuller, *The Selected Letters of Flaubert* (New York: Farrar, Straus and Cudahy, 1953), p. 211.

3. Gustave Flaubert, *Madame Bovary*, ed. Paul de Man (New York: Norton, 1965), p. 36.

4. "One should live like a bourgeois and think like a demi-god," Flaubert writes in a letter of August 21-22, 1813, in Steegmuller, *Selected Letters*, p. 161.

5. *Madame Bovary*, p. 29.

6. In speaking of the bourgeois as anyone who thinks in a low or vulgar manner, Flaubert makes him a universal character.

7. *Madame Bovary*, p. 294.

8. Ibid., p. 297.

9. To his niece Caroline, Paris, December 1842, in Steegmuller, *Selected Letters*, p. 28.

10. To Maxine DuCamp Croisset, September 1841, ibid., p. 124.

11. Gustave Flaubert, *November*, trans. Frank Jellinke (New York: Roman Press, 1932), pp. 56-57.

12. Ibid., p. 61.

13. Ibid., p. 60.

14. That Flaubert could conceive of romantic love as Bovarisme, see it not as a perversion of romantic love but as its very condition, is a symptom of that nihilistic subversive spirit that has had such a lively career in France. Flaubert gives us archetypically a cultural attitude at once French and universally modern.

15. *Madame Bovary*, p. 142.

16. Ibid., p. 201.

17. Ibid., pp. 101-102.

18. Leo Bersani, *Balzac to Beckett* (New York: Oxford University Press, 1970), p. 167.

19. *Madame Bovary*, p. 138.

20. Erich Auerbach, *Mimesis* (Princeton: Princeton University Press, 1953), pp. 482-484.

21. August 15, 1946, in Louis Conard, ed., *Correspondance*, 9 vols. (Paris: Edition du Centenaire, Librairie de France, 1921-1925), I, 174, trans. Paul de Man.

22. Roland Barthes, *S/Z*, trans. Richard Miller (New York: Hill and Wang, 1974), p. 98.

23. Jonathan Culler, *Flaubert: The Uses of Uncertainty* (Ithaca: Cornell University Press, 1974), p. 227.

24. Ibid., p. 232.

25. Hugh Kenner, *The Pound Era* (Berkeley: University of California Press, 1971), p. 126.

26. Harold Bloom has of course constructed a theory about burdens of influence.

27. See Kenner, *The Pound Era*, p. 126.

28. *Phoenix: Posthumous Papers of D. H. Lawrence* (London: Heinemann, 1936), p. 112.

29. *Madame Bovary*, p. 308.

30. Though I think it applies to the romantic tales as well, my argument is primarily addressed to Flaubert's realistic fiction. I read the romantic tales as a kind of realistic rendering of the dream life, in which mythic and historical materials are used: *St. Julian the Hospitaller* and *Herodias*, two of Flaubert's *Trois Contes*, convey the sadomasochistic aspect of the dream life. In *St. Julian* the sadism expresses itself in Julian's ferocious glorying in his power as hunter, in his god-like sense of being able to destroy life. "He only knew that he was hunting in some region or other, for an indefinite time, where everything was done with the ease one experiences in dreams." And again: "Sometimes, in dreams, he saw himself like our father Adam in Paradise, among all the beasts; by stretching his arm he made them die." The masochism reveals itself in Julian's excruciating guilt for his terrible crimes of having killed mother and father and his ultimate saintliness. Though we may feel in the romantic tales a sense of release from the inhibitions, the resistances of the detail of quotidian reality, we are overwhelmed in a work like *Salammbô* with the kind of detail reminiscent of a naturalistic novel. And the dream life, like reality, is a prison of repetition from which there is no escape. The verbs imply repeated action, characteristic activities, never unique events. In any event, the labored beauty of the tales does not provide the dimension of value necessary for art to be an authentic and convincing opposite to the squalor of life.

31. "The Pagan School," in Lois Boe Hyslop and Francis E. Hyslop, eds., *Baudelaire As a Literary Critic* (University Park: Pennsylvania State University Press, 1964), p. 77.

32. Stendhal was an admirer of Destutt De Tracy's *Ideology*, but ideology for Destutt does not quite have its modern meaning: it is the psychology of ideation. In Stendhal's *Charterhouse*, politics is still partly in the factional state. Ideas and attitudes have not fully hardened into ideological formulas.

33. Max Brod, *Franz Kafka: A Biography* (New York: Schocken, 1963), p. 68. I am grateful to Michael Platt for calling my attention to this passage. See his essay "Nietzsche on Flaubert and the Powerlessness of His Art," *The Centennial Review* (Summer 1976), pp. 309-313, a response to an earlier version of my essay on Flaubert in *The Centennial Review* (Summer 1975), pp. 157-171.

34. "The word 'religion' or 'Catholicism' on the one hand, 'progress,' 'brotherhood,' 'democracy' on the other, no longer satisfy the spiritual demands of our time. The brand-new dogma of equality, preached by radicalism, is given the lie by experimental psychology and by history. I do not see how it is possible today to establish a new principle or to respect the old ones. Hence I keep seeking—without ever finding—that idea which is supposed to be the foundation of everything." Letter to George Sand, Paris, after December 20, 1875, in Steegmuller, *Selected Letters*, p. 251.

35. *The Sentimental Education* (London: Penguin, 1964), p. 141.

36. Ibid., p. 181.

37. Quoted in Hugh Kenner, *Samuel Beckett: A Critical Study* (New York: Grove Press, 1961), p. 30.

38. Ernest Renan, Third Dialogue, *Dialogues Philosophiques*, quoted in Paul Lidsky, *Les Ecrivains contre la Commune* (Paris: Maspero, 1970), pp. 30-31, my translation. Flaubert's Renanism is expressed, for instance, in the bourgeois-baiting letter quoted at the beginning of the chapter, which continues: "It is we, and we alone—that is, the educated—who are the People, or, more accurately, the tradition of Humanity."

9. The Blasphemy of Joycean Art

1. Hélène Cixous, *The Exile of James Joyce*, trans. Sally A. Purcell (New York: D. Lewis, 1972), p. 38.

2. Richard Ellmann, *James Joyce* (New York: Oxford, 1959), p. 2.

3. Ibid., p. 226.

4. Joyce, *A Portrait of the Artist As a Young Man* (New York: Viking, 1956), pp. 171-172.

5. Joyce's rebellious attitude toward his literary heritage brings to mind Harold Bloom's view that the modern poet is engaged in an oedipal competition with his precursor. According to Bloom, the strong poet overcomes his precursor, though not his anxiety, by denying him in the act of incorporating his energies. Stephen's Sabellian heresy in the Scylla and Charybdis episode in *Ulysses*, in which he conflates father and son in his account of Shakespeare, can be viewed as a paradigm for the denial of authority to one's precursor (indeed progenitor), a "technique" of incorporating the father so as to overcome the tyranny of influence. In *A Portrait of the Artist*, however, Stephen invokes figures from his past to support his rebellion. For example, in affirming himself, Stephen denounces Tennyson (though Tennyson has found his way into Stephen's imagination through the presence of Pater). He does not have the courage simply to assert his own imagination against Tennyson. He

must associate Byron with his enterprise, a thoroughly appropriate authority figure for rebellion. Bloom does not deal with what may be an essential fact of oedipal rebellion. In killing a father one may be trading him for another. Stephen affirms himself not only at the expense of Tennyson, but also at the expense of the spiritual and worldly powers that he knows. He is not simply offering his art against the art of the past, he is pitting art against other spiritual and moral dispensations. Bloom's insistence on the poetic medium as the exclusive place for poetic development and understanding prevents us from knowing why a poet or a novelist moved toward or against a particular precursor.

6. Dante's knowledge of Homer was derivative. Homer had the *reputation* of being the greatest poet.

7. Joyce, *Ulysses* (New York: Random House, 1946), p. 38.

8. The view we take of the hell-fire sermon is an interesting instance of the problem of point of view that Joyce's work creates and which comes to be a salient feature of modernism. The episode provokes a series of questions: Is Stephen's point of view necessarily ours? If not, what is our relation to it? Are we not importing illicitly certain sentiments into a negative view of the sermon if we simply find it repulsive—for example, the sentiments of humane agnostic liberalism? Isn't Joyce perhaps presenting us with the Catholic view from the inside, an exercise in negative capability, so that we can appreciate the hold of the church on the mind of Stephen—whatever our view of Stephen may be? None of these questions can be answered with certainty. The disappearance of the authorial presence has deliberately made any particular point of view problematical. We hardly need a more convincing example of the difference between Dante's coherent medievalism and Joyce's problematic modernism than the fate of point of view in modern fiction, that is, the disappearance of the privileged point of view. Thus Joyce's tendentious heretical claim for art has implicit within it the seeds of radical doubt and uncertainty.

9. *A Portrait of the Artist*, pp. 239-244.

10. Ibid., p. 252.

11. Cixous, *Exile of James Joyce*, p. 454.

12. *Ulysses*, p. 10.

13. Samuel Beckett and others, *Our Exagmination Round His Factification for Incamination for Work in Progress* (New York: Haskell House, 1974), pp. 21-22.

14. *Ulysses*, p. 26.

15. Ibid., p. 35.

16. Erich Auerbach, *Dante: Poet of the Secular World*, ed. Theodore Silverstein, trans. Ralph Manheim (Chicago: University of Chicago Press, 1961), pp. 144-145.

17. *A Portrait of the Artist*, p. 221.

18. Lawrence provides a less generous "protestant" view: "I had a copy of *transition*, that Paris magazine—the American number. My God, what a clumsy *olla putrida* James Joyce is!—Nothing but old fags and cabbage stumps of quotations from the Bible and the rest, stewed in the juice of delib-

erate, journalistic dirty-mindedness—what old and hard-worked staleness, masquerading as the all-new!" Aldous Huxley, ed., *The Letters of D. H. Lawrence* (New York: Viking, 1932), p. 750. In his incisive, though hostile, way, Lawrence perceives the *novel* effect of parody, though this is not necessarily intended by the comment.

19. Ellmann, *James Joyce*, p. 113.

20. "Civitas," in John Freccero, ed., *Dante* (New York: Prentice-Hall, 1965), p. 141.

21. In his introduction to Baudelaire's *Intimate Journals* (New York: Random House, 1930), p. 11, Eliot makes this illuminating remark: "Genuine blasphemy, genuine in spirit and not purely verbal, is the product of partial belief and is as impossible to the complete atheist as to the perfect Christian. It is a way of affirming belief." In *After Strange Gods* (London: Faber and Faber, 1934), p. 52, Eliot notes that "no one can possibly blaspheme in any sense except that in which a parrot may be said to curse, unless he profoundly believes in that which he profanes."

22. Lawrence's Protestant anti-Protestantism leads him at moments to consider Catholicism as an alternative. "I doubt whether the Protestant Churches, which supported the war [World War I], will even have the faith and the power of life to take the great step onwards, and preach Christ Risen. The Catholic Church might. In the countries of the Mediterranean, Easter has always been the greatest of the holy days . . . The Roman Catholic Church may still unfold this part of the Passion fully, and make men happy again. For Resurrection is indeed the consummation of all the passion." *Phoenix II* (New York: Viking, 1973), pp. 573-574.

Index